THE FIGHT FOR
STATUS AND PRIVILEGE
IN LATE MEDIEVAL
AND
EARLY MODERN CASTILE,
1465-1598

MICHAEL J. CRAWFORD

THE FIGHT FOR
STATUS AND PRIVILEGE
IN LATE MEDIEVAL
AND
EARLY MODERN CASTILE,
1465–1598

THE PENNSYLVANIA STATE UNIVERSITY PRESS

UNIVERSITY PARK, PENNSYLVANIA

Library of Congress
Cataloging-in-Publication Data

Crawford, Michael J., 1970– , author.
The fight for status and privilege in late
medieval and early modern Castile, 1465–1598 /
Michael J. Crawford.
p.   cm
Summary: "In the context of legal privileges based
on status and class in premodern Spain and Europe
in general, investigates conflicts over and resistance
to the status of hidalgo in fifteenth- and sixteenth-
century Castile"—Provided by publisher.
Includes bibliographical references and index.
ISBN 978-0-271-06289-1 (cloth : alk. paper)
1. Nobility—Legal status, laws, etc.—Spain—
Castile—History—To 1500.
2. Nobility—Legal status, laws, etc.—Spain—
Castile—History—16th century.
3. Castile (Spain)—Politics and government—
16th century.
I. Title.

KKT6054.22.C73   2014
342.46'3087—dc23
2013039197

CONTENTS

ILLUSTRATIONS

ACKNOWLEDGMENTS

I would not have completed this book without the help and advice of many colleagues, friends, and family members. While at the University of Arizona, I benefited from wonderfully supportive and professionally rigorous mentors, particularly Alan Bernstein, Steven Johnstone, and Helen Nader. In particular, my adviser, Helen Nader, generously and wholeheartedly encouraged my research and writing. Her meticulous scholarship and lucid and elegant prose continue to be a model for my own work. The many members of the Division for Late Medieval and Reformation Studies at the University of Arizona fostered my intellectual growth, in particular its late director Heiko A. Oberman, and provided moral support both during and after the infamous late night seminars at his home in the foothills of the Santa Catalina Mountains. My fellow Hispanists at the University of Arizona, Aurelio Espinosa, Cristian Berco, and Stephanie Fink, set unparalleled examples of enthusiasm for research and writing on the history of Spain and early modern Europe.

I received invaluable research fellowships and grants from the Fulbright Foundation, the Newberry Library, the University of the South, and McNeese State University. I would like to thank the many archivists in Seville, Granada, Valladolid, and Simancas, whose knowledge and expertise facilitated my research. In particular, the archivists under the direction of David Torres Ibáñez at the Real Chancillería de Granada produced copies of much-needed documents when the building that housed the archive was in renovation. During daily breaks from the pages of old documents, the *funcionarios* at the Archivo Municipal de Sevilla, whom I knew simply as Juan, Manolo, Paco, and Pedro, provided kind and lively company, local knowledge, and instruction in the Andaluz accent. A hearty thanks to the members of the Association for Spanish and Portuguese Historical Studies, who have listened to what now seems like interminable papers on *hidalgos* and thoughtfully commented on and critiqued them. James Boyden read an early draft of chapter 1 and offered much appreciated and insightful feedback. I am indebted to the anonymous readers for Penn State University Press, who proposed discerning and well-grounded suggestions for improvement. Alex Crawford and Andrea Albright Crawford generously took time from their busy lives and careers to read and comment on the manuscript at different stages of its development. Not only has Andrea enriched my life and this book with her loving support and dry wit, but her studies of Louisiana civil law led to helpful comparisons and insight into the archaic legal systems of early modern Castile. She read drafts of the manuscript chapters on multiple occasions, often clarifying obscure sentences and inchoate thoughts. Above all, my parents deserve special gratitude for always supporting me, especially in my education.

An earlier version of chapter 1 appeared under the title "Noble Status and Royal Duplicity in the Crown of Castile, 1454–1504" in *European History Quarterly* 41, no. 4 (October 2011), published by SAGE Publications Ltd.

I have transcribed archival sources in the notes as they appear in the documents without modernizing spellings and forms. For greater ease of reading, however, some punctuation, capital letters, and diacritics have been added. I have also silently expanded abbreviations and contractions. Unless otherwise indicated, English translations of fifteenth- and sixteenth-century sources are my own.

INTRODUCTION:
THE STATUS OF *HIDALGO* AS A SOCIAL CLAIM

On October 4, 1477, the royal court of Castile issued a writ to the municipal councils of the city of Seville and its subject town of Gerena ordering that they respect the *hidalgo* status (*hidalguía*) of Pedro Rodríguez Gijón along with its attendant privileges.[1] Rodríguez had dutifully fought in the recent war against Afonso of Portugal, Isabel and Fernando's rival for the throne of Castile, and thereby provided military service that the Catholic Monarchs had demanded from the kingdom's hidalgos. Nevertheless, despite his military service and the claim that his family had always been in possession of hidalguía, the council of Gerena had denied him exemption from taxation. The council's resistance to what Rodríguez viewed as his requisite liberties subsequently forced him into lengthy litigation and an appeal to an ambivalent royal government for support and justice. Rodríguez was one of thousands who faced local resistance to their claims of hidalgo status during the reign of the Catholic Monarchs.

More than a hundred years later, in 1584, a prosecutor at the royal chancery court in Granada denounced Gonzalo Argote de Molina, a city councilman of Seville, charging that he falsely held the status of hidalgo and thereby fraudulently enjoyed exemption from taxation.[2] Like Rodríguez, Argote had provided loyal service to his sovereign and commonwealth. In addition to holding the office of provost of the regional militia of Andalusia, he had participated in the pacification of the Morisco revolt in 1568 and the great naval victory over the Ottoman fleet at Lepanto in 1571. Moreover, two years after the denunciation he would marry the heiress and illegitimate daughter of the Marquis of Lanzarote.[3] Unlike Rodríguez and many others, Argote ultimately avoided an appeal to the Crown and a costly lawsuit for recognition of his hidalguía. The city council of Seville, protecting one of its own members and its prerogatives, blocked the royal prosecutor's efforts to declare and list him as a common taxpayer (*pechero*).

Throughout the late medieval and early modern periods, conflicts over the recognition and possession of hidalgo status in the Crown of Castile were frequent and manifested themselves in diverse formal and informal disputes. The most conspicuous form of dispute involved the tens of thousands of lawsuits initiated by individuals at the chancery courts (*chancillerías*) to gain recognition of their possession of this status.[4] This study examines not only these lawsuits but also the full range of conflicts over hidalgo status, the contexts in which they took place, and, more broadly, the efforts to claim, deny, and manage noble legal privileges associated with hidalgo status. Through a focus on these conflicts it reveals how Castilians actually experienced legal inequality in the early modern world.

Most modern historians conventionally define *hidalgo* as the lowest rank in the Castilian nobility, below knights (*caballeros*) and seigneurial aristocrats (*señores* and *títulos*), and further assert that hidalgos as a group enjoyed a range of legal privileges, including the regularly cited exemption from taxation.[5] The small number of seigneurial aristocrats consisted of the heads of powerful families who held political and judicial jurisdiction over specific communities. The term *caballero* carried a wide range of meanings, including untitled male members of aristocratic families, cavalrymen in a royal or seigneurial service, and a rank of urban citizens required to maintain horse and arms on account of their wealth. In this hierarchy of the nobility, hidalgos formed the bottom rung as the most numerous if least materially endowed noble rank. Additionally, early modern documents used the term *hidalgo* in opposition to the term *pechero*, a commoner or ordinary taxpayer, to designate someone who did not pay royal taxes on account of status. Modern scholars have detailed how hidalgos ranged widely in wealth and occupation, but agree that they constituted a large legally privileged group that filled a liminal social space between the vast majority of the lay population and the small number of titled aristocrats.[6]

Demographic and social historians who have sought to quantify the number of hidalgos in sixteenth-century Castile have produced estimates that range from 5 percent to an extraordinary 10 percent of the population.[7] Using the conservative estimate that hidalgos made up roughly 5 percent of the population, Antonio Domínguez Ortiz calculated an astounding 108,358 hidalgo families for the year 1541, compared to the 50-odd families that held seigneurial titles.[8] In other European countries the nobility ranged from less than half a percent to roughly 2 percent of the population.[9] The purported existence of a large nobility implies the enjoyment of privileges and therefore a numerous lay elite differentiated by legal rights from the mass of commoners, who suffered legal inequalities. Early modern Castilians at times complained about such widespread noble privileges and the detrimental consequences they had for Castile's society and economy.[10] Modern scholars have noted these complaints and further argued that privileges, especially fiscal ones, acted as a source of economic backwardness because the weight of direct taxation fell heavily on the peasantry.[11] Additionally, tax exemptions compelled governments to rely on indirect taxation that handicapped economic growth and encouraged the sale of offices and honors, which led wealth to be invested unproductively in the acquisition of status. Such descriptions of Castilian society necessarily assume that noble privileges effectively conferred power and wealth on this segment of society.

This study explains that the extraordinary numbers, both of hidalgos and of the disputes over the status of hidalgo, resulted from the fact that many of those claiming hidalgo status only precariously achieved recognition of their status or failed to achieve local recognition at all. Those who succeeded in gaining some level of recognition often enjoyed few, limited, or none of the associated legal privileges. Moreover, this study demonstrates how the existence of diverse local rules governing status and the persistence of multiple sources for authorizing or recognizing the status contributed to the unstable, indefinite, and essentially rhetorical nature of hidalgo status in the early modern period.

Due to the fluid and contingent nature of hidalguía, conflicts over its recognition and disputes about its related privileges became a major and significant phenomenon in early modern Castile. Through an examination of the evolution of these disputes in the Crown of Castile, particularly in the city of Seville and its territory, this study offers new approaches to understanding elites, privilege, and social status in late medieval and early modern Europe. It questions conventional ideas about how, and the degree to which, individuals enjoyed social and legal privileges in Castile, emphasizing both widespread resistance to privilege and the fact that both status and privilege had to be actively maintained.

The rhetoric employed by those claiming noble status in Castile often explicitly or implicitly asserted that hidalgos by right of birth enjoyed uncontested legal privileges. Indeed, Castilian laws and customs existed that sanctioned privileges for hidalgos such as tax exemption, access to or monopoly over political offices, and immunity from judicial torture and debtor's prison.[12] Nevertheless, actual enjoyment of privilege did not come easily. There was widespread resistance to recognizing individual status that would confer these privileges and periodic resistance to the establishment of privileges based on status at the municipal level. This resistance took place on many levels and manifested itself in diverse ways.[13] Municipal governments and the local elites who controlled them as well as officers at the royal appellate courts acted as the primary opponents to the proliferation of privilege. This opposition seems contrary to expectation because these local elites comprised the very individuals who benefited from privileges associated with hidalgo status or sought to identify themselves as hidalgos. Reading surviving complaints made by established elites against those who claimed, assumed, or bought hidalgo status, historians in the mid-twentieth century presented such resistance as the reactionary efforts of an old nobility against the incursions of parvenus, particularly commercial and financial ones who sought ennoblement.[14]

The evidence from Seville suggests that this resistance, rather than being related to class or caste antagonisms and identity, resulted from royal and municipal concerns with maintaining revenues and the fiscal base for these revenues. But municipal governments in particular balanced these fiscal concerns with the need to uphold the status of its highest officers and their dependents and clients. Consequently, local social networks, which operated according to a range of contingent factors, heavily influenced the dynamics behind these conflicts, as did the political relations and negotiations between local municipal authorities and the monarchy. Bearing these factors in mind, this study emphasizes that the nature and meaning of disputes over hidalgo status evolved with royal and municipal efforts to elaborate and reform judicial, economic, and administrative institutions and systems.

This work is an investigation of social contests and conflict, not a study of hidalgos as a social group or class, let alone a study of the Castilian nobility. Nevertheless, it seeks to build on the considerable literature produced on these subjects and on the European nobility in general. Due to their central position in premodern society, members of the highest ranks of the nobility figure prominently in most histories, whether political, social, or cultural. Traditional scholarly treatments of the Castilian nobility before the nineteenth century range from treatises defining the group and articulating the values of its members to genealogies devoted to the preservation of the history of specific lineages.[15] While these works often addressed the full range of ranks within the nobility, modern historical studies have focused heavily, almost exclusively, on the members of the top tier of this group, the seigneurial aristocrats.[16] Not until the rise and influence of diverse currents of social history in the 1970s did historians of Spain provide direct and sustained attention to the other ranks of the nobility, particularly the far larger groups of caballeros and hidalgos, albeit as a component of histories of social elites or of specific towns and regions.[17]

Writing in the waning decades of the Franco regime, the eminent Spanish historian Antonio Domínguez Ortiz produced what has been the definitive study of the privileged classes in early modern Spanish society. For Domínguez

Ortiz, sixteenth- and seventeenth-century Spanish society was based neither exclusively on concepts of distinct legal estates nor on the social divisions of economic class. Domínguez Ortiz highlighted social mobility both into and out of the noble ranks and thoroughly rejected the notion of a closed noble estate. Moreover, his study presented abundant evidence demonstrating how separation between noble and commoner was not always clear and that there existed a multitude of intermediate situations between social groups and indeterminate boundaries dividing them.[18] In his description of the ranks that constituted the nobility and his efforts to quantify these ranks, Domínguez Ortiz identified a number of problems with categorizing the privileged classes that also challenged the historians of other national nobilities and elites: the overlapping of established nobles and those created or recognized through royal judicial writ or patent, incorporation of new elites through intermarriage, and the growth of disputes concerning noble status.[19] But while Domínguez Ortiz addressed problems of identity and status, he did not address the fundamental consequences that they had for the tangible enjoyment of privilege.

Simultaneous and subsequent social histories of the Castilian nobility sought to remedy the limits of Domínguez Ortiz's broad study of the privileged classes by applying rigorous research to particular regions and territories and thereby quantifying not only the noble population but also its economic wealth and political influence. Perhaps the most successful of these regional studies for its thorough approach to available sources and scope was Marie-Claude Gerbet's study of the nobility in Extremadura. Gerbet's study also sought to demonstrate how the nobility evolved from the fifteenth into the sixteenth centuries. She concluded that movement into the lower nobility, primarily the acquisition of the rank of hidalgo, was considerable during the wars of the late fifteenth century but subsequently slowed—even closed—in the sixteenth century, especially after Carlos I (1516–55) formally ended the royal practice of granting hidalgo status.[20] Gerbet's work recognized the growing number of lawsuits in which individuals claimed the status of hidalgo, treating them primarily as the result of efforts by nonnobles to acquire this status. Gerbet generally assumed that those who successfully proved their status in court were genuine hidalgos, while those who failed were false hidalgos. Gerbet's treatment of the hierarchy of the noble estate, despite various qualifications, repeated the tripartite division of the nobility into títulos, caballeros, and hidalgos articulated by authors of sixteenth-century treatises that sought to systematize the messy social world of Castilian elites. Gerbet concluded that this tripartite division of the nobility developed in the fifteenth century and continued—despite the growing social complexity of the early modern period—until the dramatic changes wrought by the impact of the French Revolution.[21] This presentation of Castilian society minimized the possibilities for acquisition of status by means other than royal grants or litigation.

In their efforts to quantify the nobility and its various ranks, Gerbet and other social and demographic historians faced the problem already raised by Domínguez Ortiz concerning whom to include in the group.[22] Identifying titled aristocrats was simple enough, but it was far more difficult to distinguish the large number of individuals in the lower tiers of the nobility and subsequently make supportable arguments about mobility and the political and economic fortunes of this group.[23] Similar efforts to identify and calculate the members of the lower nobility for other continental nobilities and the gentry in Britain have also proved difficult for related reasons.[24] In particular, historians of Castile have had to grapple with the problem of differentiating hidalgos from other elites, especially urban oligarchs and those termed *caballeros*.[25] Often presented as a rank superior to hidalgo, the term *caballero* during the medieval period carried multiple generic and particular meanings. Sources of the period use *caballero* both as a catch-all term for someone of noble status and to designate town citizens who engaged in mounted military service. Charters issued to towns and cities conquered or established during the thirteenth century allowed citizens with sufficient means to obtain the designation of *caballero* and with it exemption from certain taxes by maintaining warhorses and appropriate arms. The terms *caballero* and *hidalgo*, rather than being mutually exclusive designations of distinct grades in a hierarchy of nobility, could be simultaneously applied to the same person and family or combined to form hybrid designations such as *caballero-hidalgo*, as was the case in fifteenth-century Seville.[26]

Shifting usage in terminology over time and from one locale or region to another has further complicated these efforts.[27] Even as historians recognize the multiple linguistic meanings of terms such as *caballero* and the changing meaning of *hidalgo* at different places and times, they tend to present the social landscape of early modern Castile in terms derived from and defined by proscriptive laws and Golden Age literature that present neat hierarchies of distinct ranks in the nobility. This approach has shaped arguments about the roles of hidalgos and caballeros during moments of social conflict, whether of a class, religious, or racial nature.[28] Likewise, the mentalities attributed to these groups have led to extensive speculation about their roles in large-scale and long-term events such as the Spanish conquests in the Americas or the decline of Spain.[29] Americo Castro even coined the expression *hidalguisimo* to describe what he viewed as the medieval and early modern Spanish exaltation of the warrior.[30]

Despite questionable success in identifying and quantifying the full range of the nobility in Castile or elsewhere in Europe, these problems did not impede efforts to write overarching narratives concerning the history and fate of this dominant social group or to engage in national comparisons. Mid-twentieth-century historiography of the early modern European nobility focused heavily on the group's political and economic dominance and the challenges it faced from other social groups and the monarchy. In the 1960s historians of other western European national nobilities, particularly those of England and France, posited a crisis for the nobility between the sixteenth and eighteenth centuries and thereby engendered a prolonged debate about the existence, nature, extent, and significance of such a crisis.[31] Generally these historians argued that new realities of rule and production forced the nobility to change and modernize or lose their dominant positions in society. Significantly, these studies focused primarily on the top tier of the nobility and remained largely speculative about the fortunes of the lesser nobility and gentry. In a comparative study of the European nobility drawing from national and regional histories produced since the 1970s, Jonathan Dewald reviewed the debate and questioned whether the nobility faced a genuine crisis. Dewald stressed the ability of the nobility to maintain its wealth and power and adapt to new circumstances.[32] Moreover, he argued that nobles survived the changes of the early modern period by shedding their weakest members and by diversifying the sources of their wealth. Citing evidence demonstrating the diverse economic activities of the European nobility, Dewald suggested that the formation of a noble class during the period took place in terms of cultural ideals and behavior rather than by common relations to the means of production.

In Dewald's wide-ranging synthesis of the state of scholarship on the nobility, discussion of nobles shifted from a coherent socioeconomic group to cultural ideals and practices and "aristocratic social forms."[33] This shift in the subject of historical analysis paralleled the growing skepticism in historical studies concerning the objective basis of hard social structures such as class, race, and gender and the greater attention given to the ways individuals constructed these categories. As one facet of what has been termed variously the "cultural turn" or the "linguistic turn," historians, sociologists, and anthropologists increasingly since the 1980s have written extensively about the invention or construction of these social categories.[34] Once treated as firm and fixed, and representing objective groups, these social categories were presented as flexible and fluid. New cultural historians promoted an understanding of class as a discursive phenomenon and as a linguistic construct and questioned whether conceptions of class are exclusively grounded in either relations to the modes of production or the economic and social experience of the individual.[35] Historians of the late medieval and early modern periods have long recognized the problems with treating the nobility as firmly fixed and have been equally suspicious of applying strict concepts of class, Marxist or other, to the group.[36] Yet efforts to represent early modern society invariably return to social categories that require lengthy qualifications and caveats.

This study contributes to reconciling the tension between social history approaches to elites, which employ categories of social class or status as coherent groups, and cultural perspectives, which stress the discursive and rhetorical aspects of social identity.[37] To this end it explicitly addresses how individuals sought to claim status and construct and maintain identities of hidalguía in specific contexts, the constraints that limited these efforts, and the opportunities that allowed them. Sixteenth-century hidalgos did not form a unified socioeconomic class. Likewise, they did not constitute a sociolegal estate or order in the terms of medieval political theory. The diverse group of individuals and families that claimed this status generated or regenerated their social identity both in the courtroom and outside it. They did so by appropriating and reemploying discourses drawn from royal edicts, law codes, treatises on the nobility, and even—though infrequently—books of knighthood, to fashion acceptable narratives in royal appellate courts. They also achieved this end informally through the support of influential local social networks. Those who made claims to the status of hidalgo could not fashion themselves with the same freedom with which Renaissance novelists and dramatists created their characters. This study addresses not simply who claimed these identities and how they did so but, more significant, the social and political limits on the individual's ability to construct these identities and the material consequences these efforts had.

Furthermore, as an investigation of social contests and conflict that frequently required negotiation and accommodation, this study also contributes to efforts to define the limit and nature of royal authority and power in the early modern period, particularly during the transition from the Trastamara dynasty to the early Habsburg monarchs. Its treatment of contests over privilege and the Crown's role in them questions narratives about the modernizing central bureaucratic state, which is a key element of the conventional presentation of the development of absolutist royal rule in sixteenth- and seventeenth-century Spain. In this fashion the work builds on efforts to reevaluate and understand the Spanish monarchy by a wide range of scholars in the past decades and the corresponding efforts to reconcile the rhetoric of absolutism with the reality and practice of royal government.[38] These scholars have described the early modern Hispanic monarchy as characterized by the delegation of authority, institutional disaggregation, and systemic flexibility.

I. A. A. Thompson, Charles Jago, and José Ignacio Fortea Pérez have questioned older views of the relationship between the Crown and the Castilian parliament—the Cortes—that assumed a submissive assembly that readily accepted the demands of the monarchy.[39] They have emphasized the degree to which the representatives of the cities in Cortes pursued their own interests and required consent to new taxation, particularly as royal incomes declined in the late sixteenth century.[40] They have also argued for the importance of the councils as serious consultative bodies and repositories of authority that served to check the possibility of arbitrary and capricious acts by the king. From the perspective of Castile's thousands of municipalities, Helen Nader has described in detail the Crown's sale of local jurisdiction and autonomy to villages that created new towns and town councils. The royal provision of jurisdiction and political autonomy to these councils fostered an active local government at the municipal level and complex interactions and negotiations between local authorities and representatives of the royal government. Jack Owens has argued that in the realm of judicial administration, royal governments in sixteenth-century Castile were neither capable of nor interested in imposing administrative uniformity or obedience on a subject population through a monopoly of coercive force; instead, monarchs had to attract broad collaboration, which they sought to do by providing what contemporaries viewed as good government and justice. In her analysis of military recruitment in early modern Castile, Ruth MacKay reviewed not only the diverse forms of resistance to royal demands but also how these forms were part of the relationship between ruler and ruled in the early modern period. Localized opposition clothed in the rhetoric of obedience could prosper both because there was no administrative apparatus to curtail it and because there were political beliefs to legitimize it.[41]

As this wide range of scholars make clear, Castile and its empire were governed simultaneously from many sites, both in a geographic and jurisdictional sense. Among the participants in Castile's governance were local municipal elites, the seigneurial nobility, and a collection of courts and councils represent-ing the monarch. A wide range of authorities spoke in the king's name and claimed royal authority as his surrogates.[42] The multiple sites of authority medi-ated the course and resolution of conflicts over hidalgo status. Consequently, this study seeks to address disputes over hidalguía from the perspective of mul-tiple actors and levels of jurisdiction, including the negotiations between mon-archs and representatives to the Cortes, the deliberations and actions of Seville's city council, the strategies and arguments of individual litigants, and the inter-action of municipal councils with their own citizens and the myriad individuals and institutions that represented royal authority. Recognizing the importance of municipalities in the Crown of Castile's political organization, this work situ-ates both Castilian elites and disputes over hidalgo status in their municipal context rather than separate them from the political, social, and economic matrices in which they took place.[43] While the royal appellate courts played a fundamental role in the determination, and authorization, of status, they were not the sole or unchallenged arbiter one would assume them to be in an increas-ingly centralized and absolutist state.

Chapter 1 provides a general introduction to the genesis and nature of law con-cerning hidalgo status in medieval and early modern Castile and the late medi-eval practice of royal authorization of this status. The chapter focuses particularly on laws regulating noble privileges and the evolution of these laws until the end of the fifteenth century. Through a close treatment of the final years of Enrique IV (1454–74) and the reign of Isabel I (1474–1504), it analyzes the relationship between the political interests of the royal government and the granting and revoking of hidalgo status and privilege. Monarchs from the fourteenth century on used diverse qualifications to grant or deny status and privilege to recruit military troops, punish the disloyal, and maintain royal income. The chapter describes how these practices operated within existing legal and political con-texts, including rebellion against the Crown, dynastic struggle, and war against the Muslim kingdom of Granada. Moreover, it shows how royal actions autho-rizing and revoking status contributed to the articulation of new rules concern-ing privilege. Consequently, an examination of the interaction between the Castilian monarchs and the representatives to the Castilian parliament as they negotiated matters of privilege provides the context for these practices.

Royal statutes enacted in the Cortes provided prescriptive rules for the con-trol of privilege, but an examination of these statutes does not reveal information about the practice of controlling privilege or the resistance that claims to privilege faced at the local level. The second half of the chapter examines the practices of verification and confirmation of privilege employed during the reign of Isabel and Fernando, the last monarchs of Castile to make large-scale authorizations of the status of hidalgo.[44] During the reign of the Catholic Monarchs, many municipalities refused to recognize privileges for this status or refused to provide privileges to those who had received confirmation of their status from Isabel and Fernando or their predecessors. Royal grants often proved insufficient and required community acceptance. Paradoxically, on a general level, not only did the monarchs acquiesce to municipal resistance, they actually encouraged it, making use of this resistance to control the proliferation of privileges for their own ends. Rather than establishing a definitive and consistent set of rules for the recognition of privilege, Fernando and Isabel wished to reserve for themselves and their appellate courts the power to make the final decision about who could possess privilege. These monarchs elaborated legal procedures that provided local officials with the resources to deny claims to privilege in the first instance. This situation forced claimants to appeal to the royal government for verification of their status and thereby provided the royal government with the final say concerning the enjoyment of social privileges.

The second chapter shifts from a discussion of royal political practice to a discussion of hidalgo status in the city of Seville to highlight the local diversity of this status and demonstrate how changes in municipal fiscal and political regimes affected claims to hidalguía. Laws enacted in the Cortes often presented the legal "honors, freedoms, and exemptions" held by hidalgos as more or less universal throughout the Crown of Castile and ignored local variations. In similar fashion, demographic historians have described where there were greater or lesser numbers of hidalgos, but they have given less attention to where these hidalgos possessed privileges and where they did not, or what sorts of privileges they held in specific communities. In contrast to this kingdom-wide perspective, local historians of Castile's municipalities and historians of royal finances have repeatedly demonstrated that hidalgos and caballeros in different municipalities and localities did not possess the same general privileges.[45] Consequently, this chapter investigates the provision of privilege in the city of Seville and the changes in the local social designation of elite individuals and families through the sixteenth century.

In the early sixteenth century the municipal council revised the city's ordinances and thereby produced conditions that contributed to more frequent disputes over privilege and status. The city council of Seville made fundamental changes in the collection of the city's royal subsidy (*servicio*) and the requirements for public office. In this context legal privilege and status in Seville became increasingly intertwined. While the new laws and practices did not have an immediate effect on those in office, they eventually created a situation in which those who wished to enter or remain in the political elites of the city could be forced to litigate for the status of hidalgo. The change in the collection of the servicio introduced economic privileges, in the form of an exemption from taxation, into a community where none had previously existed. Despite the frequent reference to hidalgo tax exemption, no scholar has attempted to calculate the actual monetary value of this privilege in a concrete setting. This chapter not only quantifies the economic benefit of this exemption in the city of Seville but also examines the meaning of this exemption for the citizens of Seville and its relations to status and the holding of political power. In the process it demonstrates how claims to hidalguía related to the existing elites. Whether those who claimed this status were descended from genuine hidalgo lineages or not, both locals and new arrivals to the city began to appropriate this term as the most advantageous and authoritative designation for enjoying legal privileges.

Following the second chapter's review of the diversity of rules governing status and privilege in different municipalities and particularly how they were manifested in Seville, the third chapter addresses migration and resettlement as fundamental sources of conflicts over hidalguía. Political and legal identity and rights in early modern Castile were fundamentally rooted in municipal citizenship (*vecindad*), not in one's identity as a subject of a national community or kingdom. For the vast majority of Castilians the tangible legal privileges they possessed and the obligations they owed sprang from their municipality citizenship and not from being a subject of the Crown of Castile. Migration from one municipality to another required a change in one's citizenship or adoption of new citizenship and potentially distinct rights and obligations, depending on the local municipal charter (*fuero*) and ordinances. Resettlement also provided municipal councils with the opportunity to challenge hidalgo status and any accompanying privileges the status might convey in the particular community. Municipal councils viewed with hostility the claims made by new immigrants to possess extraordinary legal status and privileges, especially tax exemptions. The first section of the chapter reviews a selection of illustrative disputes over hidalgo status from outside Seville during the fifteenth and sixteenth centuries to demonstrate the pattern of reflexive municipal resistance to the hidalgo claims of new immigrants who descended from seemingly genuine hidalgo lineage or possessed authentic royal grants of status. The fortunes of these different families over multiple generations reveal that gaining recognition of hidalgo status and maintaining it was a continual process that regularly required new efforts when individuals resettled or established new households.

The second part of chapter 3 seeks to ground the fight for hidalgo status and privilege more thoroughly in the context of the unique demographic composition of the city of Seville through a presentation of the city's resettlement and specifically through a description of diverse migrants to the city in the fifteenth and sixteenth centuries. Of particular concern for future disputes are the consequences of the migration and settlement of certain conspicuous ethnic and social groups. The available sources make it impossible to determine with certainty the origin or genuine social status of the majority of those who variably came to enjoy the status of hidalgo or were forced to litigate for its recognition. Nevertheless, the city's tax records and surviving court litigation reveal a definable presence of native merchants from the Crown of Castile, as well as merchants of foreign origin, natives of the Basque territories, and the descendants of Jewish converts to Christianity among both those who litigated and those who enjoyed hidalgo status. Through a discussion of these distinct groups, the chapter traces their relative success in assimilating into the city's ruling elite and thereby positioning themselves to adopt the status of hidalgo in the sixteenth century. Simultaneously, the chapter addresses the degree to which the established descendants of members of these groups in the city and new arrivals in the sixteenth century came to engage in public disputes and litigation over claims to hidalguía.

Seville's city council challenged a broad range of claimants to hidalgo status, often with little or no knowledge about them. The city's resistance typically resulted in lawsuits adjudicated at the tribunal of the hidalgos at the royal chancery court in Granada. The fourth chapter shows how lawsuits of hidalguía during the sixteenth century ultimately served to limit the proliferation of privilege, by keeping out some newcomers and even weeding out those descended from long-standing hidalgo lineages who could not successively navigate the necessary rounds of litigation. A number of scholars have referenced these lawsuits and described the types of evidence litigants presented to substantiate their claims, but they have not provided a close analysis of the arguments the litigants, either claimants or municipal councils, made or how they made them.[46]

In the rhetoric of sixteenth-century legal disputes, there was an ongoing tension between two primary discourses concerning claims to privilege. One situated the rationale for privilege in service to the monarch, and the other justified privilege through claims to inherent qualities passed through blood. Lawyers in these disputes—arguing both for and against recognition—frequently appealed to an essentialist definition of hidalgo in their arguments and thereby strengthened the biological and racial aspects of this social status.

Regardless of the rhetoric used in these disputes and the evidence provided by the litigants, procedural factors in the lawsuits and the financial cost of litigation significantly impacted the success of the litigant. The chapter emphasizes that the burden of proof rested on the person claiming hidalgo status and the consequences this burden had for litigation. Municipal councils as defendants had a number of legal advantages. They could employ formulaic objections that then required the claimant to provide evidence of status. Litigation was expensive and grew increasingly lengthy as the century progressed, as municipalities employed the option of repeatedly appealing adverse rulings. As corporate bodies with legal experts perpetually on salary, towns and cities such as Seville had a decided advantage over even wealthy individuals or families who claimed hidalgo status.

The fifth chapter addresses how Seville's city council consciously and regularly ignored laws that defined who could enjoy the privileges of hidalguía when it proved to be in the interests of its members. Under the auspices of the city council, municipal officials provided tax refunds and the designation of hidalgo to individuals who belonged to or entered into the social networks of the dominant families of the city. During the second half of the century, the royal government periodically pressured the city to implement existing rules restricting office and privileges to hidalgos. These efforts culminated in 1583, when prosecutors at the chancery court of Granada charged dozens of the city's councilmen, their family members, and other prominent citizens with unjustly and fraudulently enjoying the status of hidalgo. This unusual initiative by the royal prosecutors dramatically revealed individuals who had obtained hidalgo status through informal means and assimilation into the city's ruling elites. The chapter examines the families charged by the prosecutor and the social networks and relations that facilitated the recognition of status. These networks and relations included marriage alliances between families, business partnerships, political patronage between members of the city council, and relations between city council officials and royal officials at court.

The sixth chapter addresses the chancery courts as the central institutions for the formal rendering of royal justice in disputes over hidalgo status and examines the courts' distinct officers and personnel and their interaction with municipal authorities. Although these different officials acted in the name of the king and with his authority, they performed distinct roles. The judges adjudicated disputes—including those involving Crown interests—and in their judicial capacity mediated potential conflicts between the royal government and municipal authorities. In contrast, royal prosecutors acted simultaneously as defenders of royal law and patrimony and as the agents for implementing royal policies. In this role they normally opposed individual claims to hidalgo status in tandem with municipal councils.

When royal prosecutors initiated charges of their own against citizens of Seville in the early 1580s, they dramatically disturbed the preexisting status quo between city and Crown. The charges made by the royal prosecutors challenged municipal and local prerogatives concerning de facto tacit power to provide hidalgo status to the city's ruling elite and their dependents and clients and generated an intense contest between officials at the chancery court and the city of Seville. The contest ended in the city's favor. For those denounced by the prosecutors, existing political relationships between the city and the royal government played a greater role in determining whether they maintained recognition of their hidalgo status than their actual descent or what existing laws said about the requirements for recognition of status. Throughout the conflict, royal prosecutors sought to apply laws restricting status as an effort to implement royal policy, but they also did so for their own personal economic interests. The second part of the chapter details the range and possibilities for malfeasance in the judicial system of sixteenth-century Castile and how such malfeasance influenced the initiation of lawsuits of hidalguía, their outcome, and the provision of justice in disputes over status.

Although fifteenth- and sixteenth-century Castilians at times used the term *hidalgo* to refer to a member of a set social group defined in terms of descent and a history of martial service, they also and more frequently used it in rhetorical claims to assert or deny the enjoyment of concrete legal privileges and enhanced social status. Employed in this fashion, the term in the early modern period had little to do with belonging to a group that exclusively engaged in military occupations, derived its economic well-being from seigneurial or landed properties, descended from established lineages, or shared chivalric values. Instead, the ability to gain recognition of this status, either through local acceptance or formal litigation, became a means to maintaining or acquiring economic privileges and access to political offices. Conversely, as a legal claim, recognizing or denying hidalguía served entrenched elites, municipal councils, and government officials as a means of resisting or controlling the provision of privilege.

THE CONSTITUTION OF PRIVILEGE:
ROYAL GRANTING, REVOKING, AND
RECOGNIZING OF HIDALGUÍA

In the fourteenth and fifteenth centuries the Crown of Castile, like other western European monarchies, experienced considerable political instability due to dynastic struggles and aristocratic revolts.[1] Both immediately and in the long term, these conflicts had profound consequences for efforts to gain recognition of hidalgo status. During these wars and in the periods of relative peace following them, Castilian monarchs created, or at least were later accused of creating, nobles, both caballeros and hidalgos. They also generated pronouncements, laws, and legal procedures intended to control their own provision of status. Thus not only did these monarchs contribute to disputes about who should legitimately be accepted as nobles, but they also armed local authorities with resources to resist the recognition of nobility.

Intense public debate about royal authorization of noble status reached a high point at the 1473 gathering of the Cortes of Castile and León. At the meeting of this assembly, the cities' representatives complained that the political conflicts of the previous decade and the subsequent juridical actions of Enrique IV (1454–74) had bred uncertainty in the determination of individual social and legal status.[2] This perceived uncertainty resulted from the royal practice of granting and confirming the status of hidalgo or hidalguía. The most notorious grants of hidalguía had occurred eight years earlier in 1465. In that year a faction of powerful magnates led by Alfonso Carillo, the archbishop of Toledo; Fadrique Enríquez, the admiral of Castile; and Juan Pacheco, the Marquis of Villena had initiated a revolt against Enrique's rule, symbolically deposing him in effigy at a ceremony in the city of Ávila and declaring his half brother,

Alfonso, the rightful monarch.[3] In response to this challenge, Enrique employed diverse means to muster military support and maintain his subjects' loyalty. As part of this effort, he issued letters providing favors (*mercedes*) to those who would come and fight on his behalf. These mercedes took many forms, including authorizations of hidalguía, which representatives at the Cortes later claimed made a commoner an hidalgo.[4] Although the petitions presented in the Cortes literally state that Enrique "made" hidalgos, the majority of the surviving chancery documents suggest that what he and his successors typically provided were authorizations of status in the form of judicial writs.

Essentially ignoring royal authority at the local level, other members of society, primarily the members of Castile's municipal councils, often refused in later years to recognize the hidalgo status of these and other claimants to hidalguía.[5] Despite the later infamy of Enrique's grants, such actions were not unique to his reign. The dual phenomena of royal grants of hidalguía and municipal resistance to them both preceded his reign and continued during the reign of the Catholic Monarchs, Isabel I (1474–1504) and Fernando V (1474–1516). More significant, acts of municipal resistance came to be carried out through appellate procedures developed by the monarchs themselves and with monarchical acquiescence. In effect, these monarchs with seemingly duplicitous intent granted status with one hand while with the other they developed juridical procedures and a legal system that could be used to resist these very grants. Local resistance to claims of hidalguía was a widespread phenomenon in the territories of the Crown of Castile during the reigns of Enrique IV and his successors, Isabel and Fernando.[6] This chapter examines how this resistance manifested itself in the city of Seville and its municipalities in the last decades of the fifteenth century.[7] Referred to in contemporary documents as the "kingdom [*reino*] of Seville," the city and its subject towns and villages constituted a major city-state and one of the principal reinos in the Crown of Castile. To understand the extent and nature of conflicts over the status of hidalgo and the role of the monarchs in these conflicts, this chapter focuses on the relevant actions and legal initiatives of Enrique IV and the Catholic Monarchs at the meetings of the Cortes and at the level of Castilian-wide politics as well as profiling disputes over status that took place at the village, town, and parish level in the territory of Seville.

Widespread conflicts over the recognition of hidalguía reveal how formal legal status in the Crown of Castile proved to be fluid and frequently indeterminate, particularly for the numerous members of the lower nobility who styled themselves hidalgos. Their unstable status resulted from the existence of diverse rules governing status and the existence of multiple sources for authorizing or recognizing it. Building on the work of historians of the late medieval period who have described how Castilian monarchs provided authorizations of hidalguía throughout the fifteenth century, this chapter addresses the resistance that royal actions engendered from the councils and citizens of Castile's municipalities.[8] In many instances these governing councils, or factions within them, ignored royal grants and confirmations and challenged individual and family recognition of status. The councils did not directly deny the monarch's right to authorize status itself but rejected the effort of the individual or the family to gain local recognition of the status and hence to enjoy privileges derived from it. Paradoxically, Castilian monarchs appear to have been complicit in this resistance. Isabel and Fernando's elaboration of legal procedures and their reform of the judiciary in regard to disputes over status suggest a deliberate policy to limit the proliferation of those who could claim hidalguía. Moreover, despite the existence of thousands of royal documents authorizing the status of hidalgo, Castilian monarchs possessed limited power to impose recognition of this status and its accompanying privileges at the local level and, in many cases, did not seek or desire to force implementation of their grants and confirmations. Despite their relative lack of interest in supporting their authorizations of status at the local level, they doggedly advanced their claim to the ultimate judicial authority in the determination of status at their appellate chancery courts in the event that disputes persisted.

Individual claimants and their families had straightforward incentives to gain formal royal recognition of hidalgo status. Throughout the late medieval and early modern periods, those claiming to be hidalgos frequently argued that their status conveyed the enjoyment of certain legal privileges. Significantly, existing laws and rules explicitly tied these privileges to the status of hidalgo and not to other higher ranks in the nobility. Despite assertions that hidalgos possessed such privileges, the actual practice of allowing the enjoyment of these privileges, whether economic or otherwise, varied considerably throughout Castile's municipalities.

In contrast to the individuals and families claiming hidalgo status who sought tangible benefits in the form of legal privilege, the Crown had complex and often conflicting reasons for seeing royal authorization of status either recognized or rejected. The divergent interests of the monarchy explain the royal government's ambivalent attitude toward its own largesse. With the rise in state expenditures in the late medieval period, accompanied by an increase in direct and indirect taxes, both municipal and royal authorities had a material interest in limiting a proliferation of individuals exempt from royal or communal taxes.[9] Depending on the community, hidalgo exemptions from taxation not only extended to royal taxes but could include municipal ones, especially as individual municipalities used diverse means to collect revenues to pay the servicio to the Crown.[10] As a means of reward, grants of hidalguía were attractive to monarchs because they were inexpensive in the short term, and, even with the proper supporting documentation, difficult for the grantee to gain recognition and enjoyment from in the long term. Moreover, in the late Middle Ages, royal claims to be able to provide and confirm the status of hidalguía served to buttress the monarch's political power. The provision and confirmation of status increased royal power precisely because of the conflicts these actions provoked, not despite them. As the primary mediator of these conflicts rather than immediate protagonists in them, the Crown secured recognition of its ultimate judicial authority in a significant facet of late medieval justice. Consequently, the equivocal support Castilian monarchs in the later Middle Ages gave to their own grants of privilege and status did not undermine their power and authority but actually served to increase it, especially as individual subjects and municipal councils broadly acknowledged the principle of Crown discretion and authority in reconciling conflicts over status that managed to arrive at the appellate courts.

NULLIFYING GRANTS AND THE UNCERTAINTY OF STATUS

Enrique IV has become the most notorious Castilian monarch for distributing grants of hidalgo status, but he did little more to deserve this notoriety than his predecessors or immediate successors. His notoriety on this score stems from his opponents' depiction of him as an ineffective, politically incompetent, and sexually impotent king and also from laws he was compelled to enact in response to his own grants. These laws had a significant legacy in the last quarter of the fifteenth century and throughout the sixteenth century as municipal councils used them to resist the efforts of their citizens to claim the status of hidalgo.[11] Nevertheless, Enrique's actions were similar in form and substance to the measures employed by other Castilian monarchs of the period. Monarchs from at least the fourteenth century had provided diverse royal favors, including recognition of the status of hidalgo or knight, to reward supporters and to encourage participation in royal campaigns. Significantly, almost the entirety of royal statutes produced at meetings of the Cortes concerning hidalgo status and its attendant privileges were formulated in periods of political conflict, when monarchs authorized hidalguía and then subsequently had to enact legislation to address the consequences of these favors.[12]

Enrique's moment of legislative activity came in the wake of a revolt by a faction of seigneurial aristocrats. After the rebels symbolically deposed Enrique on June 5, 1465, the king began sending a series of letters to the municipalities of the kingdom proclaiming favors for those who would recognize his rights to the Crown and fight on his behalf.[13] These mercedes provided a wide range of material and honorific remuneration.[14] Grants of hidalguía were only one class of these favors and not the most materially valuable. Consequently, they produced little in the way of public protest until another meeting of the Cortes could be called. Three years after the initial revolt, Enrique's half brother, Alfonso, the rebels' candidate for the throne, was dead from the plague, and the majority of cities and towns had declared themselves aligned with Enrique. With the changed political circumstances, the still influential rebels entered into negotiations with the king. While Enrique and the rebel leaders were concerned primarily with the designation of his successor and control of the royal council, the cities and towns of the kingdom were more troubled by the Crown's many grants of mercedes during the previous years.[15] Consequently, in the spring of 1469, the king, in desperate need of subsidies from the cities, took advantage of the recently terminated hostilities to call a meeting of the Cortes in the town of Ocaña.

Through the fifteenth century the Cortes operated primarily as an assembly for representatives from the cities and important royal towns (see map 1). Like similar institutions in other western European kingdoms, the Cortes facilitated the Crown's ability to secure tax subsidies and allowed municipal representatives to raise grievances and secure redress through the royal enactment of laws. Despite the rhetoric of the three estates typical of late medieval political discourse, the representatives to the Cortes did not gather in distinct groupings. The clergy and the nobility had limited presence in the institution, at least in the sense of advocates for a particular estate or order. Instead, important prelates served as members of the royal council and as spokesmen for the Crown to the representatives of the Cortes. In similar fashion, seigneurial aristocrats served on the royal council and their family members occasionally acted as representatives (*procuradores*) to the Cortes for the cities and important towns,

Map 1   The Crown of Castile in the fifteenth century

of which they themselves were citizens and often councilmen. This situation consequently led to a complex interweaving of the political and social interests of the high and middling ranks of the nobility and the councils of the dominant cities and towns in Castile. In the still tense and unsettled political situation of early 1469, six of the seventeen cities with voice and vote in the Cortes either withdrew their representatives from the meeting at Ocaña or refused to send them entirely.[16] Nevertheless, those municipalities that did attend sought to make Enrique's mercedes a central issue.

At the assembly Enrique had simultaneously to appease the representatives of the cities and towns and to avoid alienating loyal supporters whom he had provided with favors. The procuradores wanted the king to revoke the grants of lordship, which had removed communities from their political jurisdiction, and to undo his grants of hidalguía, which potentially reduced their tax revenues. The representatives appealed to the king to enact a general law in the Cortes that would deny the particular grants of privilege he had provided to individuals who had responded to his summons. Enrique responded that rebellion had forced him to provide these favors of hidalguía, but he now recognized the injustice of these mercedes and therefore declared all grants of the status of hidalgo presented since September 15, 1465, to be nullified.[17]

Despite the enactment of a general law revoking the mercedes at the Cortes, royal judges and magistrates either failed to apply the terms of the law or applied them inconsistently. Consequently, at the next meeting of the Cortes in Santa María de Nieves in 1473, the ailing king, still in a weak position politically, met renewed protests from municipal representatives that he had failed to implement the laws revoking his favors, especially the grants of hidalguía. Moreover, the representatives complained that "they knew and had seen through their own experience not only how he had ignored his promises, but also how he continued to give out similar privileges and favors." The representatives reported that when municipal councils, on the basis of the law enacted at Ocaña, refused to acknowledge the recipients' status and privileges, the recipients challenged their reading of the law in municipal and royal appellate courts. In these forums the recipients argued that the revocation applied only to those who had not really served. In response, the representatives denied this reading of the law and further asserted that the king and his officials lacked the necessary records to verify who and how many had genuinely served in the war: "and because of this uncertainty and to alleviate confusion, it is just and better that the few deserving compensation for their service should suffer than to leave exempt a great number that do not deserve such reward and deceitfully strive to obtain it through great treachery and prejudice to your majesty, reduction of royal taxes, and harm to the communities where they live and the poor and disadvantaged who live in them."[18] The king ultimately acquiesced to the demands of the representatives and sanctioned their interpretation of the law.

Both Enrique's original promises of the status of hidalgo and the representatives' response expressed an understanding of hidalguía as a status dependent on an individual's achievements and merit and not exclusively on blood or birth. This understanding reflected the royal practice of authorizing status in return for service that had become widespread during the previous century and a half. Significantly, the representatives did not deny the monarch's authority to make and consequently nullify such grants. In fact, the representatives' description of events and demands for justice readily accepted the monarch's ability and authority to confer and revoke such privileges and exemptions. Historians of Spanish law have described how monarchs in the High Middle Ages appealed to Roman and canon law to rearticulate the idea of the king as maker of laws and not simply the adjudicator of existing laws.[19] To achieve this end, Crown jurists rationalized the king's creation and nullification of laws as incumbent on furthering the "common good," even when monarchs issued legal pronouncements in the form of privileges that violated general laws. Consequently, as possible future beneficiaries of such individual or corporate privileges and favors, the representatives at the Cortes had tangible interests in acquiescing to such royal powers.

MULTIPLE LEGAL REGIMES

The representatives' petitions in the Cortes and Enrique's responses to them occurred in a complex legal environment. Parallel to royal grants of hidalgo status and apparently preceding them, there existed a long tradition of the local genesis and recognition of hidalguía. Enrique's juridical actions, both the authorizations of status and the enactments of laws in the Cortes, joined a diverse body of existing rules dealing with the recognition of hidalgo status and the granting and revoking of related privileges. Like other medieval kingdoms, the Crown of Castile had a multitude of legal regimes inscribed in diverse texts and local customs instead of a single systematized one. In addition to enactments of general law made in the Cortes (*leyes* and *ordenanzas*), there existed collections of judicial precedents (*fazañas*), local customs and practices (*costumbres* and *usos*), numerous municipal charters, and specific royal orders in the form of judicial writs and letters of privilege.[20] Produced with different intentions and often to serve particular ad hoc needs, these texts and rules provided a range of evolving positions on the status of hidalgo and the privileges tied to it.

Despite the diversity of legal pronouncements concerning hidalguía, historians of the Castilian nobility have emphasized certain texts that define various ranks within the nobility, giving little attention to others that often had more practical relevance. These historians most frequently cite the *Siete partidas*, a massive encyclopedic compilation of law commissioned by Alfonso X (1252–84). This source, however, poses significant problems for recreating late medieval attitudes and practices.[21] Produced in the late thirteenth century, the text does not appear to have been in use as a means for reconciling disputes until the sixteenth century, and even then jurists and judges used it in a contingent fashion, regarding it as subsidiary to existing charters and dependent on royal interpretation.[22] As an ideological work that advanced and emphasized the judicial and legislative preeminence of the monarch, the text minimized or ignored local custom and charters, imposing a standardized hierarchy on a complex social landscape.[23] Moreover, as a work that strove to achieve a comprehensive legal synthesis for all the territories controlled by the Crown of Castile, the *Siete partidas* sought to rationalize diverse local practices, laws, and even terminology. Relying on the *Siete partidas*, modern historians have defined an hidalgo as someone of noble birth and hidalguía as hereditary nobility acquired through one's lineage.[24] Beyond articulating this hereditary or racial component, the text did not seek to define a noble or the quality of nobility in the sense of essential characteristics or requisite criteria for possession. Similarly, the text did not address how hidalguía as a rank in the nobility could be acquired or lost, and, perhaps more important, it did not indicate what privileges, if any, came with this status.

In contrast to the *Siete partidas*, the compilation of law titled the *Fuero viejo de Castilla* provided late medieval and early modern claimants to status with some of the fundamental statements about privileges tied to hidalguía. In particular, the text provides the earliest assertions that *fijosdalgo/hijosdalgo* (the archaic forms of the word) possessed exemption from royal taxes and immunity from arrest or seizure of property for debt. Although the origin of the text is obscure, the extant version dates from the mid-fourteenth century. Compiled at the behest of Alfonso XI (1311–50), the text contains rules that may have originated as early as the eleventh century.[25] The *Fuero viejo* is a compilation of rules regulating the relationships between hidalgos and between persons of hidalgo status and Castilian magnates (*ricos omes*), of whom the king was the most powerful. In addition to laws derived from custom, the text contains numerous judicial precedents originating from rulings of the royal court and itinerant royal judges. Articulated in the Castilian frontier society of the eleventh and twelfth centuries, many of these rules arguably had become obsolete in the social and political conditions of the late fifteenth century.

Whether or not the majority of rules set out in the *Fuero viejo* continued to have any judicial consequence by the late Middle Ages, the brief passages concerning exemptions and freedoms made the text an attractive reference in claims to privilege well into the early modern period. The *Fuero viejo* recognized the exemption that royal monasteries, military orders, and hidalgos held from royal exactions and taxes (*pechos*). It also suggested that the economic benefits of this status were tied to service and merit and not to descent. It stipulated that an hidalgo who failed to fulfill his obligation to provide martial service to his lord not only had to repay his stipend but also had to pay double the amount he had received.[26] The text also provided a simple procedure for recognizing the legitimacy of a person's hidalguía in the event it was challenged. It stipulated that the person whose status had been challenged should provide five witnesses, three hijosdalgo and two farmers (*labradores*), or the reverse, to verify his or her claim. Other than a person's individual act of relinquishing the status, the *Fuero viejo* did not provide any grounds or criteria for granting or revoking this status by other parties, including the monarch. When read collectively, the rules included in the *Fuero viejo* suggest that the privileges of hidalguía resulted from military service and that community estimation, not the dictates of the monarch, provided the essential means to confirm one's social status.

More pertinent for the actual enjoyment of privileges based on the status of hidalgo were regional customs, municipal charters, and evolving municipal ordinances that stipulated local positions on privileges. In practice, diverse municipal fueros and ordinances created localized understandings of the connection between status and privilege, which varied considerably from the relationships articulated in compilations such as the *Siete partidas* and the *Fuero viejo*. The medieval fueros of some Castilian towns specifically sought to limit the privileges claimed by hidalgos.[27] Conversely, in certain towns and cities in Old Castile and León, all citizens possessed the status of hidalgo by virtue of their municipal citizenship and consequently any exemptions tied to the status were frequently ignored. In opposition to the commonplace historical assertion that all natives of the Basque provinces of Vizcaya and Guipúzcoa were hidalgos, Domínguez Ortiz argues that the pretension to universal hidalguía was an aspect of Basque resistance to the incursions of absolutism in the late sixteenth century.[28] Additionally, the citizens of the cities of Burgos in Old Castile and Toledo in New Castile held exemption from direct royal taxes, such as the servicio, by virtue of their municipal citizenship.[29] In contrast, many of the towns and cities in the regions of Andalusia and Murcia possessed charters or subsequent ordinances that required all citizens, regardless of their status as hidalgos or pecheros, to pay royal and municipal taxes.[30] Demographic studies of the distribution of hidalgos in the sixteenth century have revealed a greater presence in northern parts of the peninsula and fewer numbers in the south.[31] This distribution appears to have resulted from ordinances in the municipalities of Andalusia and Murcia that restricted the privileges that could be enjoyed by hidalgos and consequently limited interest in claiming the status in a public or formal manner.

Diversity of practice in the provision of privileges to hidalgos could even exist within the same jurisdiction. While the city of Seville denied hidalgos any exemptions from taxation until the early sixteenth century, many of its own subject towns and villages allowed exemptions to citizens who possessed hidalguía. From the late thirteenth century the cities and larger towns of the Crown of Castile produced ordinances with royal confirmation that restricted access to positions on the city council and created, or at least formalized, closed regimes composed of members of the dominant families. In the city of Seville this involved the eventual introduction of rules that designated half of the city council seats and certain offices to those citizens who were caballeros hijos-dalgo.[32] Conversely, small towns and villages within Seville's jurisdiction generally did not restrict access to municipal office based on social status.

Contrary to the presentation of hidalguía in the *Siete partidas*, which defined a racial nobility, the rationales provided in the Castilian parliament for granting and revoking hidalgo status reinforced discourses that linked privilege to service, merit, and maintenance of the commonwealth (*república*). These discourses were readily employed by the cities' representatives in their efforts to nullify Enrique's grants and came to be used by the Catholic Monarchs as means for controlling the numbers of hidalgos and encouraging their active service. Efforts to encourage service to the Crown preceded the Catholic Monarchs and can be seen in the laws concerning hidalgos enacted in the Cortes meetings of the fourteenth and early fifteenth centuries. Late medieval Castilian monarchs, particularly Alfonso XI, legislated privileges for hidalgos that sought to ensure their ability to provide military service. At the Cortes of Alcalá in 1348, Alfonso enacted a law that the military weapons, armor, and horses belonging to hidalgos could not be seized for debts.[33] He subsequently extended this privilege to provide hidalgos with immunity from imprisonment for debt. In addition to enacting laws beneficial to those who secured recognition of hidalgo status, late medieval Castilian monarchs periodically revoked or threatened to revoke the status of hidalgo and caballero from those who failed to provide service.[34]

Nevertheless, the emphasis on service as the basis of hidalgo privileges evident in the laws enacted through the Cortes meetings was not always consistent. The tendency to blend conceptions of hidalguía as both grounded in one's lineage and in military service is shown in the brief statements that addressed the possession of hidalguía by women. The law issued by Enrique III at the Cortes of Toro in 1398 reiterated that hidalgos should be exempt from contributing to the pecho and added that a widow who had been married to an hidalgo should continue to enjoy her husbands' "franqueza y hidalguía," provided she remained chaste and did not remarry.[35] Conversely, the law stipulated that if a woman who was an hidalgo (*hijadalgo*) in her own right should marry a man who was not an hidalgo she should pay the pecho while her husband lives, but if the husband should die then she should again enjoy freedom as an hijadalgo. The section on hijasdalgo suggested that the status accrued by a woman's ancestors passed to her by blood, but her enjoyment of this status and its associate privileges depended on her marrying a man possessing hidalguía. The law further implied that in the event she married a commoner, her status did not pass to their children. Through these stipulations, the law sought to limit the enjoyment of privilege to those who actively provided the monarch with military service.

Due to disputes over the recognition of status, especially status granted or authorized by Castile's monarchs, these same rulers also sought to introduce formal procedures to adjudicate status.[36] As early as 1371 Enrique II (1369–79) ruled that in disputes over the possession of hidalgo status the case should be determined by judges of the royal court and chancery, with a legal representative of the claimant's municipality and the royal prosecutor present. A subsequent law enacted by Enrique III (1390–1406) in 1398 at the Cortes of Toro provided the manner by which hidalgos could establish their status and the evidence that should be considered. Claimants should demonstrate that their father and grandfather had not paid the pecho. Presumably, this would be done through a review of the municipality's tax lists (*padrones*) or through testimony from local officials responsible for the collections, though such measures were not listed. Of great subsequent importance, the law provided individuals and municipal councils with the right to appeal rulings on the status of one of their citizens, but they had to do so before the judges of the hidalgos. The appointment of extraordinary judges to decide disputes over status and eventually the creation of a special tribunal at the chancery court appears to have resulted from growing disputes at the local level. Despite the creation of this tribunal, the continuing practice and resulting problems of local judges issuing rulings on status prompted Juan II (1406–54) to issue a law in 1447 declaring the status of hidalgos to be dependent exclusively on the ruling of chancery judges.[37] In the event of a dispute, rulings by local judges would be invalid.

Nevertheless, on the eve of Isabel's reign few other procedural rules had been articulated, and judging from the haphazard manner with which complaints were brought to the Crown and adjudicated, those in place were not necessarily followed in a consistent fashion, especially in times of political instability. For example, in 1477 the council of Trujillo protested the confirmation of hidalguía provided two years earlier to Alvar Sánchez and his three brothers on the grounds that Isabel had not appointed the judges of the city's appellate court who had ruled on the case and that the court had not been properly reformed.[38] Left unsaid was the fact that the town had been controlled at the time by one of the monarchs' fiercest opponents, Juan Pacheco, the Marquis of Villena. Moreover, the council alleged that the brothers had paid the judges "45 doblas" for a favorable sentence. Even after the political instability of the late 1470s came to an end, the multitude of legal pronouncements, laws, and favors provided petitioners and courts alike with ample legal precedent and resources for diverse arguments both for and against the validity of individual claims to possession of hidalguía.

The disputants who made these arguments about hidalgo status found ready models in treatises of the period. The fifteenth century proved to be a fertile time for the production of written works debating questions concerning nobility, knighthood, and chivalry. This literary production arose from diverse sources: efforts to grapple with the realities of social mobility experienced throughout Europe, as individuals and families moved into and out of the ranks of the dominant elites; and the impact of new intellectual perspectives, as Renaissance humanists and those they influenced read and were inspired by the historical, ethical, and juridical works of the ancient world.[39] The authors of these works debated the relative claims of letters versus arms and birth versus achievement. Diego de Valera's vernacular treatise *Espejo de verdadera nobleza* (Mirror of true nobility) revealed the range of contemporary positions on nobility and how they intersected with the legal and political realities in Castile.[40]

Valera's view of the nobility was grounded not simply in the reading of diverse abstract or theoretical works on the subject but in a lifetime of interactions with nobles from the lowest ranks to the most eminent rulers. The son of a physician, Valera managed to climb from relatively humble origins to be an honored knight and official for three successive monarchs, Juan I, Enrique IV, and finally Isabel I.[41] Although his father's ancestry is uncertain, his mother descended from hidalgos in the city of Cuenca, and her family had important connections with prominent títulos. Through these noble patrons Valera came to serve as a page at the royal court of Juan II. At the age of nineteen he participated as a squire in the 1431 royal campaign against the Muslim kingdom of Granada. In the following years Valera distinguished himself as a true knight-errant, fighting with other Spaniards on behalf of the Holy Roman Emperor against the Hussites in Bohemia. He would also serve on diplomatic missions to the Burgundian and Danish courts for Juan II.

Produced in the last years of Juan's reign, Valera's *Espejo de verdadera nobleza* described the different types of nobility, their origin, and how or whether one could attain and lose nobility. In this discussion he explicitly equated what he called civil or political nobility with what in the Castilian vernacular was called hidalguía. The sources for civil nobility included both one's lineage and royal grants of dignities and office. In this manner—and contrary to the *Siete partidas*—he acknowledged that some hidalgos legitimately obtained their nobility through the favor of their lord or monarch. This occurred when one through virtuous acts obtained dignities and honor from a prince; such dignities thereby made the recipient noble. Moreover, Valera expressed criticism of those who claimed hidalguía from their lineage alone without following noble customs. Citing the jurist Bartolus de Saxoferrato (1313–51), he acknowledged that by common law, nobility derived from lineage lasts to the third generation for those who may be born noble but are not held to be so.[42] But this limitation on transfer of nobility did not apply to kings, dukes, counts, or others, who from the dignity of their office or title derived nobility.

His sole mention of disputes over hidalguía appeared in an unfavorable comparison of nobility in Spain with that of other countries, in which he further criticized contemporary Castilian practices for determining status:

> In Germany nobility lasts as long as the nobles live "honestly" without meddling in base jobs; in Italy all legitimate descendants of nobles are nobles until they sink into poverty. These matters are the least refined in Spain, especially in Castile, where even if they are bastards who have not been legitimized by the prince, or even if they have sunk into base occupations, or are the least adorned with good customs, as they should be, yet

for the most part everyone allows them to be *hidalgos* as long as they can prove that their fathers and grandfathers were exempt from taxation.[43]

In this passage Valera objected to the formal recognition of a person's status, and consequently the privileges tied to this status, on the exclusive basis of the family's past possession of privileges. Valera asserted that hidalguía should be closely tied to the ideal of knighthood and legally required "good customs," understood as continued activity in accord with knightly status as defined in such texts as the *Siete partidas*. Although individuals in his day gained recognition of their status in the manner he described as spurious, to do so, he claimed, actually violated the laws, "which require that nobility should be lost as a result of bad customs, base occupations, or defective birth."[44]

PROCEDURES FOR CONFIRMING AND VERIFYING STATUS

The dynastic struggle following Enrique's death and the subsequent war against the kingdom of Granada (1482–92) led to additional monarchical actions that further complicated the laws on hidalguía and the legitimacy of claims to hidalgo status. The issue of succession, one of the major sources of conflict through the second half of Enrique's reign, remained contested at his death on December 12, 1474. The ensuing conflict between his daughter Juana and her betrothed, Afonso V (1448–81), king of Portugal, and their opponents, Enrique's half sister, Isabel, and her husband, Fernando of Aragon, led both sides—but particularly the eventual victors—to imitate Enrique's earlier promises of reward for support and loyalty.

In addition to recognizing the legitimacy of some of Enrique's nullified grants and confirmations of hidalguía, Isabel and Fernando also threatened to revoke the status of hidalgo from those who failed to support them and from those who neglected their martial obligations. For instance, Isabel confirmed the status of Alfonso Fernández Jimón, a citizen of the village of Frexno in the jurisdiction of León, who had been made an hidalgo by a "letter of privilege" from Enrique in 1465.[45] In contrast, she threatened to revoke the hidalguía of Lope Vásquez de Cabreja and other citizens of Cuenca unless they provided martial service.[46] In 1475, as challenges to her succession began to mount, Isabel issued letters promising to confirm the status and privileges of those who had served Enrique IV if they served her at their own cost.[47] Through this promise the queen seemingly overturned the laws enacted and interpreted by Enrique at the Cortes meetings of Ocaña in 1469 and Santa María de Nieves in 1473. Although the queen's promises explicitly referenced those individuals who previously had served Enrique, the letters provided an opportunity for ambitious individuals who had not fought for Enrique to now provide service and claim hidalgo status for themselves. Likewise, families that had attained local recognition of hidalguía in the past treated the call as a welcome opportunity to formally confirm and maintain their status.

Isabel's pronouncements and subsequent juridical actions produced an almost immediate opposition from municipal representatives at the Cortes of Madrigal in 1476. Not surprisingly, the representatives cited the law enacted by Enrique in 1473 at Santa María de Nieves to deny the validity of Isabel's promises to confirm status. Moreover, they claimed that the new confirmations had led to further conflicts between municipalities and their citizens.[48] In response Isabel acknowledged that she had issued letters confirming some of Enrique's grants, but she had issued them to those who faithfully had fought for her or provided her with significant funds during the war. She ordered that these individuals should continue to possess their hidalgo status as long as they maintained the martial trappings of a knight, specifically a horse worth at least 3,000 *maravedís* and arms worth 1,000 *maravedís*.[49] Seemingly, not only did this pronouncement quash the laws enacted by Enrique, but in the event that would-be hidalgos who had received letters of confirmation failed to comply with this criterion, it nullified the very confirmations Isabel had issued only a year earlier.

While still battling domestic revolt and Portuguese incursions into Castilian territory, the new monarchs sought to implement the measure. Two months after the Cortes, on November 2, 1476, Isabel sent a letter to the municipalities of Castile, ordering them to announce to hidalgos living in their communities that they had to confirm their status formally. The law she now enacted required those who desired confirmation to provide continued service to her as rightful ruler and to attend a military muster to secure necessary documentation of this service. Presumably, with the proper letters of confirmation these hidalgos could enjoy their status, but lacking them, the laws enacted by Enrique would apply. The order directed these individuals to present themselves before royal magistrates within the next three months to confirm their privileges. If they should fail to do so, the letter informed them that they would revert to being common taxpayers.[50] The regulations and procedures the Catholic Monarchs elaborated in 1476 constituted a conscious attempt to limit the number of hidalgos. Only those with the necessary letters of proof, that is, those who had loyally served in the recent war, could receive the letters of confirmation. Additionally, the deadline removed those who lacked the means or initiative to press their claims through attending the muster.

Despite the legislative efforts of the Catholic Monarchs, the limited nature of the royal government, which effectively lacked a bureaucracy, and the delegated manner of tax collection made direct Crown regulation of status not only impossible but unnecessary. In fact there is little evidence that Isabel and Fernando actively sought to implement the law or that they required adherence to it. They ultimately left the policing of status to the local municipal governments. Efforts to revoke status during these years continued to originate from the initiatives of municipal councils or local citizens rather than the preemptive actions of the Crown.[51] This was especially true once the hostilities with Afonso of Portugal ceased.

Efforts to implement the law and require service from hidalgos—both new and old—resumed with the monarchs' war against the Muslim kingdom of Granada. In November 1484, in preparation for the following year's spring campaign, Fernando issued a general summons including specific mention of hidalgos created by Enrique and Isabel.[52] Despite earlier requirements that hidalgos should serve at their own cost, the king promised payment for their service as an added inducement for participation in the campaign. He supplemented this promise of rewards with threats and ordered municipal governments not to recognize the exemptions and privileges of those who failed to serve and thereby did not receive the necessary letters of confirmation.

Four years later, during the siege of the strategic city of Baza in the summer of 1489, the Catholic Monarchs followed through on their demands and sought to forcibly induce Seville's city council members and its other hidalgos to participate in the campaign.[53] While some of these men ignored the summons, others made a brief appearance at the siege but deserted within a month. Consequently, Isabel contacted the Crown's chief magistrate in Seville (*asistente*) and directed him to begin actions against the recalcitrant and the deserters. She ordered him to penalize them with loss of office and exemptions. The officer reported to the queen the presence of numerous deserters in the city and declared his concern that the great number of those who had returned without permission made it impossible for him to send them all under guard and by force to the front. In response, Isabel directed him to apprehend and bring those whom he felt were most guilty and those who would best serve as an example to deter any future challenges to royal commands.[54]

The Catholic Monarchs' legal pronouncements and actions concerning hidalguía during the war of succession and the subsequent conquest of Granada repeatedly sought to tie the enjoyment of privileges associated with status to service to the Crown. Regardless of whether they intended to apply these pronouncements, they faced significant logistical problems in implementing mechanisms for confirming service, punishing noncompliance, and validating legitimate claims to status. More significant, as with Enrique's laws, the legal efforts of the Catholic Monarchs contributed to local disputes that persisted for decades, if not longer. After the capitulation of the kingdom of Granada in 1492 and after a decade and a half of responding to disputes over the status of hidalgo, the Catholic Monarchs issued an edict (*pragmática*) to their chancery court officials outlining the procedures to govern the adjudication and determination of claims to this status.[55] This edict, referred to subsequently as the Pragmática de Córdoba, essentially left the policing of status to the local municipal authorities in the first instance, while providing the chancery judges with criteria for determining status in the event of appeal.

LOCAL RESISTANCE IN THE LATE FIFTEENTH CENTURY

At the meetings of the Cortes the cities' representatives did not directly oppose the legitimacy of the Crown's authorization of hidalguía. Instead, municipal councils typically refused to recognize the status of hidalgos at the local level, effectively preventing the claimants from enjoying tangible privileges. These councils made use of the uncertainty created by the grants of hidalguía as a rationale to deny the status of new recipients of hidalguía as well as the status of those from established hidalgo lineages. Statutes enacted by Castilian monarchs—both Enrique's laws revoking grants of hidalguía and the Catholic Monarchs' laws requiring service and confirmation to maintain hidalguía—provided municipal councils with the necessary pretext for refusing recognition of status. Perhaps more significant, these laws and subsequent procedural rules shifted the burden of proof and litigation to the claimant. Even as Castile's municipal councils resisted the recognition of hidalgo status and the easy enjoyment of accompanying privileges, the Catholic Monarchs elaborated procedures of appeal that

served their own interests and those of municipal councils in limiting the proliferation of privilege.

Conflicts over status that erupted during the late fifteenth century reveal
that many of those claiming hidalgo status, and seemingly with good cause,
often had to engage in multiple rounds of disputes with municipal councils,
both within a single generation and over multiple ones (see map 2).[56] During
the reign of the Catholic Monarchs, surviving documents reveal at least seventy-
three separate conflicts concerning hidalgo status taking place in the city and
subject municipalities of Seville alone.[57] Since these conflicts typically involved

Map 2   Municipalities in the territory of Seville with disputes over hidalgo
status, 1475–1506

multiple members of a single family or of related families, the total number of litigants was much higher. For instance, in a case concerning contested status from the town of Alcalá de Real in 1502, the clerk recorded that twenty-seven of the town's citizens had entered a dispute with the council claiming to be knights and hijosdalgo.[58] In this case, and in many like it, the claimants were often relatives connected through blood or marriage and consequently constituted significant factions within their own communities.[59]

Municipal resistance to hidalgo status in these disputes took two forms: the denial of privileges and appeals against authorizations made by the Crown. As we have seen, the process of formal appeals to overturn royal rulings concerning status predated Isabel and Fernando, but the procedural rules for such disputes remained unclear even at the time of their succession. Nevertheless, evidence that the Catholic Monarchs sought to regularize these procedures can be seen early in their reign, even as they fought to maintain their hold on the Crown. In 1476, the village council of Alanis in the territory of the city of Seville demanded that eight of its citizens, six men and two women, contribute in the community's pechos and other taxes, which they had refused to do.[60] At the ambulatory royal court in the town of Toro, the plaintiffs' advocate explained that his clients and their ancestors were all publicly known hidalgos, as the letter of privilege he presented described at length. He recounted that ever since the late king Enrique had died, the village council had tried to violate their freedoms as hidalgos because they had failed to confirm their privilege. According to the advocate, the council rejected their status to force them to pay taxes and deny them use of the village's commons. On December 9, 1476, after reviewing the documentation presented by these citizens of Alanis, the monarchs found in favor of the petitioners and ordered the council to acknowledge their exemptions and rights. Furthermore, the king required the council to return any securities or property it might have seized from these citizens. The royal clerk set the customary penalty of 10,000 maravedís for anyone who failed to comply with the royal writ.

Despite this seemingly unequivocal order, a formulaic clause at the end of the letter provided the possibility for further resistance by the council. This clause explicitly allowed the municipal council the right to contest and appeal a royal ruling recognizing hidalgo status in the event that the community had additional grounds to object.[61] Present in letters and writs through the late 1470s, the clause became a standard component of royal documents concerning the recognition of hidalguía in the following two centuries. Significantly, in this case and others, the clause provided the municipality with the right to contest a ruling even after royal review of the claimant's evidence. Although the writ specified a deadline by which the village council had to respond, the council did not have to produce evidence against the claim but only notify the court that it objected. In many cases in which the plaintiffs had not previously presented evidence, the burden of proof now fell on them rather than the municipal council.

Like almost all litigants who claimed to possess hidalguía, these citizens of Alanis did not allege a moment at which they had been granted the status. Instead, they stated that they were publicly known to be hidalgos and that the town had moved against them only because they had failed to gain confirmation from Isabel and Fernando after Enrique's death. The charges suggest that the town officials either expected them to get this confirmation or were using the fact that they had not provided service to the new monarchs as a rationale to deny or deprive them of privilege. Whether the claims to status were based on legitimate grounds or not, the council's refusal to recognize status and its citizens' responses to this resistance suggest local conflicts in which the disputants strategically used decrees and laws enacted in the Cortes to their own advantage against rivals. Not surprisingly, both sides in these disputes did so regardless of actual descent or actual service.

In part, the nature and form of the so-called grants of hidalguía contributed to the confusion and difficulty contemporary authorities encountered, and modern historians continue to face, in determining the exact status of these individuals. Although historians often refer to royal letters of privilege and favor as grants or patents of hidalguía, they were almost never addressed to the individual on whom they bestowed social status or privilege.[62] Instead, these grants were typically judicial writs stating that the monarch or the royal court had judged or recognized a person or persons to be hidalgos. The writs informed municipal councils—specific ones and generically those of the kingdom of Castile—and tax collectors and tax farmers that the individual in question was an hidalgo and should enjoy whatever privileges, honors, freedoms, and exemptions that other hidalgos held.[63] Whether or not the Crown was recognizing the person as an hidalgo for the first time, the documents presented the individual and his family as already holding this status. The distinction between concessions (first-time grants) and confirmations is primarily the result of the language used in the acts of the Cortes, which refers to the king as creating hidalgos and is not based on contemporary documents that authorized the status.[64]

Although Castilian monarchs occasionally provided favors that literally transformed the status or estate of the individual, such acts were rare and required them to invoke their absolute powers to contravene existing laws. The Catholic Monarchs provided just such a privilege in 1477 to Sancho Gonçáles Trapero, a citizen of the city of Seville, as reward for his loyal service. Given the occupational title Trapero (rag monger), which served as his second surname, either Gonçáles himself or one his ancestors had been a dealer in used cloths. The document explicitly stated that the royal favor ennobled (*sea noblecido*) Gonçáles by making him an hidalgo.[65] In making the grant, the monarchs called on their absolute royal authority to accomplish the deed.[66] Significantly, the document recognized the monarchs' violation of common law and custom by anticipating possible objections to the grant. The letter stated that the action should be valid despite any law or edict that declared that letters of hidalguía should not be given to anyone or that stated that in the event they are given they should not be valid.[67] These clauses reveal an explicit acknowledgment of contending legal authorities originating from the Crown itself and provide evidence of the tensions between general legal pronouncements and documents that stated exemptions to these pronouncements.

Not surprisingly, given this legal environment, in many of the disputes between local authorities and would-be hidalgos, genuine textual proof of royal service proved insufficient to avoid local resistance, and claimants often required additional court orders. In the case from 1477 referenced in the introduction, the royal court ordered the city of Seville and the town of Gerena to recognize the hidalguía of Pedro Rodríguez Gijón.[68] The order confirmed that Rodríguez had recently served in the war against Afonso of Portugal and consequently had provided the service demanded by the Catholic Monarchs. Additionally, he had produced a letter testifying to his service and documents of his family's status as hidalgos. Like the citizens of Alanis, Rodríguez explicitly claimed that his family had been in possession of hidalguía long before the recent conflicts and that he should have his possession respected. In this instance, it appears that Gerena, like many other municipalities in the late fifteenth century, used the mass nullification of the grants from Enrique's legislation to deny those who had been recognized as such for generations. This resistance occurred despite Rodríguez's possession of legal documents supporting his claims. Presumably, failure to produce either evidence of service or documents and testimony supporting his family's status as hidalgos would have kept him from securing royal recognition and allowed the council to continue denying Rodríguez any accompanying privileges.

Similar municipal resistance in the face of supporting royal documentation of status occurred repeatedly in cases of claims to hidalguía. In 1485, multiple citizens of the village of Zufre faced opposition from their council despite possessing a wealth of documentation, including letters of privilege, a court ruling, and certificates of service in the war of succession and the ongoing war in Granada.[69] It was during this year that Isabel and Fernando mounted a major offensive to capture the towns, particularly Ronda, which provided a ring of defense for the Muslim port city of Málaga, a crucial link to the Maghreb. The offensive led to the first general call-up of Castile and extraordinary levies to finance the campaign, which subsequently produced disputes over status.[70]

These cases suggest that without periodic efforts to maintain one's status through royal service and formal reconfirmation of status, an individual's and a family's hidalguía could be denigrated or ignored by local authorities. Those who wanted to avoid the loss of their status had to actively maintain it and engage in preemptive efforts to secure evidence to support their claims. Such efforts occurred repeatedly in the mountain town of Fregenal during the reign of the Catholic Monarchs. This frontier municipality was situated in the Sierra of Aracena northwest of Seville and in an area of Portuguese military incursions during the late 1470s. In October 1477, immediately following the succession struggle and war with Afonso of Portugal, the sons of two of the town's hidalgos, or so they claimed their fathers had been, sought reconfirmation of privileges their families had received from Juan II and from Enrique IV. In their petition, the descendants of Gonzalo Ferrándes Campón and Ferrando Rodrígues Campón insisted that the privilege from Enrique IV was itself a confirmation of earlier confirmations, and not a new grant of status.[71] Despite obtaining the royal court's authorization of their status in 1477, members of these families continued to face resistance from the local council. In 1484, the Crown again had to order Fregenal's council to recognize the status of the members of these related families. In the dispute that preceded this order, the claimants produced evidence in the form of judicial records. Their fathers had been forced to initiate a lawsuit before the judges of the hijosdalgo during the reign of Juan II some fifty years earlier. At that time the judges had given them a favorable ruling and provided them with an executive writ against the council. In 1484, they also presented the letters they had received from Isabel and

Fernando seven years earlier. The plaintiffs stated that the council had respected these letters until recently, when the monarchs had ordered an extraordinary levy to support the siege of the city of Málaga. The town officials had required them to contribute in this levy, claiming that on the orders of the monarchs themselves, "in those things pertaining to the war, everyone—both the exempt and the non-exempt—should pay."[72]

In the case of extraordinary forms of taxation, especially when first introduced, municipal councils did not always observe privileges derived from hidalguía, or they used such situations as an opportunity to ignore hidalgo status. In the case of the Malagan levy, the city of Seville had obtained the Crown's approval to disregard the exemptions held by the hidalgo citizens of its subject towns and villages. This royal sanction was the result of an appeal made by the city a year earlier. Seville's council had petitioned the Crown, protesting the fact that some of the wealthiest citizens of the city and its territory claimed to possess privileges exempting them from the levy, and consequently the Crown's demands weighed heaviest on the poor.[73] In their response to the petition, the monarchs justified the violation of tax exemptions by citing the holy nature of the war and the fact that in other places where there were similar privileges everyone was contributing to the war effort. They then empowered Seville's council to require all those with such liberties and privileges to pay in the levy. Magistrates in Fregenal subsequently used this general order to ignore the privilege of exemption held by the Ferrándes Campón and Rodrígues Campón families, which had been repeatedly confirmed by the royal government. Importantly, such forced exactions set precedents that a family had contributed in taxation, an important criterion for determining status throughout the sixteenth century. During the next two decades, at least five other disputes occurred in Fregenal over recognition of hidalgo status, each involving distinct families. These disputes prompted the Catholic Monarchs to issue another letter to the town in 1489, ordering it to respect the exemptions of known hidalgos.[74]

As in the previous case, the antiquity of the family's possession of hidalguía often failed to deter the municipal council from denying them the enjoyment of privileges. In 1485, a number of municipal councils in the territory of Seville refused to recognize the status of multiple related families who held citizenship in Seville itself and the city's subject villages of Cortegana, La Nava, Bodonal, Higuera, and Cumbres Mayores. The families claimed possession of hidalgo status extending back in time to before the reign of Pedro I (1350–69). Related to what was most likely the Malagan levy of 1484 that provoked disputes in Fregenal, the city of Seville ordered all citizens of these subject municipalities to pay the royal tax. When the council of Cortegana seized property from one of the families, which had refused to contribute, the family appealed the matter to the Crown. The family's representative, Diego López, told the court how his great-great-grandfather, Ferand Pérez de la Nava, had been forced to litigate before Pedro's judge of the hidalgos when his municipal council had refused to recognize his status. This long-dead ancestor had won his suit and secured supporting documentation from the royal notary for the province of Andalusia. López also claimed to have letters of privilege from Juan II and Enrique IV ensuring the recognition of this ruling.[75] In the first case of the families' recorded litigation—during Pedro's reign—and the most recent one under the Catholic monarchs, royal officials had produced documentation as a result of municipal resistance, but these documents proved insufficient to restrain subsequent challenges. In the disputes from Seville's subject towns and villages we repeatedly find multigenerational efforts to gain or maintain recognition of status as well as resistance to these efforts.

These cases reveal repeated resistance not only to those who supposedly had received recent grants of status but also to those with long-standing and seemingly legitimate claims based on descent from established hidalgo lineages. The municipal councils and even local citizens made strategic use of royal decrees and pronouncements to resist claims to status. In addition to these legal actions, changes in royal and local mechanisms for gathering taxes and levies provided local authorities with opportunities and rationales for resisting claims to status.

Late medieval Castilian monarchs used diverse means to recruit military forces, punish the disloyal, and maintain royal income, including authorizing and revoking hidalgo status and its associated privileges. These actions and the disputes they generated led to demands in the kingdom's parliament for laws to regulate status and provided an impetus for elaborating legal procedures for its determination. Nevertheless, the monarchs of the late fifteenth century did not attempt to harmonize the diversity of laws governing privilege. Instead, they sought to hold the position of ultimate arbiter of the law. They held an interest in perpetuating a situation of legal uncertainty that provided them both with a rationale for being, as the final provider of justice, and with disputes they could exploit for their own ends. Moreover, through judicial procedural reforms these monarchs not only acquiesced to municipal resistance against those claiming hidalgo status but actually encouraged it. By doing so they limited the ability of Castilians to successfully claim privileges and thereby maintained the number of those subject to taxation.

Castilian monarchs throughout the late Middle Ages repeatedly seized on the role of authorizer and adjudicator of status. By the end of the fifteenth century Fernando and Isabel did not simply enact laws concerning status on the populace. During the war of succession and again during the war against the kingdom of Granada, they recognized the status of supporters whose grants of hidalguía had been previously revoked by their predecessor Enrique IV, effectively violating royal laws established in the Cortes. Through their recognition of status by mercedes they contravened existing laws and employed their absolute powers as monarchs. Just as they invoked the public good to violate earlier laws when it proved expedient, they repeatedly responded to local disputes concerning status and in some cases abrogated their own grants. The exercise of royal power in this manner reveals another area in which absolutist doctrines came to be accepted through their practical application. In the context of late medieval Castile, such actions further enhanced royal judicial power. These monarchs in fact strengthened their political position by creating the potential for disputes that they claimed the authority to adjudicate.

Nevertheless, the Crown's practice of granting and revoking concessions of status and its negotiation with local authorities over these grants suggest that neither these monarchs nor their contemporaries viewed royal authorizations of hidalguía as absolute or sufficient in themselves. For monarchs, mercedes of hidalguía constituted only one form of reward for supporters who participated in royal military campaigns or remained loyal to the Crown in times of civil conflict. Castilian monarchs also provided grants of royal annuities (*juros*) to important supporters and paid stipends to others. For recipients, royal grants and confirmations served as a means or resource for claiming status. Nevertheless, they were not the only authoritative sources for claiming hidalguía, nor were they unchallengeable. A grantee also had to gain or maintain local recognition of status, which in the face of resistance meant recourse to the monarchs themselves or to the royal appellate courts.

Regardless of the monarch's authorization of status, the enjoyment of privilege in the first instance depended on local recognition and local norms for most of the fifteenth and sixteenth centuries. Compilations of medieval law, such as the *Fuero viejo de Castilla*, presented hidalgo privileges, at least within the boundaries of the realm, as universal.[76] In the Crown of Castile, however, the enjoyment of privileges based on the status of hidalgo and the meaning of the status itself varied significantly between communities. Local practices and rules affected whether a person could or could not enjoy privileges and the exact nature of these privileges. When citizens attempted to claim privileges based on the status of hidalgo that their community did not observe or chose not to provide, they provoked conflicts with local authorities, which increasingly led to the royal appellate courts. Such appeals provided frequent opportunities for the exercise of royal power. Whereas the Catholic Monarchs could not guarantee that local authorities would always accept their authorizations of hidalgo status, they gained a broad acceptance of the Crown as judicial mediator when conflicts over status arose.

2

THE ECONOMIC AND POLITICAL VALUE OF STATUS

The debates at the meetings of Castile's Cortes and the laws enacted at these assemblies concerning the Crown's granting and revoking of hidalgo status reveal little about what possession of this status meant at the local level. Prior to the year 1515, hidalgos in the city of Seville enjoyed no special economic privileges in the form of tax exemptions. Although municipal ordinances reserved certain seats on the city council for hidalgos, there were no rules prohibiting pecheros from holding even the highest council offices. While the dominant elite families of the city controlled these offices, this elite was not itself a closed group. Individuals from diverse backgrounds had entered and exited this dominant group throughout the fourteenth and fifteenth centuries.[1] The absence of formal privileges tied to hidalgo status ended in 1515, when the city—with the approval of the royal government—instituted seemingly mundane but ultimately contentious and conflict-producing changes in its tax regime. At this time it abolished the existing direct property tax (*pecho*) used to pay the servicio to the Crown and replaced it with a single excise tax (*sisa/imposición*), for which hidalgos and clergy were exempt. Within months of instituting these fiscal changes, the council also introduced formal prohibitions against common taxpayers holding any of the major political offices on the city council, exclusively reserving them for those the city recognized as hidalgos.

In subsequent decades both long-established and recent citizens of the city—whether they descended from hidalgo lineages or not—sought to identify themselves as hidalgos, because recognition of this status became formally tied to the enjoyment of economic and political privileges. Thus, concern with maintaining or acquiring recognition of the social status of hidalgo shifted with the evolution of local fiscal structures and political norms of the city. The reform of the servicio also provided the council with greater control over the provision of privilege, as its officers now directly oversaw exemption from the excise tax and consequently control over public recognition and institutional documentation of status. The city council, or factions within it, with growing frequency denied recognition of hidalgo status to local rivals, opponents, and new citizens, forcing them to initiate lawsuits, and in doing so sought to restrict the enjoyment of economic privileges and limit potential access to political office.

The sixteenth-century historian and native son of Seville Luis de Peraza likened his city's council to the Senate of Rome and its members to the patrician elders who presided over the ancient republic (see fig. 1).[2] As a veritable city-state with governing authority not only over the populace of the largest city of early sixteenth-century Castile but also over sixty-eight towns and villages in its territory, Seville and its council warrant Peraza's claims.[3] The council managed a wide range of aspects of local life, including local markets, religious institutions, charity, education, public health, the city's infrastructure, the muster of militias, and military fortifications in its territory.[4] In practice the city government operated as a fusion of local and royal authority and political power.[5] Traditionally, the Crown appointed the city's chief appellate judges (*alcaldes mayores*), who were members of the great regional seigneurial families. The alcaldes mayores served over the judges (*alcaldes ordinarios*) appointed by the city council itself. The Crown also appointed an outsider—often an aristocrat— as asistente, the office of *corregidor* in other Castilian cities, to serve as a representative of the monarch and co-governor with the council. The councilmen, referred to as *regidores* in other municipalities, were called *veinticuatros* in Seville after their original eponymous number. In actual practice the number of councilmen greatly exceeded twenty-four, and through the 1480s and 1490s their numbers fluctuated around the high seventies and low eighties. By that time the position of veinticuatro was essentially a hereditary office with perfunctory royal confirmation, and the men who held it typically came from the dominant elite families of the city or from families that had successfully integrated with them. Unlike the veinticuatros, who held the power to vote on council decisions, the parish representatives (*jurados*) served as both community and royal oversight of the council and held the right to voice their opinions in council meetings and the duty to alert the Crown of local abuses of power or

Fig. 1 Facade of the sixteenth-century city hall (*ayuntamiento*) of the city of Seville. Photo: author.

violations of the law. Traditionally, each parish elected two of its citizens to serve as jurados, but this position had also become hereditary by the early sixteenth century. While the council served as the local instrument for implementing royal directives, it did so as its members saw fit and at times resisted unwelcome royal demands or policies.

Although the city council, through its alcaldes, handled criminal and civil disputes in its territory, it did not oversee lawsuits of hidalguía. The chancery court in Granada adjudicated the lawsuits arising from the city and its subject towns and villages as well as all similar disputes in municipalities south of the Tajo River.[6] Documents from the court of Granada provide evidence of a substantial growth in the amount of litigation to gain recognition of the status of hidalgo involving citizens of Seville during the course of the sixteenth century (see fig. 2). For the first two decades of the century, the archive possesses records of only a handful of cases; in the third decade the number of cases rose to eighteen.[7] In the 1530s and 1540s the number of lawsuits went into the twenties and then jumped to forty-eight in the 1550s. More dramatically, the incidents of litigation doubled by the 1580s, when the total number of lawsuits for the decade reached ninety. These figures do not provide the total number of lawsuits either initiated or concluded. The surviving documents in the chancery archive of

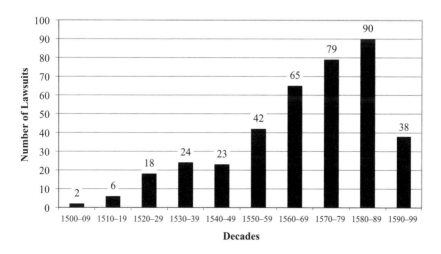

Fig. 2 Lawsuits between citizens and the city council of Seville over the status of hidalgo by decade for the sixteenth century. The number of lawsuits includes only the cases with surviving rulings (*sentencias*) and executive writs ordering the implementation of a judicial ruling (*cartas ejecutorias*) at the Archivo de la Real Chancillería de Granada.

Granada concerning litigation over this status are fragmentary and incomplete. Seville's municipal archive possesses documents of lawsuits and judicial rulings for individuals that have no surviving legal records at the chancery court, suggesting that many records have perished.[8] Although the chancery archive provides an incomplete count of the number of lawsuits, the surviving documentation reveals a clear and dramatic pattern of increase in litigation after 1515. Moreover, the number of lawsuits jumped substantially in the 1550s, when the generation of councilmen who governed the city in 1515 would have been completely replaced.

Historians of Seville have explained the tax reform in general terms as an attempt by the city to maximize its revenues in the face of an influx of immigrants who flooded the city in the early decades of the century, especially those who came to participate in the Indies trade.[9] They have also described it as a means to limit the diversity of exemptions, especially those arising from occupation, held by the city's residents. Acknowledging the subsequent rise in litigation over hidalgo status, these scholars explained the growth in lawsuits exclusively in terms of the economic benefits that hidalguía bestowed on those who could gain recognition of their status, but they have not assessed the actual economic value of this exemption. Moreover, previous treatments of this reform did not address how it affected the structuring of legal inequalities among the city's citizens, access to public office, or social identity.

The changes in Seville's tax collection, while initiated by the city council, resulted from overlapping yet distinct interests of the local governing elites and the royal government. Seville, like other cities and larger towns of the Crown of Castile during the early decades of the sixteenth century, sought to take greater control of local taxation previously managed and collected by tax farmers and private financial entrepreneurs.[10] Simultaneously, these decades witnessed royal initiatives to restructure finances to increase and regularize revenues. These developments came in the wake of fifteenth-century disruptions in the regular provision of the servicio, especially during the civil wars of Enrique's reign and the years of periodic warfare under the Catholic Monarchs, which disrupted the regular collection of royal revenues. Notably for Seville, the servicio in Andalusia between 1476 and 1500 had been collected in an ad hoc manner through allocations provided for the regional militia forces (*hermandades*).[11] During this period, a committee for the hermandad determined the allocations for contributions (*repartimientos*) from each city and town to support the hermandad and the war against Granada. These repartimientos served as a substitute for the servicios previously arranged in the Cortes. Efforts to regularize and simplify the collection and payment of the servicio and other taxes to the Crown, concretely through the procedure of *encabezamiento*, provided the local elites who controlled municipal government the opportunity to implement economic privileges to their own benefit.[12] Encabezamiento allowed municipal authorities to collect royal taxes communally rather than being subject to tax farmers. Consequently, issues of tax collection became intertwined with and impinged upon issues of social status and its recognition. Ultimately, changes in tax collection generated both collective and individual resistance in the form of complaints against municipal reforms and lawsuits seeking recognition of denied status.

In the case of Seville a review of justifications given by both the city council and the royal government for the 1515 changes reveals that reform in tax collection led directly to the introduction of formal rules requiring hidalgo status for holding political office. These rules did not result in the loss of office by incumbent councilmen, nor did they substantially affect who could obtain a council seat or office; instead, these rules altered the manner in which the city elites came to identify themselves and the way the council tracked and identified its citizens.

CHANGING FISCAL REGIMES: THE BLANCA DE LA CARNE]

In sixteenth-century Seville the mundane activities of buying meat for the household larder and petitioning for the city's annual tax refund on these purchases served to create and reproduce group identities and set social boundaries. In 1530, a witness in a lawsuit between a claimant to the status of hidalgo and the municipal council of Seville described how the city's citizens no longer paid the servicio through a direct property tax but through an excise tax on meat: "On each pound the buyer pays a *blanca* [a half maravedí coin] more than the value of the meat. Everyone pays this tax, hidalgos as well as pecheros and clerics, and at the end of the year by order of the city the accumulated sum of this tax is refunded to those hidalgos, clerics, and other people that, for whatever privilege, are free from contributing in the dues of the common taxpayers."[13] The witness's declaration to the chancery judges expressed what was common knowledge to citizens and residents of Seville concerning the refund and the weight it held for the determination of status. The social importance of this tax was still evident 150 years after its introduction, when the veinticuatro of Seville, Diego Ortiz de Zúñiga, gave a lengthy review of its introduction and significance in his history of the city.[14] In 1530, the witness noted that the imposition, known as the *blanca de la carne*, had been levied for fifteen years and that previously the city council had apportioned the pecho among the good citizens of Seville to pay the servicio. Importantly, the witness's statement provided the chancery judges with a brief history of Seville's 1515 reform in the collection of its incomes and the payment of its subsidies to the king about which they might well have been ignorant. While some municipalities in the region, such as Jerez de la Frontera and Medina Sidonia, implemented similar excise taxes to pay their servicio, many others did not.[15]

A municipality's founding fuero and subsequent grants of municipal privileges and favors from the royal government—or loss of these favors—strongly influenced the nature and structuring of local taxes. Sales taxes (*alcabalas*) on diverse commodities and goods had traditionally been important sources of revenue for the royal government and constituted a major percentage of the Crown's income.[16] Authorities leveled alcabalas and sisas on items as diverse as cloth, raw wool, vinegar, wine, cheese, dried and fresh fish, dried and fresh fruit, meat, and many other goods.[17] Notably, the most lucrative excise tax on a single commodity was often from the meat sold at municipal butcher shops. In Ciudad Real the average revenue from the tax on meat between 1557 and 1561 was 442,600 maravedís.[18] During the fifteenth century, the Crown set the alcabala in Castile's major cities at 5 percent, but monarchs occasionally raised it in moments of emergency. In small villages the rate was as low as 3 percent. The collection of the alcabala was done as a tax on the seller rather than the consumer and was typically arranged and paid in advance to tax farmers (*arrendadores*) by associations of retailers, who simply passed these costs along to consumers in higher prices for their goods.[19] Hidalgos did not have exemption from the alcabala, but some municipalities, especially those situated on the frontiers, often held exemptions from the alcabalas on certain products.[20] In contrast to the alcabala, a sisa or imposición was an excise tax leveled by the municipal government on a commodity and paid directly by the consumer.

Seville's 1515 reform in taxation involved the introduction of a permanent sisa on meat to pay the city's servicio and established a fiscal regime that provided limited economic privileges to a small minority. The city council of Seville, not the royal government, initiated Seville's reform in tax collection. The reform effectively changed the local rules governing exemption from taxation. Significantly, it freed those who could claim the status of hidalgo, including the council members themselves, from contributing to the royal servicio. In other municipalities in the Crown of Castile, though not all, recognition of the status of hidalgo exempted a person from paying the direct taxes collected locally to meet the servicio. In fact, during the fifteenth and sixteenth centuries a number of the towns and villages subject to Seville's jurisdiction and lordship provided exemptions to people they recognized as hidalgos. Despite this practice in some of Seville's own subject municipalities and in other parts of Castile, Seville never provided tax exemptions to hidalgos prior to this reform.[21] Moreover, the lack of hidalgo tax privileges was widespread in late medieval Andalusia.[22] Records from the meetings of the Cortes during the period stated that "in Andalusia all pay their taxes, the rich, as well as caballeros hijosdalgo and all other people."[23] While this blanket statement applied to municipalities such as the cities of Seville and Córdoba and the town of Carmona, which all taxed their hidalgos, caballeros, and resident seigneurial lords, actual local practices in the region were more complex and diverse depending on the trajectory of local history. For instance, in the town of Úbeda, hidalgos held the privilege of paying a set nominal amount of five maravedís in each tax apportionment.

In some Andalusian communities in the late fifteenth century, municipal councils defended local practices and resisted attempts by hidalgos in their communities to assert their claims to economic privileges. These efforts came in the midst of intense pressure from the royal government to secure income for the military campaigns against the kingdom of Granada and after decades of dynastic struggle had interrupted the regular collection of the servicio. In the town of Carmona, the municipal council required all its citizens and residents to pay the pecho except the members of the council itself. In the early 1480s the hidalgos of Carmona collectively initiated a lawsuit against the town council to force it to recognize their privileges and allow them exemption from the servicio.[24] In 1483, the royal government ruled in favor of the council supporting the position that all Carmona's citizens, pecheros and hidalgos, had to pay this tax. Despite the fact that the Crown ruled against the hidalgos of Carmona as a group, the same monarchs provided various documents to individual hidalgo families of Carmona in the 1490s, in which they required the council to respect the privileges of these particular families.

In Seville, before the introduction of the blanca de la carne freed those who could successfully claim to be hidalgos from the economic burden of the pecho, the city had allocated the distribution of the pecho on a progressive basis according to a household's wealth. A pair of officials made up of one jurado and one veinticuatro visited each parish, collected information, estimated each householder's wealth, and placed them in a tax rate (*cuantía*) or bracket.[25] The estimates for a citizen's cuantía excluded their house of residence, clothing, weapons, staple foodstuffs, or adornments.[26] The city set the highest rate, the "cuantía of a thousand," on those citizens whose wealth amounted to 200,000 maravedís, for which they contributed 1,000 maravedís—1,000/200,000 or 1/200—of their wealth. This was the maximum rate and the cuantía did not increase after this point. The minimum rate was 10 maravedís for those who had no property and "live by their labor and toil, are of the age that they can work, and are healthy in body."[27]

The ordinances established that for the "magnates, masters of the military orders, counts, and likewise the magistrates, judges, constables, and councilmen," the councilmen themselves set the amount of maravedís that each one would pay. This method was a direct estimation and did not involve the application of the cuantía. This method actually placed a greater tax burden on the elite, because they often had property worth much more than the 200,000 maravedís limit, and to follow the cuantía system they would have paid a small amount of their wealth.[28] For the seigneurial nobility the amounts paid ranged from 1,500 maravedís for Pedro Ponce de León, first Count of Arcos, to 4,000 for Juan Alonso de Guzmán, third Count of Niebla, whereas the amounts for the urban knights, hidalgos, and councilmen ranged between 100 and 500 maravedís. In the mid-fifteenth century Pedro Ponce de León and Juan Alonso de Guzmán were the heads of the two dominant and rival noble clans in southwestern Andalusia. Moreover, these men and their successors, particularly the heads of the different Guzmán families, came to control Seville's city council in the years of civil strife during Enrique IV's reign.[29] Nevertheless, through the fifteenth century they and their many relatives contributed to the pecho. Only a small segment of Seville's population referred to as *francos* were free from paying this tax. The officials, servants, and artisans at Seville's royal mint, the king's palace, and the Crown shipyards almost exclusively constituted the group of francos, not the elites of the city.[30]

The ability of the city to collect its own taxes had been a matter of political debate in the thirteenth and early fourteenth centuries. By the fifteenth century the city of Seville, like most of the cities of Castile, had secured the right to collect the yearly servicio it owed the Crown and actively administered the collection of this tax itself.[31] In contrast to Seville's administration of this tax, many royal and seigneurial towns before and during the sixteenth century often chose not to take a role in the collection of royal taxes and left the task to individual or group entrepreneurs, who bid for the tax-farming contract (*arrendamiento*) from the royal treasury.[32] For the city of Seville the reform of 1515 brought a final conclusion to this process by definitively placing collection of the servicio in the hands of the council. Due to the city government's control of Seville's public butcher shops, the introduction of an excise tax on this staple good not only allowed the council to continue overseeing the collection of the servicio but required it.[33] The reform of taxation served the interests of the city elite and members of the city council.

Other municipalities in Andalusia made similar changes in the collection of incomes for paying the servicio during the early decades of the sixteenth century. Nevertheless, efforts to implement change elicited diverse responses and had distinct consequences depending on the municipality's particular local histories, customs, and relations with the Crown. In the city of Jerez de la Frontera in 1511, the switch from the collection of a pecho on the property of each household in favor of a number of excise taxes led to a lawsuit between the knights who served as the city's councilmen (*caballeros veinticuatros*) and the rest of the city's knights, squires, and citizens who sought to deny their exemption.[34] Testimony from the lawsuit suggests that before 1511 Jerez's councilmen had held various informal or tacit exemptions from paying property taxes due to their control of municipal government and their manipulation of tax collection.

Occasionally, the extraordinary demands of Castile's monarchs, particularly in times of war, forced the councilmen to contribute money, through excise taxes, levies, or material support, along with the other citizens of Jerez. When the council implemented its reform in the payment of the servicio in 1511, the councilmen took the opportunity to claim formal exemption from the new excise taxes. They justified their exemptions from these taxes on the basis of a privilege the city had received from King Pedro in 1354 that allowed for the creation of a closed city council. According to the privilege, the commune of the city had the right to nominate thirty caballeros to hold the office of councilman, and the king chose thirteen of them to form the municipal council. Various witnesses testified that on the basis of past privileges the caballeros veinticuatros had never contributed in the pecho or been placed on lists of taxpayers. Nevertheless, other witnesses testified that the veinticuatros contributed allotments of wheat to the Catholic Monarchs during Gonçalo Gomes de Cervante's tenure as corregidor. In opposition to the veinticuatros' claim of exemption, the city's other caballeros alleged that the councilmen had also been required to contribute in the taxes imposed to maintain the siege of Baza during the conquest of Granada. Whatever the preceding situation had been, the council's efforts to formalize their exemption from taxation generated resistance from the other citizens of the town, who initiated a lawsuit to oppose the establishment of this financial inequality.

Similar fiscal changes in the city of Córdoba generated a series of conflicts that led to a lawsuit in 1497 and related disputes that continued for two decades. In the original suit the city's caballeros de premía demanded that the caballeros hijosdalgo contribute in the royal subsidy along with the other citizens of property.[35] In the thirteenth and fourteenth centuries towns in the Crown of Castile, particularly in Castilla Nueva, Andalusia, and Murcia, witnessed the development of a class of urban knights, composed of townsmen who on account of their wealth were either required to maintain horse and arms or could choose to do so to gain economic privileges.[36] Depending on the locality, these knights were called *caballeros de premía, caballeros de alarde,* or *caballeros de cuantía.* A tax list from Córdoba in 1497 lists caballeros de premía who were engaged in a wide range of occupations, such as cloth merchant, shopkeeper, tanner, dyer, silversmith, furniture maker, and even a tenant farmer. The genesis of the dispute in Córdoba began in 1495 or 1496, when the caballeros de premía, perhaps in response to efforts to tax them more heavily than less wealthy citizens through a direct tax on property, pressured the council to introduce the use of excises to pay the city's allotment of monies to the Crown.[37] This effort led to the introduction of a sisa on meat and fish. The council subsequently exempted Córdoba's caballeros hidalgos from paying either this sisa or a related pecho and thereby sparked the lawsuit adjudicated by the royal council in 1497.

In the lawsuit the caballeros de premía eventually argued that caballeros hidalgos should contribute along with those de premía, on the grounds that the two groups overlapped and that they were of similar social distinction. The caballeros hidalgos responded that only those who were hidalgos should be exempt. The hidalgos insisted that if there was a time when some of their number had been included among the caballeros de premía it had occurred when the magnate Alonso de Aguilar controlled the city and factional feuds and divisions had divided Córdoba's dominant seigneurial families.[38] Aguilar held the lordship of ten communities in the territory around the city and possession of the office of alcalde mayor for Córdoba. His efforts to control the city government clashed with those of his rival, the Count of Cabra, who was the city's chief constable (*alguacil mayor*).[39] The witnesses asserted that during this contentious time partisans of Aguilar had listed some hidalgos as caballeros de premía against their will because they followed the faction opposed to this powerful lord.[40] Although the caballeros de premía received an initially favorable ruling, the case dragged on for many years through appeals and resurfaced in 1514, when hidalgos in the city demanded that the city council investigate the inclusion in the tax lists of the parishes of Saint Marina and Saint Lawrence of various individuals who, they claimed, were hidalgos and therefore exempt from inclusion.[41]

In the city of Jaén the introduction of a new tax regime overlapped with existing factional tensions and economic burdens and grievances to cause some citizens of the city to join the Comunero Revolt against the government of the new Habsburg monarch, Carlos I. The burdens and costs of the conquest of Granada, the suppression of the first revolt in the Alpujarras in 1500, and expeditions in North Africa fell heavily on the municipalities of Andalusia. The fiscal demands for these enterprises left Jaén deeply in debt and prompted the city to appeal for relief from the royal government at the meeting of the Cortes in Seville in 1501, at the very time the monarchs sought to reintroduce the servicio payments in Andalusia.[42] The city's representatives explained that during the war the hidalgos of Jaén had contributed to the pecho used to pay the city's contribution to the hermandades and they had also served the monarchs in person. Consequently, they requested that the city's hidalgos be exempt from the reimplemented servicio, just as the hidalgos of Old Castile were exempt. Concerns and grievances over the payment of the servicio troubled Jaén's entire citizenry and prompted Jaén's corregidor in 1502 to order the councilmen to arrest anyone who should instigate a disturbance. He also advised the council to ask permission from the monarchs to collect the 320,000 maravedís the city owed for the servicio by means of a sisa. The sisa was not established and payment of the servicio remained a difficult burden for the following years, especially during the poor harvests of 1506 and 1507. In the latter year the royal government even remitted the city's payment of the servicio. These fiscal challenges finally drove the city to implement the encabezamiento of the alcabalas in 1517. The city continued this system until the outbreak of the Comunero Revolt in 1520. Prior to the revolt, citizens of the city had sent petitions to the royal council, complaining how the city council provided privilege and favors to false hidalgos with ties to Jaén's regidores and jurados.

The caballeros of Córdoba, the citizens of Jerez and Jaén, and the individual claimants to the status of hidalgo in Seville after 1515 were genuinely concerned with the economic consequences of changes in tax regimes and explained their actions primarily in terms of economic ends. These litigants, however, also knew that the outcomes of these contests held significant political and social consequences. In Córdoba and Jerez, court decisions would set precedents on local tax exemption, and, for the individual citizens of Seville, judicial rulings would mark claimants as either belonging to or excluded from the city's elite.

Although some litigants in Seville after the 1515 reforms definitely sought to establish their status through legal action in the chancery court for economic reasons, the material benefit for the majority of recipients was modest, especially compared with the heavy cost involved in litigation. When calculated on a yearly basis, individual hidalgos in the short term obtained relatively small economic benefits from the city's change in tax collection. In the 1515 account of Seville's sales tax on meat, the blanca de la carne, the two largest returns went to the heads of dominant regional seigneurial families. Juan de Guzmán, the Count of Ayamonte, received 3,303 maravedís and Rodrigo Ponce de León, the first Duke of Arcos, received 5,040 maravedís.[43] Neither of these refunds was for the entire year. Guzmán's was from the beginning of the year until the end of August and Ponce de León's until the end of September. Only four other recipients received returns greater than 1,000 maravedís or 3 *ducados*.[44] Evidence from the records of the tax refund through the sixteenth century indicate that the value of the returns in 1515 at the inception of the blanca de la carne were roughly equivalent to those paid at midcentury and in the 1570s and 1580s (see table 1).[45] Not surprisingly, the wealthiest of the local seigneurial aristocrats and resident Crown officials received the most significant benefits. In the 1577 refund, the largest amount the city treasurer provided any one hidalgo was 14,600 maravedís for the period of three years and four months (roughly 4,380 maravedís a year), to Don Francisco Zapata de Cisneros, Count of Barajas, the asistente for the city.[46] As in the case of the Count of Barajas, recipients did not always collect their returns on a yearly basis, and the sums they received reveal the long-term value of the exemption, such as the 1582 refund of 18,576 maravedís for the period of eleven years to Don Juan Ponce de León or the refund, also given in 1582, to Doña Clemencia de Guzmán of 9,340 maravedís for the period of five years.[47]

Even the largest of these returns was only a tiny percentage of the average income of a seigneurial aristocrat, which in 1577 ran just over 28,000 ducados or 10,500,000 maravedís.[48] Excluding the Count of Barajas, the average return for the year 1515 was 715 maravedís. While not a paltry sum, the refund did not

Table 1 Value of refunds from Seville's blanca de la carne in the sixteenth century

Year	Average refund (maravedís)	Median refund (maravedís)	Largest refund (maravedís)	Number of recipients
1515	318	195	5,040	207
1542	735	500	3,750	139
1547	829	400	5,900	50
1583	1,072	871	1,991	108

Source: For 1515, see AMS, sec. 1, carp. 175, doc. 48; for 1542, see AMS, sec. 1, carp. 178, doc. 95; for 1547, see AMS, sec. 3, tomo 3, doc. 40; for 1583, see AMS, sec. 3, tomo 4, doc. 4.

Note: These figures are based on the refunds provided to recipients listed as hidalgos, including hijadalgos, the widows of hidalgos, and individuals who held political offices that required the status of hidalgos. The table excludes all returns given to those who held exemptions for other reasons, such as church canons, monks, workers at the royal mint, and so on. The refund for any given year did not include all hidalgos resident in the city, because individuals often did not choose to collect the refund on a yearly basis or were impeded from doing so. The table also excludes those returns given without a specified amount of time for which the sum had accumulated. Surviving records do not always include the refunds for all the city's parishes, as is clear in the returns for the year 1547.

constitute a substantial amount of even the average Castilian's finances. For most recipients the return would have amounted to a week or two of earnings, perhaps 3 to 4 percent of one's yearly income. A miller in Andalusia in 1576 received annual wages of 6,636 maravedís, an average of 140 maravedís a week. In the same year a nurse in Old Castile received annual wages of 2,040 maravedís, and a hired laborer in New Castile earned 76 maravedís a day. The wages of these workers constituted only a part of the material remuneration they received from their employers, who also typically provided an allowance of meat, bread, and wine, or monetary commutations of these items, and either lodging or a dwelling.[49] In light of the incomes of average Castilians, the refund would have been a modest but welcome boost in cash for those who could obtain it. Some recipients, most likely in need of liquid funds, did not wait for the conventional yearly return but sought disbursements multiple times through the year.

The worth of the refund increased for those with larger households and greater expenditures for staple goods such as meat. The value of the refund, while not insignificant, did not amount to a substantial portion of the income of Seville's urban elite and for many meant more as a clear designation of their status. Certainly the long-term and collective value of the exemption over many years and for multiple members of a family served to increase its appeal and the desire to obtain it. Excluding the blanca de la carne, hidalgos in Seville continued to pay the rest of the royal and council taxes, including various sisas on other commodities.[50] In the lawsuits for hidalguía made by citizens of Seville, the litigants demanded only the return of the sales tax on meat, and the council provided these monies only to those who gained recognition of their status.[51]

From the perspective of royal finances, the servicio was just one of the incomes the Crown drew from the city of Seville and its territory.[52] After 1515 a substantial amount, if not the entirety, of the servicio came from the city's excise tax on meat. For the year 1542 the city paid the royal government 1,245,708 maravedís from the blanca de la carne.[53] This sum did not increase significantly through the century. Considering the rise in inflation in the second half of the century, the sum of 1,250,733 maravedís paid to the royal government in 1577 from the blanca constituted a decrease in revenue.[54] From the perspective of royal finances, the better part of the Crown's income from Seville and its territory came from three sources: the customs dues paid on goods entering and leaving Seville's territory (*almojarifazgo mayor*), the ordinary sales taxes (*alcabalas*), and the royal portion of the church tithes (*tercias*).[55] Unlike the servicio, the revenues from the almojarifazgo mayor increased dramatically through the century. Fixed at about 17,000,000 maravedís annually through the 1520s, this state income increased to almost 40,000,000 in the 1540s and exceeded 100,000,000 maravedís a year by the 1560s.[56] The ordinary sales taxes were leveled on more than eighty different commodities, ranging from foodstuffs to building materials in both the city and its subject municipalities.[57] These alcabalas produced almost 160,000,000 maravedís annually.[58] Hidalgos in Seville held no privilege that exempted them from paying these other diverse taxes.

NEW RULES FOR PUBLIC OFFICE

Despite its relatively modest economic value, the tax came to have a meaning and significance distinct from immediate financial concerns. The petition that the city refund the tax on the purchase of meat became the moment when citizens advanced their claims to the status of hidalgo. Gaining the refund became a tangible sign of this status. Seville's tax collection was intrinsically connected to the city's recognition or denial of status and consequently involved the council in litigation. Since the city controlled who received the tax return, it held first-instance determination of its citizens' privileges and status. City officials, specifically the parish jurados, now possessed the responsibility for deciding whom the city would exempt from taxes.

As the assessors of the parish tax lists, traditional collectors of the royal pecho, and arbiters of their fellow citizens' status—including other members of the city council—jurados held the power to provide privileges both before and after the changes implemented in 1515. Consequently, their decisions and actions produced objections and disputes. In 1515, Fernando Díaz de Santa Cruz, citizen in the parish of Santa María and one of the city's stewards (*mayor-domo*), refused to pay the pecho amounting to one gold ducado worth 375 maravedís.[59] He claimed both that he was an hidalgo and that he had never paid any pecho for the twelve years he had lived in the city. Disregarding his protests, the jurado for his parish, with an order from the city council, had the local constable seize movable property—one armchair and two bags full of wool—in lieu of the payment. On the eve of the reform in the servicio, the forcible impounding of Díaz's property in 1515 would have been for the sums apportioned to him for the previous year. Díaz immediately filed a suit that dragged on until 1532, by which time he himself had acquired the office of jurado. By the end of the suit, opposition to Díaz's claims from within the council must have shifted significantly in his favor, as he also served as one of the city's two procuradores to the Cortes of Madrid in 1528.[60]

Díaz's claim suggests that through either a form of collusion among the officials of the council or agreements with local jurados, members of the city government had succeeded in evading the payment of their taxes prior to the reform. Whether the cause resulted from a falling out with his parish jurado or with others on the council, or some other reason, the council in 1515 required him to pay the pecho. In the face of these demands, Díaz sought to continue his tax evasion by gaining recognition of the status of hidalgo. A similar dispute involving Diego Jaymes illustrates local concern with the often seemingly arbitrary power of jurados to determine the social status of the citizens in their parishes. As a citizen of Seville, Jaymes initiated a lawsuit in 1526 against the city council's refusal to recognize his status as an hidalgo. In his initial petition to the judges of the court, Jaymes complained particularly about Juan Aguado and Francisco Pinelo, the jurados of the parish of Santa María la Mayor, where he lived, singling them out as responsible for the unfair denial of his status.[61]

The city's implementation of an excise tax made it easier for the council to act against obstinate claimants to the status and privileges of hidalguía who refused to pay the pecho, because the city no longer had to seize property.

Unlike the situation with Francisco Díaz, the city already held the monies that the individual had paid at the public butcher shops and simply refused to provide claimants with a refund of these sums. Moreover, after 1521 the city began to demand that those who sought the refund of this tax (*refracción*) had to provide their parish representative with a royal letter in the form of a court ruling to establish their status.[62] As collector of its own servicio, the city became a principal participant in disputes over privilege. These disputes, which in other municipalities and at different times in Seville's own history had generated lawsuits between municipal citizens and tax farmers, now placed Seville's citizens against their own municipal council.

Even as the status of hidalgo allowed a person to receive the refund, the refund itself served to establish and prove one's hidalguía. Seville's innovation in its payment of the servicio allowed the council to partially exempt its officers, but, more significant for local understanding of status, this innovation and associated accounting practices conflated possession of public office with the status of hidalgo. The association of municipal office with hidalgo status became explicit and conspicuous when the city implemented new rules requiring hidalguía to hold the positions of jurado, veinticuatro, and *fiel ejecutor* (municipal inspector and regulator) in the year following the introduction of the blanca de la carne. Through these new ordinances the tacit and illicit exemptions enjoyed by officials of the city council became formally established and legitimate. The introduction of the blanca de la carne appears to have resulted from local complaints to the royal government, which forced Seville's council to address its practice of tacitly providing illicit tax exemptions to officeholders. Consequently, the city government responded by introducing new ordinances, which either required municipal officeholders to possess the social status of hidalgo or simply denied pecheros the office.[63] So even as the city required the status of hidalgo to fill these positions, it began to provide tax returns to those holding council offices.

The changes to the city's rules for holding public office introduced a formal legal requirement that excluded pecheros and constituted a radical break from the city's past. Since the Christian conquest of Seville in 1248, the city's ordinances had used diverse and changing terms to refer to the dominant elites and the larger body of citizens that comprised the city's population, but these rules had never formally excluded commoners from access to positions in the city's government. In 1251, Fernando III granted the new settlers the charter of Toledo as the basis for the rights and obligations they had to the Crown.[64] The fuero itself did not designate who could hold specific offices, nor did it provide quotas based on status for these offices. References to the early gatherings of the city's assemblies mention participation by both caballeros and good men (*omes buenos*). Modern scholars have defined *omes* or *hombres buenos* as propertied and tax-paying citizens.[65] As discussed earlier, the term *caballero* had a range of meanings, from a member of a seigneurial family to urban knights. The exact meaning of these terms in the documents of the period remains somewhat ambiguous, and scholars have suggested that there was overlap between the two groups as omes buenos entered the ranks of the caballeros de cuantía.[66] Subsequent city ordinances authorized by the Crown, but often at the instigation of the city's government, elaborated the nature, composition, and regulation of Seville's council and its political offices. As early as 1286 Sancho IV confirmed the establishment of a municipal council (*concejo* or *regimiento*) of twenty-four regidores, drawn from twelve of the city's caballeros and twelve of its omes buenos. By the fourteenth century the main body of the council had coalesced in the form it would have through the sixteenth century.[67]

Local elite families controlled Seville's highest council offices from at least the fourteenth century, but the composition and membership of Seville's elite through the late Middle Ages proved fluid with the addition and disappearance of families from this ruling elite.[68] The members of these families, typically referred to in late medieval documents as caballeros, came from both long-established lineages and families of new prominence who initially entered the ranks of the elite as caballeros de cuantía.[69] Although these caballeros filled the offices of councilman in the first centuries after conquest, no established rule designated a particular status for council members until the mid-fourteenth century. In 1351, the royal government of King Pedro attempted to reduce the number of Seville's veinticuatros, which exceeded thirty-six, and reform the membership of the council, ordering that "there should be twelve *fijosdalgo* and twelve *ciudadanos* (nonnoble citizens)."[70] Whether the introduction of hidalgo in the regulation was intended to provide a means to control the number of regidores or simply reflected a linguistic shift, the number of councilmen remained well in excess of twenty-four through the late Middle Ages and continued to be composed of individuals from diverse origins.[71] María Concepción Quintanilla Raso argues that during this period the caballeros who controlled the municipal councils of southern Castile and Andalusia sought to emphasize the distance between themselves and other caballeros—de cuantía or de premía—by taking advantage of their status as hidalgos to call themselves caballeros hidalgos.[72] By the fourteenth century the position had become one for life and by the fifteenth century was accepted as hereditary.[73] The only other reference to hidalgos in the city ordinances pertained to the office of mayordomo. A letter from Alfonso XI dated 1346 stipulated that for the two city treasurers one had to be an hidalgo and the other a ciudadano.[74]

The 1515 change in the city's ordinances concerning the status of jurados was particularly significant due to the historical functions and duties of this office and the prior lack of requirements of formal status to hold it. Described in royal letters as representatives of the common people and guardians of community interests, they were supposed to watch for and oppose council abuses. Simultaneously, as officers of the city and the royal government, they served to implement council orders and the demands of the monarch. Certain decisions of the city government could not be made without the presence of the jurados, particularly those dealing with the fixing and collection of taxes.[75] They were also responsible for generating the city's tax and militia lists, through commissions composed jointly of jurados and veinticuatros. In the fourteenth century the city's ordinances required only that the citizens choose a good and honorable man of impeccable reputation. Additional ordinances originating from Juan II (1406–54) stipulated that the person elected should be "a citizen of means and a capable man of good reputation."[76] Despite these regulations, by the early fifteenth century the practice of election came to an end, as the office gradually became the patrimony of its holders.[77] However, not until 1515 did a royal letter issued in Queen Juana's name add the requirement that a pechero could not hold the office.[78]

Despite the absence of formal economic privileges based on status in Seville before 1515, evidence suggests that the council tacitly provided exemptions to its own members. This favoritism and the council's implicit claim to the right to exempt its officials produced complaints from anonymous sources and an ongoing dispute between the city council and the royal government in the early decades of the sixteenth century. In 1502, in the wake of the reintroduction of the servicio, the Catholic Monarchs responded to complaints from segments of the city, possibly from individual jurados on the council itself, that the city was illicitly exempting many of its officials from paying the pecho.[79] In a letter directed to the city, the monarchs accused the council of providing these exemptions without proper authority and ordered it to desist from allowing its officers such economic privileges. Specifically, they commanded that the jurados of the city include all city officials, presumably jurados as well, on the lists of taxpayers and require them to contribute to the pecho. Moreover, they ordered that this be done regardless of any exemptions these officials might possess. The language of the royal order suggested that Isabel and Fernando wished to reserve final say on the matter to their own ruling. Despite the fact that the Crown ordered the city not to give any more exemptions to its officers, they included a clause that would allow such grants in certain instances: "We order that henceforth the city cannot give exemptions or liberties from any royal or council taxes, except those that by law should be given."[80] The ordinance, however, did not specify the instances that the law allowed. Litigation during the early years of the century supports the complaints made to the Catholic Monarchs that Seville's city council, or individual council members, provided exemptions from the pecho to city officials. Among others, the case of Fernando Díaz suggests that city officials did not always receive these exemptions in a consistent or regular manner, and the possibility that they might lose these exemptions existed.

The city council continued to provide exemptions to its own members, eventually prompting the royal council in the name of Queen Juana (1504–55) to issue an order on May 19, 1515, establishing that pecheros could not fill the office of jurado or constable.[81] Like earlier correspondence, Juana's letter claimed to respond to complaints from the city, but it did not designate who made these complaints or who requested royal intervention. Two months later another letter from the queen stated that on account of the great benefits the first order had produced for the city's citizens and residents, Seville's representatives requested the royal favor of extending this rule to the more powerful position of veinticuatro and the office of fiel ejecutor.[82] The letter provided convincing evidence that pecheros held council offices before 1515, but no indication about what actions the city was supposed to take against pecheros or the descendants of pecheros who were then holding office.

The new ordinance had little to do with royal interests in strengthening hidalgo or noble control over the government and more to do with the relationship between royal and municipal authorities and their respective powers. The law was part of an existing contest between the royal government and local elites concerning who had the prerogative to provide privileges of tax exemption and who could control entrance to political office. Aware of the council's growing provision of tax exemptions to its own members and officers—and the practice of refunding the excise tax on meat to its officers—the royal government made a tacit compromise by changing the requirements for office rather than insisting that these city officials pay the tax. Juana's letter stated that the royal government had received reports and complaints about how the city allowed pecheros to be appointed as parish representatives and constables. Furthermore, the reports had indicated that by virtue of their offices these men were exempt from paying and contributing to the city's taxes. The authors of the letter then claimed that providing pecheros with the privilege of exemption would harm the welfare of the city as a whole. Using this appeal, the letter declared that Juana wanted such persons to pay so that these offices not be a burden on the poor, the widows, and the citizens of the city. The queen's letter related that in fact the city itself had petitioned the queen to provide an order that from now on "no pechero would be provided with this office, but only hidalgos notorios, because in this way the harm to the city would be remedied."[83]

The change in Seville's rules concerning jurados and a subsequent extension of these rules to veinticuatros formally provided the Crown with greater power over appointment to these offices by limiting the right of possessors of council office to dispose of their offices as they wished. The new ordinance effectively invalidated the conditions of earlier royal grants to municipal offices, which had provided the recipient with the right to designate the office to the person of his choice, leave it to his heir, or hand it over to another party and left the final decision about who should possess the office in the hands of the monarch.[84] The letter specifically acknowledged the monarch's rights to appoint the person of her choice, in the event that the law was violated: "If any pechero should be provided with any of these offices, I order that they should not be recognized and that such election should be invalidated, and I declare this so that I should be able to provide the said office to persons exempt from the pechos."[85] In terms of implementation and practice, the ordinance provided the city council with the informal power to continue to provide exemptions to those it chose to recognize as hidalgos. Instead of excluding individuals of pechero status from the city council, Juana's ordinance allowed members of the city council to surreptitiously assume the status of hidalgo regardless of their lineage. That is, these individuals and their heirs subsequently succeeded in identifying themselves as hidalgos through the precedent of receiving the refund. There is no evidence that royal officials initiated litigation against council members or officers in the years following the ordinance, that councilmen had their offices seized, or that councilmen were kept from transferring their office to the person of their choice. The long-term effect of these novel city ordinances was to provide a useful justification for denying the office of jurado and veinticuatro to political rivals who could not demonstrate that they were hidalgos. These rules simultaneously gave the Crown greater freedom to control the appointment of candidates to these positions.

REFASHIONING ELITE IDENTITY

Whether or not these new rules kept people of pechero descent out of city council office, within a generation they significantly changed both the way the city council represented why it provided privileges and how the city's elites represented themselves. A close examination of Seville's fiscal records detailing the tax refunds provided in the years 1515 to 1520 reveals that the status of hidalgo initially played little part in who received an exemption from the excise tax on meat. The city clerk recorded the person's name, the amount of meat consumed, the amount of the refund, the amount of time it had accumulated or the ending date for the amount refunded, and the person's office if he held one. During the first year of the blanca, the city clerk recorded that the city paid refunds to 207 lay recipients, excluding those laymen who received refunds because they worked at the royal mint or the royal palaces.[86] Of these 207 recipients, 94 held some sort of municipal or royal office (see table 2).

Table 2   The recipients of the refund for the year 1515 listed by office

Office or reason for refund	Number	Percentage of lay recipients in the year's return
Councilmen (veinticuatros)	18	8.70
Parish representatives (jurados)	39	18.84
Constables (alguaciles)	13	6.28
City clerks (escribanos públicos)	12	5.80
Court clerks (escribanos de la justicia)	3	1.45
Judges (alcaldes/jueces)	4	1.93
Lieutenants to the royal magistrate (tenientes de asistente)	2	0.97
Military commanders (comendadores)	2	0.97
Chief constable (alguazil mayor)	1	0.48
Total holding office	94	45.41
By review and certification of their jurado (por cédula de su jurado)	113	54.59
Total	207	100.00

Source: AMS, sec. 1, carp. 175, doc. 48.

Among those who received the refund but did not hold office, the majority were relatives of members of the city council.[87] A high number of these had family members listed as jurados, the very officials responsible for authorizing the refund. At the beginning of the sixteenth century, the city had twenty-seven parishes and consequently fifty-four jurados. By the end of the century the council had incorporated two additional parishes, raising the number of jurados to fifty-eight.[88] In fact, the number of jurados in the city was greater than simply two per parish, as both council and Crown bestowed the office as a material and honorific reward. At the completion of the new city hall in 1564, Seville boasted seventy-two jurados.[89] In the extant records of the refund from 1515 until the outbreak of the Comunero Revolt in 1520, city clerks continued to record its provision of fiscal privileges in this manner. Evidence from the city of Jaén for the year 1523 reveals the same correlation between jurados and the recipients who received a refund from the town's sisa. Those who came to be designated as hidalgos were related to the city council officials, especially jurados.[90] Notably, Jaén, like Seville, had not required jurados to be hidalgos before this time.

A generation later, in 1542—the first year with surviving records of the refund after 1520—the description of the recipient changed significantly. The city clerk, in addition to providing the amount returned and the period of time it had accumulated, provided a brief statement explaining why the city had given the refund. The clerk expressed the reason with the simple phrase "for being [por ser]." Some of the men recorded as receiving the refund "for being an hijodalgo" also held city council offices, including the positions of veinticuatro, jurado, and alguacil. The clerk also recorded disbursing refunds to men who held these offices without mentioning whether or not they were an hidalgo or whether they had received the refund for being one. Among those who were now listed as hidalgos in the 1542 refund were many of the family names that lacked any designation of status in the first five years of the refund.[91]

Certain laywomen from elite families, like their male counterparts, also succeeded in appropriating the status of hidalgo to secure tax advantages from the council. Studies of women from the titled nobility, particularly the extensive and powerful Mendoza clan, have revealed that aristocratic women in early modern Castile, as widows and in the place of absent husbands, managed, bought, and sold family property.[92] They also exercised guardianship over their fatherless children, chose the spouses of their sons and daughters, and—in an environment in which the private estate of the aristocrat was a public lordship and jurisdiction—engaged in a wide range of informal political activities. Consequently, it is not surprising that these women and their counterparts among the lesser nobility made clams to hidalgo status to secure material and honorific benefits for themselves and their families.

In the 1515 account of the refund, the city clerk listed 12 women out of a total of 210 recipients. He provided 10 of these women with the title *doña*, and they came from some of the most prominent families in the city, including the Esquivel, Fuentes, Guevara, Martel, Melgarejo/Cervantes, Mendoza/Peón, Ponce de León, Ribera, Saavedra, and Valderama.[93] Of these entries, 3 listed the recipient as a wife and only 1 listed the recipient as a widow. Twenty-seven years later the 1542 refund listed 132 recipients as hidalgos, and 28 were women. Because of the new ordinances and tax impositions, both men and women who served as the heads of their households found it more advantageous to identify themselves as hidalgos. Among the women who received the refund in 1542, the clerk distinguished between those who possessed this privilege through their husband, sometimes indicated as deceased, and those who possessed the privilege in their own right as an *hija dalgo*. The clerk listed 16 women who held the privilege to the refund in their own right, and 9 who held it through their husbands.[94]

Although the medieval martial demands placed on hidalgos connect this term of designation with the sex that went to war, one of the earliest recorded uses of the word survives in *El poema de mio cid* (*The Poem of the Cid*) and references Rodrigo de Vivar's wife rather than the epic's hero himself: "Veremos vuestra mugier membrada fija dalgo" (We shall see your worthy and noble wife).[95] Despite these early uses, when Seville's clerks and stewards applied this identity to elite women of Seville, they introduced a term that locals had not previously used in this manner. Prior to the sixteenth century the authors of royal letters and narrative chronicles employed the designations *dueñas* and *doncellas* for women of Seville's elite classes, those who controlled property and possessed political influence or stood to inherit such authority. The new use of *hijadalgo* paralleled the use of *hijodalgo* for men. Unlike the designations *caballero*, *dueña*, and *doncella*, existing laws that tied various privileges to status made the identity of hidalgo advantageous to claim.

Despite references to hidalgos in the division of city properties, after Fernando III's conquest of Seville and in late medieval municipal ordinances, few hidalgos were recorded in the fiscal records of the city before the sixteenth century. Moreover, there appears to be little continuity between early hidalgo settlers and the city elites of the late fifteenth century who claimed this title and the veinticuatros of the fifteenth and sixteenth century who styled themselves caballeros hijosdalgo. Only 10 of the original 200 families listed as hidalgos in the original apportionment of properties after the conquest can be connected with any certainty to families in the city in the fifteenth century.[96] Through the fifteenth century the city's padrones record a meager 150 hidalgo households, many of relatively humble means.[97] Rafael Sánchez has explained the erosion of the original hidalgo segment of the population as the result of their abandonment of the city and the failure of their lineages to reproduce.[98] While Sánchez has convincingly detailed the extinction of some of these families, an additional cause for the seeming disappearance of these hidalgos in the two centuries after the city's conquest was the political and economic practices in the city. In a context where the status of hidalgo afforded no economic privileges, few sought to maintain it. This situation led to relative disuse of the term as a designation for elite status until its revival in 1515.

In Seville during the early decades of the sixteenth century, the dominant families used their control of the city government to maintain and extend their hold on public offices by requiring possession of a social status that the council had the power to effectively provide their dependents and clients and recognize in the first instance. Moreover, the council instituted fiscal privileges to increase the economic benefits derived from this status. In the wake of these changes in the city's tax regimes and qualifications for municipal office, litigation over the status of hidalgo increased. In the city of Seville council elites refashioned existing legal structures and norms to enjoy greater economic privileges and to control entrance into the municipal government. These changes established a situation in which those who lacked sufficient connections with the dominant local elites could not easily gain recognition of the status necessary to enter the political class of the city. Inequalities in Seville in the sixteenth century were not founded in distinct legal rights linked to estates. Instead, those with material advantages—patronage and wealth—were able to appeal to such legal rights to gain and perpetuate their superior social and economic positions.[99] Most individuals who claimed the status of hidalguía gained recognition of their status tacitly through the operations and favors of the city council; only those that faced opposition from the council had to achieve recognition of status through litigation at the royal chancery court.

3

MIGRATION, RESETTLEMENT, AND STATUS

On May 30, 1528, a new citizen of Seville named Alonso Caravajal initiated a lawsuit at the chancery court in Granada against Seville's city council to gain recognition of his hidalguía. Alonso's family originated from the town of Ocaña, roughly four hundred kilometers north of Seville on the northern fringes of La Mancha. While Alonso had been born in Ocaña, he had migrated to Seville at least a decade earlier, settled permanently in the city, and eventually became a municipal citizen (*vecino*). Once a citizen, Alonso sought to gain recognition of his hidalgo status to enjoy the limited tax privileges it afforded. Seville's city council summarily rejected his initial claim to hidalguía, so he turned to royal justice at the chancery court. The city's denial of Alonso's status came despite his possession of a royal letter issued in 1468 testifying to Enrique IV's grant of hidalgo status to his grandfather Pedro Gonçalo de Caravajal and a confirmation of this grant provided to his father by Isabel and Fernando in 1499.[1] Thirteen years after Alonso presented his original complaint at the chancery court in Granada, and after multiple rulings and appeals, the court definitively ruled in his favor on September 2, 1541. This was not the only time a member of his family had to litigate for hidalgo status. While Alonso's litigation dragged on, a relative named Francisco de Caravajal had a lawsuit in 1536 against the council of Villarubio, a small municipality roughly fifty-five kilometers east of Ocaña. Another relation named Bernardino de Caravajal also had a lawsuit with the council of Ocaña itself in 1539.[2]

As the basis of a sixteenth-century Castilian's political identity, municipal citizenship was an essential first step in litigation for hidalgo status. In all lawsuits of hidalguía the court clerk listed the claimant as a citizen of the city, town, or village that opposed recognition of his or her status. In these cases the litigant was usually either a new citizen who had acquired citizenship after maintaining a household in the municipality for a set number of years—ten years for sixteenth-century Seville—or the descendant of a family that had acquired citizenship a generation earlier and had been unable to acquire recognition of the status of hidalgo in their first generation of residence in the municipality.[3]

In early modern Castile an individual or family could move easily from one municipality to another, but the status and privileges they possessed could not.[4] For Castilians who enjoyed the recognition of hidalgo status, moving and settling in a different municipality often led to challenges to their status and the beginning of legal actions.[5] Alternatively, propertied families of nonhidalgo lineage who had accumulated wealth in one locality could seize the opportunity provided by moving to a new municipality to claim hidalguía. Municipal councils viewed the claims of these new immigrants to possess legal privileges, especially tax exemptions, with hostility. For municipal authorities and officials, resettlement provided the opportunity to deny a family the privileges they claimed. Consequently, migration rendered status unstable and placed the enjoyment of privilege in jeopardy. The litigation that Alonso Caravajal had to initiate against the city of Seville in 1528 highlights the troubles encountered by hidalgos who tried to move to and settle in new communities.

As the first chapter suggests, gaining recognition of hidalgo status and maintaining it in the late medieval and early modern periods was a continual process that required the cultivation of community recognition and the acquiescence of local authorities; it was not a one-time event realized solely through a royal grant or a royal judge's ruling and subsequently fixed for perpetuity. Successive generations of a family often had to obtain authoritative recognition of their possession of hidalgo status multiple times in different locations and even at different times in the same municipality.

To understand the fight for privilege and status in Seville, this chapter addresses two distinct but related issues: first, the dynamics between migration and disputes over status in general, and second, the consequences of Seville's particular resettlement for later disputes, especially the ethnic and occupational diversity of migrants to the city prior to the beginning of the sixteenth century. Seville's position both as a traditional site of royal administrative authority and as a growing commercial center increased the opportunities and likelihood for disputes over status due to the influx of migrants and settlers, which was considerable in the late fifteenth and sixteenth centuries. Nevertheless, during this period, the city was not unique in its economic expansion or in the arrival of new residents. Migration and resettlement throughout the territories of the Crown of Castile was common and unimpeded. Likewise, municipal resistance to new citizens claiming hidalgo status was pervasive, whether the municipality was a major city with representation at the Castilian Cortes or a small village. To illustrate the widespread consequences of migration and demonstrate the general nature and form of municipal resistance to the claims of new residents and citizens, the chapter examines a series of cases from outside of Seville ranging from the fifteenth century until the late sixteenth century.

The second part of the chapter lays the groundwork for understanding disputes over hidalgo status in sixteenth-century Seville by situating them in the broader urban life of the city. It does this through a review of Seville's medieval resettlement and repopulation after its conquest in the mid-thirteenth century. It particularly examines the demographic composition and origins of its citizenry and residents. The diverse groups that settled in the city contributed to the nature of later disputes over status. The chapter traces some definable groups among the many who migrated to and ultimately settled in Seville and later variably enjoyed the privileges of hidalguía or became embroiled in disputes over the status. As reviewed in the previous chapter, hidalguía as a source of privilege was inconsequential in late medieval Seville and became significant only in the second decade of the sixteenth century. By this point some Sevillian families, who ostensibly did not conform to existing legal or cultural discourses defining hidalguía, possessed the necessary political and economic influence to adopt this identity. At the same time other individuals of similar origins already resident in the city or arriving in the sixteenth century sought to do so and faced the resistance of local authorities.

MULTIGENERATIONAL LITIGATION AND DISPUTES OUTSIDE OF SEVILLE

Other than the current examination of Seville and Marie-Claude Gerbet and Janine Fayard's study of southern Extremadura, no systematic research of lawsuits of hidalguía for other municipalities and territories exists.[6] Nevertheless, anecdotal evidence reveals both the resistance that families faced for the recognition of status when they resettled and the multigenerational nature of litigation over hidalguía. The story of the litigant Hernando Mexía de Chirino and his ancestors and descendants aptly demonstrates this process, as members of the extended family moved from New Castile to La Mancha and ultimately to Andalusia. The extensive records of the family's litigation reveal how the Mexía de Chirinos engaged in multiple lawsuits and appeals over a seventy-year period and perhaps even longer. Originally from the town of Guadalajara, Mexía de Chirino's great-great grandfather, Alonso de Guadalajara, resettled in Cuenca during the early fifteenth century. Witnesses later testified that Alonso's son Hernando Alonso Chirino held the office of regidor in Cuenca, defended the city during the civil wars of the late fifteenth century, was locally recognized as a caballero, and did not pay taxes.[7] His sons and grandsons later moved to the town of Úbeda in Andalusia on the frontier with the kingdom of Granada and finally established themselves in the city of Jaén. While authorities in Cuenca exempted members of the family from paying the pecho, the councils in Úbeda and Jaén resolutely resisted the family's repeated assertions of their status as hidalgos and demands for tax exemption. The earliest suit with the councils of Jaén and Úbeda began during the reign of the Catholic Monarchs, and the Mexía de Chirino family received a series of rulings denying their status. Not until the reign of Felipe II in 1567 did Hernán Mexía de Chirino's daughter Doña María de Narváez regain recognition of her and her family's hidalguía. After resistance to the Chirinos' claims to hidalgo status in their newly adopted municipalities, the family ultimately triumphed, at least in the surviving documentation. While the Mexía de Chirinos' success after repeated failure was unusual, the fact of repeated challenges was the norm.

The example of the related families of the Sande, Carvajal, and Paredes provides similar evidence from Extremadura.[8] Originally from Galicia in the northwest corner of the peninsula, where they claimed they were recognized as hidalgos, members of the Sande family established themselves in Extremadura in the mid-fifteenth century. After multiple generations in the region, Pedro de Sande, a citizen of Caceres, began a lawsuit in 1551 to force recognition of his status and faced council opposition. He continued to appeal adverse rulings without success. Sande's sons continued his efforts in the 1570s and eventually succeeded in gaining recognition of their hidalguía more than twenty years after their father's first efforts.

In the case of the Diosdado family, whether its members moved to a municipality a day's journey from their native town in Extremadura or traveled thousands of kilometers to settle in a newly discovered continent, they faced repeated obstacles and resistance to their claims to hidalgo status (see fig. 3).[9]

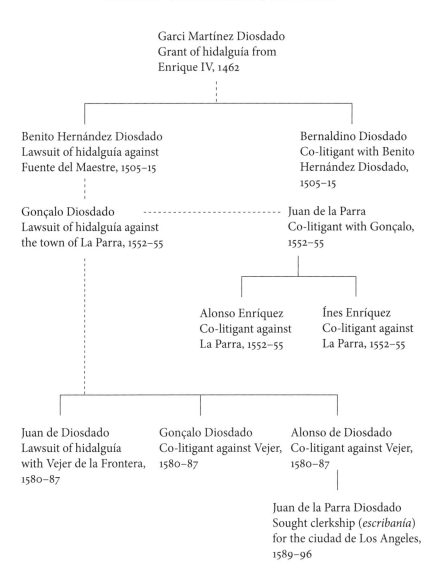

Fig. 3 Members of the Diosdado family and their litigation for hidalgo status. Direct
lines of descent are represented by solid lines; dashed lines represent kinship relations
that are indirect or unspecified in the documents.

Members of the family had to litigate at least three different times in the sixteenth century—in 1505, 1552, and 1580—in small municipalities in Extremadura and Andalusia despite seemingly irrefutable evidence supporting their status. The Diosdados based their assertions of hidalguía on the status granted their ancestor Garci Martínez Diosdado. Enrique IV had rewarded Garci Martínez, vecino of La Parra, with hidalgo status on October 29, 1462, while on campaign in the town of Agreda near the frontier with Aragon. Notably, the king made the grant three years before the rebellion against his rule in 1465 and the notorious grants of hidalguía of the same year. Enrique's letter expressly announced how the monarch possessed the power to provide nobility and hidalguía and included the legal formula by which he appealed to his absolute royal authority to make Garci Martínez Diosdado and his descendants hidalgos in perpetuity. Martínez received a formal confirmation of the royal favor two months later in Segovia from the king's senior accountant and his secretary of privileges. Some of the more esteemed witnesses to the grant included Don Fadrique, the king's cousin and admiral of Castile; Juan de Guzmán, Duke of Medina Sidonia; and Alonso Pimentel, Count of Benavente.

In the family's earliest recorded dispute over their hidalgo status in 1505, the brothers Benito Hernández Diosdado and Bernaldino Diosdado, citizens of the town of Fuente del Maestre in southeastern Extremadura, refused to pay their contribution to the servicio. The two men were the sons of Esteban Martínez Diosdado, who had moved from the town of La Parra, roughly thirty-two kilometers to the west. Esteban's exact relationship to Garci is unstated in the document. In response to the brothers' resistance to the royal tax imposed by the municipality, the sheriff of Fuente del Maestre seized household tools and implements valued at 900 maravedís as security for their tax obligation. The brothers then filed a complaint with the chancery court. In the subsequent dispute, the council employed a range of procedural and substantive arguments against the Diosdados, alleging that they had failed to announce their status by the deadline set by the town and that the family's privilege was based on a letter issued by Enrique IV for which the legal basis was no longer valid. Additionally, the council stated that the Diosdado brothers were obligated to maintain horse and arms, and they had failed to do so and consequently should not be acknowledged as hidalgos. Not least among the objections, the council claimed that they were of illegitimate birth. The Diosdado brothers responded by asserting the legitimacy of their ancestor's privilege. Nine years after the original complaint, on September 9, 1514, the chancery court in Valladolid ruled in favor of the Diosdado brothers. The royal prosecutor (*fiscal*) and the council of Fuente del Maestre immediately appealed the ruling.[10] As part of their appeal, they asserted that the privilege had been revoked by laws issued in the Cortes and royal edicts.[11] They also stated that the privilege was never recognized in the town and that the family had always paid the pecho. Despite the efforts of council and prosecutor, the court's judges again ruled in favor of the brothers on March 15, 1515.

A little over thirty years later, another dispute arose in the town of the family's origin.[12] In this instance, the town council of La Parra, rather than seizing property, took the unusual step of presenting a complaint at the chancery court of Granada against Gonçalo Diosdado and his relatives Juan de la Parra and Juan's son and daughter, Alonso and Ínes Enríquez. The council's attorney alleged that the family were common taxpayers and had always contributed to royal and council taxes like other pecheros but recently had wanted to avoid paying the pechos and sought recognition as hidalgos. As evidence of their status, the members of the Diosdado family presented not only a copy of the privilege accorded to Garci Martínez Diosdado but also the judicial ruling and writ won by the Diosdado brothers in 1515. Witnesses' testimony confirmed the relationship of the litigants with the earlier Diosdado and revealed Juan de la Parra's connections with powerful local figures. For many years Juan de la Parra had served the fourth Count of Feria, Pedro Fernández de Córdoba y Figueroa, as steward and accountant for the nearby town of Zafra, one of the count's seigneurial properties. Moreover, Juan de la Parra's own father had been secretary to the previous Count of Feria, Lorenzo Suárez de Figueroa. Juan had lived most of his life in Zafra and briefly in Badajoz, his wife María de Enríquez's native city, and had only returned to Zafra after her death and shortly before the dispute. Significantly, La Parra was also one of the count's towns. On October 13, 1553, the judges in Granada ruled that the prosecutor and the town council had failed to prove their claims against Gonçalo Diosdado, Juan Parra, and Juan's son and daughter. The council and royal prosecutor twice unsuccessfully appealed the ruling, which the court definitively confirmed in March 1555.

Other descendants of Garci Martínez Diosdado, the brothers Juan de Diosdado, Gonçalo Diosdado, and Alonso de Diosdado, all natives of La Parra, engaged in additional litigation over hidalgo status with the town of Vejer de la Frontera between 1580 and 1587.[13] Far from the Diosdado hometown of La Parra in Extremadura, Vejer de la Frontera in southwestern Andalusia perches on a hill about ten kilometers from the Atlantic coast and about halfway between the port of Cádiz and the strategic town of Tarifa at the Strait of Gibraltar. Vejer's council had demanded that Juan de Diosdado maintain a horse and attend the town's militia musters. Although the court records do not mention contemporary events, the Duke of Medina Sidonia, serving as captain general of Andalusia, was aggressively levying troops for the occupation of Portugal and for coastal defense against Ottoman raids immediately prior to and during these years.[14] When Juan de Diosdado failed to comply with the town's demands, the council assessed taxes against him as a pechero and penalized him 3,000 maravedís. The council also seized goods from the brothers in one of the town's assessments of taxes on its pecheros. Although the brothers had presented the judicial writ supporting their status to the local authorities in 1578, the town council refused to recognize it. By 1580 they presented their complaint to the chancery court. Four years later the judges found in favor of the Diosdado brothers. Again the town appealed the ruling, only to have the judges reconfirm the earlier decision in 1587.

Only two years later, thousands of kilometers across the Atlantic Ocean in the city of Los Angeles in the viceroyalty of New Spain (modern-day Puebla, Mexico), Alonso de Diosdado's son, Juan de la Parra Diosdado, granted his father and uncles authority and power of attorney to obtain evidence and certification of his "descent, purity of lineage, and the nobility of his parents and grandparents."[15] Not only did Juan de la Parra's eventual evidence (*probanza*) of his status reference his distant ancestor Garci Martínez Diosdado, it also cited another relative named Juan de la Parra, who had allegedly served as a secretary to Fernando during the conquest of Granada, had been a knight of the Order of Santiago, and held the *encomiendas* (seigneurial territories of a military order) of Montemolin and Bienvenida. In 1589, Juan de la Parra Diosdado sought formal recognition of his lineage and hidalgo status as a means to obtain the favor of an office of royal clerk in the Indies for the city of Los Angeles.[16] He further empowered his relatives to submit his petition for the office before Felipe II and the council of the Indies. In this instance, even though Juan's efforts to substantiate his status lacked an active opponent, success in the effort to obtain office required him to gather the full complement of evidence and present it before authorities in Castile and in New Spain. He formally gained possession of the office in 1596. Ten years later Juan went to the expense of copying and notarizing the documents testifying to his hidalgo status in the event of future disputes or necessity.

The example of Juan de la Parra Diosdado reveals how claims to hidalgo status continued to arise in Spain's colonies in the Americas in the sixteenth century, even though the Crown largely succeeded in restricting the extension of fiscal exemptions to hidalgos there. For Juan de la Parra, the status of hidalgo was nominally necessary for certain administrative and judicial offices, or at least facilitated acquisition of them, especially when there were multiple competing candidates. Other migrants to the Americas, whether initial conquistadores or later settlers, produced *probanzas* or *relaciones de meritos y servicios* (reports of merits and services) as a means for claiming favors from the royal government and interwove their accounts with claims to elite lineage and hidalgo status (see fig. 4).[17] Such claims had to be managed and maintained and the legal privileges tied to them frequently faced opposition. On November 23, 1580, authorities of the municipal council in Mexico City arrested García de Contreras Figueroa for failure to pay his creditors despite repeated court orders to do so. In García's petition to the royal appellate court (*audiencia*) of New Spain, he claimed that on account of his status as an hidalgo he should not be imprisoned for private debts.[18] Individuals claimed hidalguía to escape incarceration for debt in Castile and the Americas well into the seventeenth century, as in the example of Domingo de Salcedo, who was arrested in Mexico City in 1627 for a debt of 350 gold pesos. Unsurprisingly, the men to whom García de Contreras owed the most substantial sums, Juan Gutíerrez de Bocanegra, Pedro de Prada, and Juan de Olid Peralta, adamantly rejected his claim to hidalgo status and his petition for release. Consequently, the dispute, which had begun as a suit to collect overdue loans, had now transformed into a lawsuit over hidalgo status and one that revealed multiple efforts to maintain this status (see fig. 5).

While García languished in the municipal prison, his brother Juan Alonso de Contreras, the vicar of the silver mines at Guanajuato, gathered evidence to support the family's claim to hidalgo status, including witness depositions, records of past lawsuits, and petitions to the Crown. This evidence revealed that their father, Alonso de Contreras, a native of Segovia, had arrived in New Spain in 1520 with the Panfilio de Narváez expedition and joined Hernán Cortés. Alonso survived early setbacks and defeats to take part not only in the siege and capture of the Aztec capital of Tenochtitlan but in the subsequent conquest and pacification of the territory of Jalisco. Settling in the newly founded Mexico City, Alonso held a number of political and administrative positions as city

Fig. 4 The cover of the *relación de meritos y servicio* produced by Domingo de Salcedo to prove and support his hidalgo status and gain release from debtor's prison. The cover displays the coat of arms of the Urbino family, to which Domingo claimed to be related. Reprinted with permission from the Latin American Library, Tulane University, New Orleans.

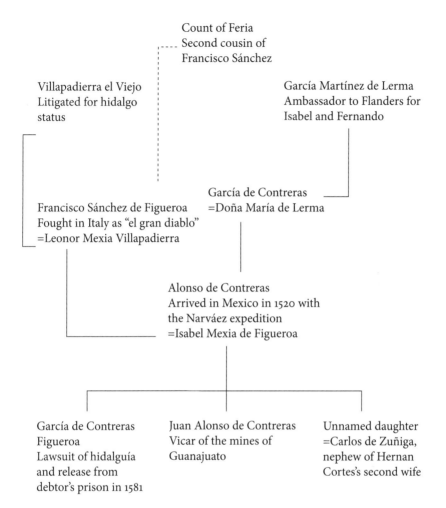

Count of Feria
Second cousin of
Francisco Sánchez

Villapadierra el Viejo
Litigated for hidalgo
status

García Martínez de Lerma
Ambassador to Flanders for
Isabel and Fernando

García de Contreras
=Doña María de Lerma

Francisco Sánchez de Figueroa
Fought in Italy as "el gran diablo"
=Leonor Mexia Villapadierra

Alonso de Contreras
Arrived in Mexico in 1520 with
the Narváez expedition
=Isabel Mexia de Figueroa

García de Contreras
Figueroa
Lawsuit of hidalguía
and release from
debtor's prison in 1581

Juan Alonso de Contreras
Vicar of the mines of
Guanajuato

Unnamed daughter
=Carlos de Zuñiga,
nephew of Hernan
Cortes's second wife

Fig. 5 Members of the Contreras Figueroa family and their litigation for hidalgo status. Direct lines of descent are represented by solid lines; dashed lines represent kinship relations that are indirect or unspecified in the documents.

judge, as councilman, and as judge of the city's black inhabitants. Alonso had direct connections with principal leaders in New Spain, even serving as a factor for Hernán Cortés in the early years of the conquest and later marrying one of his many daughters to Cortés's nephew.[19]

More significant for García de Contreras's hope for release from imprisonment, witnesses and judicial documents testified that his father, Alonso de Contreras, and his father's parents were widely esteemed as caballeros hidalgos in Segovia. One witness even described a feud between García de Contreras, grandfather of the litigant, and Luis Cerón de Pineda, a knight from Toledo, that led the Segovian authorities to jail them both. Other witnesses noted the service Alonso's maternal grandfather, García Martínez de Lerma, an alcalde mayor for the city of Burgos, had provided as an ambassador to Flanders for the Catholic Monarchs. The witnesses testified not only to the hidalgo lineage of García de Contreras's paternal line of descent but also to his lineage on the maternal side. Alonso's wife, Isabel Mexia de Figueroa, was a native of Badajoz, where it was publicly known that her father, Francisco Sánchez de Figueroa, held the epithet "el gran diablo" for his ferocity and bravery in battle, especially in the wars in Italy. Witness testimony also alleged that "the great devil" was the second cousin of the Count of Feria. Other witnesses explicitly recognized that Isabel's mother, Leonor Mexía Villapadierra, received the designation of hijadalgo in her own right, and her family's status had been formally proven through the litigation of her father.[20]

Alonso de Contreras had originally gathered the information about his own deeds and his family's lineage for a petition in 1558 to protect his property and obtain additional encomiendas and favors from the Crown. He emphasized how his participation in the conquest expeditions had always been at his own cost and had been done as an hidalgo and person of quality. As a participant in the early conquests in New Spain, Alonso had received half of the tribute for the Mixtec town of Tamazola and another half of the tribute from Zenzontepeque. Alonso asserted that these grants had never been sufficient compensation and provided meager rents. To his further financial detriment, a general royal edict had deprived him of the labor of the Indians of his encomiendas.[21] In 1557 the audiencia in Mexico City had adjudicated a suit between the inhabitants of Tamazola and the Spanish settlers who held rights to tribute and labor from their community (*encomenderos*), Alonso de Contreras and Juan Vázquez, concerning a reduction in annual payments of the encomienda, in which the court had lowered the tribute the towns owed. It is unclear from the surviving documents whether Alonso secured additional grants from the Crown, but his son Juan Alonso made sure to copy the documents in 1567 and other depositions taken in 1547 from natives of Segovia to verify Alonso's hidalgo status. These documents proved essential for establishing García de Contreras's status and ultimately for bringing about his release from prison in 1581, but it did not resolve his financial difficulties with his creditors. The Contreras Figueroa family provides evidence of multigenerational appeals and disputes over hidalguía in Iberia and in New Spain. It also illustrates continued interests in cultivating and maintaining the status of hidalgo in the Americas and challenges to such efforts.

THE LATE MEDIEVAL RESETTLEMENT OF SEVILLE

The previous chapter addressed how changes in the rules for holding office in Seville and reform in the city's tax regime affected claims to hidalgo status. In addition to changes in the political and fiscal structures of the city, Seville's demographic composition significantly shaped the nature and development of disputes over status. From the moment Christian forces conquered Seville in 1248, inhabitants of the many territories of the Crown of Castile seized the opportunity to settle in the ancient city and its surrounding hinterland. The conditions of the city's surrender required the evacuation of the existing Muslim population and the transfer of immovable properties to Fernando III, whose government allocated property and lands in the city and its surrounding territory to participants in the campaign and royal supporters.[22] While the stream of settlers was initially slow and the numbers fluctuated in the early decades, as the first arrivals did not always make permanent roots, the city's new population continued to grow until the pandemics of the mid-fourteenth century. The population decline experienced throughout western Europe during this period began to reverse itself in Seville by the second half of the fifteenth century.

The settlers who arrived during the 250 years following the Christian conquest of Seville came from territories and municipalities throughout the Crown of Castile and even from outside Castilian territory. A small but significant number of these new settlers and migrants and their descendants later engaged in disputes over hidalgo status in the late fifteenth and sixteenth centuries. Some of these migrants, due to their occupations or to their ethnic origin, more readily initiated disputes over status or became conspicuous to their contemporaries, and subsequently to modern historians, for claiming hidalgo status. Due to the nature of the surviving evidence from lawsuits of hidalguía, which is often fragmentary and incomplete and lacking evidence from both parties, it is difficult to determine or verify the occupation, social status, or origin of the litigants and their ancestors. While the documents sometimes reveal the municipality of previous citizenship, these municipalities are not always the family's place of origin, which at times was detailed and at other times was not. Moreover, the litigants on occasion deliberately obscured this information or falsified it. In addition to the surviving records of litigation, other sources from the period allow a rough identification of the litigants into distinct demographic groups who proved to be conspicuous in the political and economic life of the city and who can be readily identified because of their commercial and political activities, their distinct ethnic origin as revealed by their surnames, or their religious background. Prominent among these groups were merchants and traders of diverse Iberian and non-Iberian origin, naturalized Genoese and other Italians, natives of the Basque territories, and the descendants of converted Jews (*conversos*).

Paradoxically, among those families involved in disputes over hidalguía were natives of the Basque territories, a group that modern historians conventionally present as being readily accepted as hidalgos. Also, seemingly in opposition to contemporary discourses on nobility and hidalguía, the descendants of converted Jews and foreign merchants in Seville who entered into Seville's elite ruling class came to be recognized as hidalgos. While some of these new elites from converso and merchant families faced opposition to their claims to hidalgo status, others easily enjoyed their relatively newly obtained hidalguía.

From the late thirteenth century individual traders and even colonies of merchants from the different kingdoms of the Iberian Peninsula and from outside it established themselves in the city on both a temporary and more permanent basis.[23] The city held a unique position in the lower Guadalquivir valley that allowed easy access to the Atlantic down one of the peninsula's few major navigable rivers. Seville's location kept it secure from naval attack and piracy and gave advantageous access to regional overland routes. While Seville's predominantly Christian population and the number of resident merchants declined in the face of epidemic disease and a depressed economy in the second half of the fourteenth century, economic recovery beginning in the mid-fifteenth century led to a transformation of the city into one of the major commercial metropolises of Europe. The agricultural wealth of Seville's surrounding territories, which produced diverse commodities for international trade, particularly olive oil, wine, grains, animal hides, and leather, contributed to its transformation and development. In addition to the commodities from Seville's immediate hinterland were goods, such as mercury and raw wool, funneled through the city from the interior of the southern half of the peninsula. Seville also held a strategic geographic position in terms of trade routes and networks both traditional and new—between the Mediterranean and the Atlantic and between Europe and North Africa. It served as the point of entry and redistribution of Mediterranean, Atlantic, and North African goods for much of the southern half of the Crown of Castile. Moreover, the city joined together a developed network of communication and transport by river and land routes. As a major commercial crossroads, Seville not only marketed local commodities and redistributed imports but also funneled them into a range of local craft and manufacturing enterprises for the production of goods, including wood containers, ceramics, tiles, and cloth, as well as ship construction. Due to these factors and its own growing market of consumers, Seville drew petty traders as well as international merchants. By the late fourteenth and fifteenth centuries the most prominent communities of foreign merchants in the city came from Galicia, Burgos, the Basque territories, Catalonia, Portugal, and Genoa.[24]

The Genoese and Other Foreign Merchants

While Italian merchants from a number of the different republics and cities lived and worked in Seville, the Genoese had the longest and most substantial presence. Traders from Genoa not only visited the city but also were resident in Seville as early as 1160, when the Almohad Berber dynasty briefly made Seville its capital city. The Genoese presence increased in the immediate wake of the 1248 conquest due to generous grants from the Castilian king, Fernando III, and his successors, who provided Genoese merchants with permanent facilities, their own neighborhood, and a range of privileges. The Genoese community in Seville held the right to adjudicate its own civil disputes, and it received royal guarantees of protection for commerce and reduced customs dues. In the late thirteenth and early fourteenth centuries the Genoese lent crucial naval support for Castilian territorial expansion, particularly during the capture of the port city of Tarifa in 1292 and the later capture of Algeciras, which allowed tentative control of the Strait of Gibraltar and greater security from North African military expeditions and raids. The military, commercial, and financial roles that the Genoese played for the Crown of Castile contributed to the formal establishment of a trading colony with recognized privileges.

In the second half of the fifteenth century the Genoese colony doubled in size.[25] A 1474 letter from the Republic of Genoa to the city council of Seville noted more than one hundred resident Genoese merchants.[26] While most Genoese merchants did not maintain permanent residence in Seville, a minority did and some eventually became naturalized and even entered the ranks of the city's elite. Members of the Cataño (Cattaneo) family became citizens by the late fourteenth century, while members of the active and prominent Centurión, Castaño, Italiano, Gentil (Gentile), Salvago, Spínola, and Grimaldo (Grimaldi) families entered the ranks of Seville's citizens by the last third of the fifteenth century.[27] These Genoese engaged in both private and public commercial and financial activities. Some naturalized Genoese even came to hold significant administrative and political positions in Seville's municipal government. For example, Jorge Cataño held the office of jurado, which he passed to Diego de Céspedes in 1478, while Rodrigo Cataño later served in the same office for the parish of Santa María la Blanca in 1485.[28] In a position of greater consequence for the running of the city's affairs, Juan Cataño filled the office of veinticuatro during the 1470s.[29] The merchant Marco Cataño married a daughter of Pedro de Fuentes, Señor of Fuentes, and his wife, María de Guzmán.[30] Either through successful integration with local elites, royal favor, or both, the Cataños had successfully entered the city's ruling elite.

Another Genoese family that thoroughly assimilated and successfully established themselves as citizens of Seville and members of the city's government were the Pinelos (Pinelli). One prominent member of the family, Francisco Pinelo, became a citizen of Seville in the last decades of the fifteenth century. During these years Pinelo helped finance the campaigns of the Granadan war for the Catholic Monarchs, especially providing needed funds for the siege of Baza.[31] He also played a significant role in Atlantic exploration when he loaned 1,400,000 maravedís to the Catholic Monarchs to cover the costs of outfitting the ships for Columbus's first voyage.[32] In addition to holding the offices of jurado of his parish and fiel ejecutor for the city, Francisco Pinelo became one of the first managing factors of the House of Trade (Casa de Contratación) when it was established in 1503. Francisco married María de la Torre, who belonged to one of Seville's established caballero families. Francisco had two sons, Pedro and Jeronimo, who remained prominent in Sevillano society.

Carlos Negrón, the son of another naturalized Genoese merchant, also successfully assimilated into Castilian society. Born in 1507, Carlos earned a law degree at the University of Salamanca, served as a legal adviser to Seville's tribunal of the Inquisition, and was named as prosecutor to the councils of the Indies and the treasury by Felipe II in 1572. In addition to his judicial activities, he owned two galleons that ran slaves between Africa and Veracruz in New Spain. Carlos married Ana de la Cueva, whose family were local notables and arranged a favorable marriage for his eldest son, Julio, to Leonora Zapata Osorio.[33] Leonora was the daughter of Francisco Zapata de Cisneros, the Count of Barajas and asistente for Seville from 1573 to 1578. Julio eventually became Lord of Villa del Casar in Extremadura. Despite Carlos's success and the advantageous marriages of his children, a relative, Jorge Negron, found it necessary to litigate for his hidalgo status in 1550.[34] Carlos's son Camilo and a relative, Juan Negron, also had lawsuits and eventual confirmations of their status in 1589.[35]

Among the Genoese who established themselves in Seville were some who belonged to Genoa's elite ranks, including the city's nobles or at least those with noble pretensions. Among these nobles were members of the Bocanegra family. The Seville-based branch of the Bocanegras descended from a Genoese admiral and ship owner, who had contributed to the capture of the Muslim port city Algeciras and subsequently settled in Seville during the reign of Alfonso XI. At least two notable members of the family were naturalized by 1384, Alonso de Bocanegra, Lord of Palma de Rio, and Luis de Bocanegra, veinticuatro of the city.[36] As with other late medieval Italian city-states, the distinction between old nobility and the elite merchant class was often unclear. Efforts to define the established noble families culminated in 1528, when the city council of Genoa, at the instigation of the admiral Andrea Doria, passed a law designating the twenty-eight families that formed this rank. Of these twenty-eight families, twenty-one of them had representatives in Seville in the early sixteenth century.[37]

Considering the success that some of the Genoese families, or at least branches of these families, had in assimilating into Sevillano society, it is unsurprising that they sought and obtained privileges reserved for hidalgos. In 1515, the first year of the blanca de la carne, recipients of Genoese descent included Juan and Diego Cataño, Niculosa de Spinola, and Cristóbal and Bernardo Pinelo.[38] Among these men, Cristóbal Pinelo was listed as a city jurado, the very office responsible for assessing status. For the Genoese and other groups in Seville, access to the office of jurado facilitated recognition and confirmation of social status.

While the Genoese were certainly not the only foreign merchants in Seville, they were without question the largest and most evident non-Castilian community. Although Portuguese and Catalan traders were also present in high numbers through the first half of the fourteenth century, they declined in num-

ber and virtually disappeared in the fifteenth century, without leaving conspicuous established assimilated families. Despite their virtual disappearance, the
street that housed the shops of Catalan merchants still bears their name. In
contrast to the declining presence of the Portuguese and Catalans, traders from
other territories of the Crown of Castile became more active in the city in the
1400s, particularly those from the Old Castilian city of Burgos and the coastal
towns of Galicia and the Basque territories.

From the mid-fifteenth century the simultaneous transformation of Seville
into one of the major commercial centers of Europe and the increase in the
level of national and international trade in the North Atlantic contributed to
more significant numbers of Burgalese and Basque merchants in the city. Merchants from the northern half of the peninsula had previously focused their
efforts in shipping Castilian wool and Basque iron to Flanders and other northern European markets. Building on their late medieval trade in the North
Atlantic, the number of merchants from Burgos who were resident in Seville
grew substantially in the second half of the century. These traders played a crucial role funneling shipments of grain to Andalusia during years of severe wheat
shortages in the second half of the fifteenth century. The Guadalquivir valley
proved to be a grain house for other regions of the peninsula in good years,
while having to import wheat in years of poor harvests. In the bad years the city
turned to the Burgalese colony of merchants, particularly between 1467 and
1469, in 1473, and in the long crisis of 1503–8. The last of these crises affected the
entire Mediterranean, but was worse in Seville due to the pestilence of 1507 and
a plague of locusts that prolonged shortages until 1510. Consequently, in the
period between 1467 and 1510 there were around 191 merchants from Burgos
operating in Seville. Roughly one-fifth of these merchants established themselves definitively in the city. Through the purchase of juros and the investment
of part of their capital in land, these merchants sought not only to diversify
their risks but also to imitate the activities of Seville's local elites and seigneurial
families. Among the Burgalese merchants who followed these strategies, the
more successful in the late fifteenth century were Tomás de Palenzuela, Bernardino de Isla, and Álvaro de Valladolid.[39] The last of these men even married
Isabel de Saavedra, the daughter of Fernando Arias de Saavedra, one of the
city's councilmen and member of a regional knightly family.[40]

Once established in Seville, or other Andalusian municipalities, the Burgalese came to dominate the trade in wool from Córdoba to North Africa as
well as the import of manufactured textiles from northern France and Flanders.

They also traded in commodities produced in the newly colonized Atlantic islands such as hides, dyes, dried fruit, and sugar. While these merchants used both land and river routes, they relied heavily on maritime shipping. For this reason they, like their Genoese and Basque counterparts, collectively sought to own ships in part or entirely. In this respect they engaged in the same strategies as members of Seville's local elite, including resident seigneurial families and the Genoese.[41] Among the men of Burgos who bought ships was the merchant Álvaro de Briones.[42] Like other Burgalese merchants, Briones gained citizenship in Seville, eventually served on the city council as a jurado, and was one of the recipients of the blanca in 1515.

Among the foreign and Castilian merchants and their respective descendants who became citizens of Seville shortly before and after the turn of the century, some succeeded in assimilating into the ranks of the city's elites while others sought to do so and failed. Works of literature from the period amply testify to the city's social mobility, the intermarriage of commercial and financial elites with traditional landed nobles, and the criticisms and satires of these phenomena.[43] Successful merchants, especially those who held council offices or had family members who did, came to enjoy privileges based on the status of hidalgo. Those who less successfully assimilated, and yet continued to covet these privileges, chose the route of litigation at the chancery court. Among these naturalized merchants and their descendants, some sought recognition as hidalgos in the early sixteenth century and even initiated lawsuits against the city of Seville. Even prior to the city's change in its tax regime, the Burgalese merchant Pedro de Carrión sought recognition as an hidalgo in 1489 to avoid the city's property tax. Likewise, another citizen of Seville and native of Burgos, Fernando Castro de la Hoz, also litigated for his hidalgo status to avoid paying the pecho.[44]

Another significant problem for determining hidalgo status in the sixteenth century that was related to the issue of migration was the diversity of municipal practices for providing privileges to hidalgos. Some municipalities, most notably the cities of Toledo and Burgos, did not provide fiscal privileges such as tax exemption to hidalgos exclusively.[45] Instead, all citizens of these two major municipalities enjoyed the tax exemptions accorded to hidalgos. The citizens of the city of Burgos as a community possessed the privilege of exemption from the servicio originally granted by Alfonso X. The city maintained this privilege through the Trastamara period and the reign of Carlos I. Felipe II also recognized the privilege but required that it be reconfirmed every three years when the servicio came due.[46] Notably, these privileges were not extended to the citizens of Toledo's and Burgos's subject towns and villages. When the Crown began efforts to sell the status of hidalgo during the reign of Felipe II, the purveyor of patents of hidalguía in Toledo tried to interest potential buyers by pointing out that they would be considered common pecheros if they left the city and sought to resettle elsewhere.[47] Consequently, efforts to prove or to challenge claims of hidalguía for individuals and families from these municipalities lacked evidence in the form of distinct tax rolls or lists for hidalgos and pecheros.

Among the Burgalese and Genoese who obtained citizenship in Seville—including those who succeeded in gaining local political office—some faced resistance to their claims to hidalgo status and enjoyment of associated privileges. In 1515, Burgalese native Bernaldino de Isla held the office of jurado. Despite initial opposition to his claims, he finally succeeded in gaining exemption from the tax when the council ordered that his name be removed from the list of common taxpayers and his property returned to him.[48] The council did the same for Bernaldino's relative García de Isla. The same year the Genoese merchant Jeronimo Salvago complained that the jurado Diego Bernal de Girona had violated the privileges bestowed on him by the Crown.[49] In this instance, Salvago appeared to be contending against the traditional property taxes the city used to pay the servicio and not the blanca excise tax, which was just being implemented. Moreover, it is not clear whether he based his demand for exemption on his privileges as a Genoese merchant or if he claimed hidalgo status. As the next chapter addresses in greater detail, individuals commonly used evidence of past tax exemptions enjoyed by themselves personally or by relatives as evidence for the possession of hidalguía, whether or not the exemptions enjoyed had been the result of hidalgo status. The exact basis for Salvago's complaint is unclear from surviving records. In contrast, a dispute initiated a number of years earlier by the Genoese merchants Esteban and Gaspar Centurión against Seville's city council explicitly asserted the brothers' status as hidalgos.[50] The dispute with the city became a multiyear lawsuit that eventually arrived at the tribunal of the hidalgos at the chancery court in Granada, was appealed to the court's president, and drew the attention of Fernando of Aragon, who at the time was acting regent of Castile for his daughter Juana.

Between 1513 and 1517 Gaspar Centurión was one of the most active capitalists and financiers of Genoese origin in Seville, especially for the provision of essential sea loans for the acquisition, transport, and security of merchandise in the western Mediterranean and Atlantic trade.[51] Gaspar's brother Esteban was primarily a resident of the city of Granada but spent a few months each year in Seville, where he had various commercial enterprises and owned the ship *La Victoria*. In the court documents the plaintiffs avoided the typical legal designation of resident (*morado*) or citizen and described themselves instead as *habitantes* of the city of Seville. More significant, they claimed that their father was an hijodalgo according to the standard Castilian formulary. As part of the evidence for their claims, they submitted to the court their letter of naturalization (*carta de naturaleza*), recognizing that they belonged to the community of the kingdom of Castile. This letter, dated April 13, 1508, and issued in the name of Queen Juana, stated that she bestowed native status on members of the Centurión and Doria families and provided them with various privileges, notably rights to trade in the Indies.[52] In addition to Esteban and Gaspar, the letter conveyed *naturaleza* (nativeness) to their brothers Martín and Melchior Centurión and the Genoese banker Francisco Doria. Not only did members of the family actively trade with the Indies, but one relation, Benito Centurión, served as the family agent on the island of Santo Domingo. Decades earlier a young Christopher Columbus had worked for the Centurión family. Although the Centurións did not directly invest in Columbus's voyages of exploration, they served as personal creditors for the admiral and his descendants and funneled monies for his third voyage.[53]

Seemingly unconcerned with their foreign origin and their very public commercial activities, the Centurións' witnesses testified that Esteban and Gaspar's father and grandfather were hidalgos and were publicly held as such. The witnesses themselves were mostly Genoese, including Andrea Doria.[54] This Andrea Doria was either the famous Genoese admiral, who decades later provided crucial naval support for Carlos I, or a relative of the same name. A subsequent ruling from May 10, 1514, again issued in Juana's name, declared that naturalized foreigners should enjoy the privilege of hidalgo and that the plaintiffs had proven that they and their ancestors were *hijosdalgo notorios*. The courts' ruling made mention of a similar and earlier grant to Bernaldo Pinelo, another of Seville's citizens of Genoese origin.[55] The court president and judges ordered the city council to return seized property to the Centurión brothers and strike their names from the lists of taxpayers. The council appealed the ruling. After review the court upheld the earlier decision and ordered the city to comply with the previous orders and not to harass the Centuriónes any longer. To ensure the city's compliance, the court threatened monetary penalties and placed a deadline for the city to implement the order.[56]

Despite considerable opposition, the Centuriónes ultimately succeeded in gaining recognition of their status as hidalgos. The Centuriónes were not unique in their claims to status and privileges associated with it, or to resistance against these claims. Numerous other Genoese and Italians had lawsuits of hidalguía in the course of the sixteenth century, including members of already settled and hispanized families, as well as members of families, or branches of families, that did not have established predecessors.[57] Some of these litigants were prominent traders and maintained business and martial relations with other Genoese. One of these hispanized would-be hidalgos of Genoese origin, Luis Spinola, established a company with a group of Genoese merchants in 1550 for the trade of merchandise and slaves between Seville and the Americas.[58] The same year he began a lawsuit at the chancery court to obtain recognition of hidalgo status.[59] As we will see in subsequent chapters, some of these disputes left records at the tribunal of the hijosdalgo at the chancery court and others did not.

Basques and Their Descendants

Among the new migrants to the city of Seville and its many subject municipalities, settlers from the Basque territories of Vizcaya and Guipúzcoa and their descendants initiated a high number of lawsuits in their efforts to obtain economic privileges. While considerable cultural, linguistic, and social diversity existed among the Basque peoples populating these two small territories, Basque natives and their descendants in the course of the sixteenth century came to be united by a common claim to being hidalgos.[60] Recent scholarship has demonstrated that Basque claims to universal hidalgo status were the result of a process of cultural and political identity formation that culminated in the sixteenth century and that the status had not been recognized for all natives of the Basque territories during the Middle Ages. In the eleventh and twelfth centuries these territories had been part of the kingdom of Pamplona and its successor state, the kingdom of Navarre, which had close relations with the county of Castile. With Castile's expansion and growing political influence, especially after its union with León, the Basque territories gradually came into Castile's sphere of influence, and its prominent noble families (*parientes mayores*) developed ties with the Castilian royal court and the major Castilian magnates.

By the beginning of the thirteenth century the Crown of Castile successfully annexed the Basque territories of Alava, Vizcaya, and Guipúzcoa. Nevertheless, these territories, especially the latter two, preserved significant political independence and successfully obtained the Castilian monarchs' acceptance of their local customs and freedoms. In the course of the fourteenth and fifteenth centuries Castilian monarchs further formally recognized Basque freedoms through the redaction and royal confirmation of municipal and eventually regional charters.[61] From the time that the monarchs of Castile took the title of Lord of Vizcaya, they were expected to visit the territory and swear to uphold the fueros, customs, and liberties of Vizcaya at the tree of Guernica, where the general assembly of the Vizcaínos was held. Notably Fernando of Aragon performed this act in July 1476 in the midst of Castile's succession struggle and to ensure continued Basque loyalty prior to an imminent French invasion of Guipúzcoa.[62]

During the fourteenth and fifteenth centuries the designation of hidalgo was used in Basque territories, but it did not extend to all inhabitants nor did Basque hidalgos enjoy privileges in all localities.[63] In contrast to twelfth- and thirteenth-century charters issued to towns in Vizcaya, which did not recognize distinctions among their citizens and even required hidalgo settlers to forgo any privileges, charters produced in the late medieval period acknowledged distinctions even as the towns as a whole pressed for the extension of privileges to all citizens. Outside the jurisdiction of the new townships, there continued to be a large number of Vizcaínos designated as taxed farmers (*labradores censuarios*), who provided an annual tax to the Lord of Vizcaya, and other Basques referred to as estate cultivators (*labradores solariegos*), who worked the lands of the parientes mayores. While the *Fuero viejo de Vizcaya* produced in 1452 explicitly declared the privileges held by Basque hidalgos—exemption from tributes that hidalgos in the rest of the Crown of Castile enjoyed, the right to construct fortified houses, the freedom to enter into alliances with other hidalgos, the inviolability of their homes, and immunity from arrest for debt or judicial torture—it also complained that Basque labradores who fled to the towns were obtaining privileges equivalent to those held by hidalgos. In Guipúzcoa during the fifteenth century, the towns likewise played an equivalent and perhaps even greater role in extending the status of hidalguía, as liberties and privileges held by municipal citizens were transferred to all natives as a unified province, and provincial institutions emerged from the collective of municipalities.[64]

The process of ceding unique legal status to all natives of Vizcaya culminated early in the reign of Carlos I with the remarkable and novel statement of universal hidalguía among Vizcaínos and the extension of Basque privileges and freedoms outside of their native lands to the other territories of the Crown of

Castile. This was done through royal recognition of a revised version of the fuero of Vizcaya produced in 1526, which recognized a universal hidalguía for all natives of the territory.[65] The relevant passage stated that "any native son of Vizcaya, or his dependents, who should marry or become municipal citizens or residents outside of the territory of Vizcaya in any other place or province of the kingdoms of Spain, demonstrating and providing proof that they are native Basques, should be allowed their hidalguía and should have kept for them the privileges, freedoms, and liberties that an hidalgo should completely enjoy according to the fuero de España."[66] Prior to this pronouncement, it is not clear whether or not Basques had widely expected to receive recognition as hidalgos.

Despite the apparent royal recognition of universal Basque hidalguía in 1526, municipal governments throughout the territories of the Crown of Castile frequently had proven unwilling to recognize the hidalgo status of Basques who settled in their communities in the fifteenth century, and they largely continued to resist such claims throughout the sixteenth century. Even when the councils nominally conceded hidalgo status to Basque claimants, they frequently refused to provide them with accompanying privileges. The disjunction between local municipal determination of status and royal confirmation of Basque privilege generated numerous disputes and lawsuits. The novel and innovative claim to collective Basque exemption from any taxes or dues imposed on hidalgos was further complicated by the fact that not all Vizcaínos or Guipuzcoanos enjoyed legal and economic privilege—or the same privileges—in their own native provinces.

As the previous chapter reviewed, in the fifteenth century the city council of Seville refused to provide tax exemptions to any of its citizens—regardless of their status—especially those of foreign origin. The denial of privilege included natives of the Basque territories. Despite the council's resistance, Basques in the late fifteenth century repeatedly appealed to the royal government to enjoy tax exemption. In the case of the related Almansa and Guerrero families, Fernando and Isabel ignored or overruled the city's customs and issued a royal letter in 1497 supporting their claims to the status of hidalgo.[67] The royal letter responding to the Almansas and Guerreros' complaint did not specify from which tax they sought exemption. Given the timing, it is likely that it was from an extraordinary levy called the *pecho de peones* leveled in 1496 and applied to resident foreign merchants and naturalized ones.[68] Both families were Basque in origin, but citizens of Seville at the time of their dispute with the city. Despite the monarchs' letter of support, the Almansas and Guerreros did not succeed in gaining exemption from the pecho at the time of their complaint or even in the years following the city's tax reform in 1515, as there are not records of members of these families receiving a refund of the blanca. By the end of the century, when Melchior and Hernando de Almansa held seats on the city council, Bernaldo de Almansa received 3,200 maravedís for a four-year period ending in 1583.[69]

The Guerreros and Almansas were not unique, and other Basques who had become citizens of the city faced resistance from the city council both before and after the city's tax reform in 1515 allowed hidalgos exemption from the excise tax on meat.[70] Among the more notable Basque litigants was the well-to-do merchant Miguel Martín de Jauregui, who litigated twice, first in 1520 and again in 1537. At least seventeen citizens of Seville of Basque origin or descent had to litigate for recognition of their hidalguía in the first thirty years after the introduction of the blanca de la carne in 1515. Seville was not unique in its opposition to Basque claims of hidalguía. Between 1443 and 1520, more than 165 Basque natives and citizens of cities and towns throughout Old and New Castile sought recognition of their hidalgo status through litigation at the chancery court in Valladolid. The municipalities challenging hidalgo status included major cities as well as small towns. Some of the municipalities with high numbers of suits included Medina del Campo, Segovia, Calahorra, Ciudad Real, Soria, Siguenza, Haro, Nájera, Valladolid, and Miranda de Ebro.[71]

The litigation of the Vizcaíno and citizen of Seville Ortuño de Avendaño provides evidence that neither the royal government nor Basques themselves viewed all natives of the province as legally equal in terms of privilege.[72] Moreover, the attorneys for the city appealed to this difference to deny claimants the privileges of hidalguía. The evidence from the case indicates that in their native homelands, some Basque families enjoyed privileges that the royal government did not accord to all Basques. In Avendaño's efforts to secure the tax refund in Seville, he provided the chancery court in Granada with evidence of his family's privileges and exemptions in Vizcaya from an earlier lawsuit adjudicated in Valladolid in 1533. The evidence consisted of depositions of witnesses from the town of Durango in the province of Vizcaya, taken by the receptor from the chancery court of Valladolid with the assistance of the judge of the fuero in the district (*merindad*) of Durango. The first questions in the 1533 depositions sought to substantiate the standing of the house and estate (*casa y solar*) of Viquiça over which Ortuño's grandfather, Juan de Avendaño, was alleged to be the lord. The witnesses were asked if the estate of Viquiça was a well-known solar of caballeros hijosdalgo and considered a lordship of vassals outside of Vizcaya in the province of Alava.[73] Later questions asked about the local privileges held by hijosdalgo of powerful estates and the arrangements that existed between the powerful families of the province and the Castilian Crown.[74] The questions revealed how the Crown held certain incomes from rights to the commons of the province and from its iron mines. Not only did the Crown collect dues on the iron mines and iron foundries, but it also received special annual dues from the towns of Vizcaya and the merindad of Allendebro, which included Guipúzcoa and part of Alava.[75] Moreover, the court official asked about the annuity (*censo*) the king received from his rights in the provinces' common lands on households built after the lordship of Vizcaya had transferred to the Crown of Castile.[76] Specifically, the court official wanted to know whether Ortuño de Avendaño belonged to one of the houses free of this censo. The questions reveal not only the types of taxes and tribute that Basques paid to the Crown of Castile but also that claims to universal Basque hidalguía were evaluated in terms of a family's history of exemption from taxation in the Basque homelands.

The investigation of another Basque who resided and acquired citizenship in Seville decades later reveals that inequality in terms of legal privileges among Basques in their own provinces continued until the end of the century. The Basque native and citizen of Seville Pedro Ortiz de Abeçia had to litigate at the chancery court in Valladolid in 1572, but not initially to obtain exemptions in the city of Seville. The opposing parties in the dispute in Valladolid included the judges of the valley of Zuya and the municipal council of the village of Abeçia in the province of Vizcaya.[77] Significantly, the council of Abeçia actively participated in the litigation and supplied evidence and witnesses against Ortiz. Moreover, Pedro Ortiz de Abeçia and his relatives, Diego Ortiz and Pedro Ortiz de Eguiluz, sued for recognition of their status to recover securities they claimed that the village council Abeçia had seized from them to pay the royal pecho. The family won the case in Valladolid, and six years later Pedro Ortiz used the executive writ from the court in Valladolid to gain recognition of his status in Seville. The city's attorneys thoroughly examined the document and required Ortiz to provide witnesses to substantiate his identity before they accepted his evidence.[78] In the cases of both Avendaño and the Ortiz, the litigants succeeded in gaining the refund from the blanca not simply because they were Basques, but because they proved that they were members of distinguished Basque lineages who had enjoyed tax exemptions elsewhere and because they had the means to pursue extended litigation.

Conversos

The last set of disputants to form an identifiable group in contests over the status of hidalgo in the fifteenth and sixteenth centuries were the descendants of converted Jews (*conversos*). In surviving municipal and chancery sources, converted Castilian Jews and their descendants are less easily identified through their surnames in the manner that reveals Genoese and Basque families. Other factors serve to obscure the Jewish origins of families in Seville, particularly the converso practice of changing names at the time of conversion and the tendency of converts or their descendants to adopt the names of established Old Christian families with whom they married. The very prominence of converso families in Seville and the degree to which they intermarried with old local noble families led to widespread assertions in the early seventeenth century about the lack of blood purity among the city's elites.[79] Despite the obstacles to differentiating conversos from "Old Christians," the intense scholarly study of this ethnic group in the last century and corresponding studies of the Spanish Inquisition, which had its first tribunal in Seville, have provided considerable information about Jews and conversos in Castile as a whole and in Seville in particular.[80] Consequently, detailed information about particular families and individuals makes it possible to identify as conversos individuals who effectively shed any public reputation of their Jewish past and even successfully obtained council offices and hidalgo status in the sixteenth century.

Castilian Jews joined the ranks of migrants to Seville after its conquest in 1248 and by the fourteenth century created the second largest Jewish community (*aljama*) in the Crown of Castile, with more than four hundred families and perhaps two thousand individuals.[81] Some of these new settlers were in fact the descendants of natives of Seville who had fled Muslim rule in the late twelfth century during the period of Almohad persecution. In the initial division of the city's properties among new settlers, twenty-seven Jews were listed as receiving grants and several influential Jewish courtiers and financiers of the Castilian Crown received especially generous ones.[82] Much like foreign merchant communities, Castile's religious minorities in the thirteenth century had the right to live under their own law and adjudicate their own internal civil disputes, and these rights were extended to the new Jewish community in Seville. The leaders of the aljama also had the obligation to collect a yearly tax for the Crown from their community. The standing and wealth of the Jewish population ranged widely, but included affluent and influential members who served as bankers, financiers, and tax farmers for the Crown as well as others of somewhat lower rank who served as administrators, estate managers, and stewards for the regional noble families. The Jewish quarter in Seville occupied a highly visible location in the city's geography in the neighborhoods immediately adjacent to the western side of the royal palaces. By the fourteenth century a wall surrounded the quarter, but many Jews lived in other neighborhoods throughout the city.[83]

The pogrom of 1391 dramatically ended the relatively peaceful and tolerant period of coexistence for Seville's Jews.[84] The previous year Seville's archbishop had died without a designated successor. Three months later the reigning monarch, Juan I, had a fatal accident and left as heir to the throne the eleven-year-old Enrique III. The resulting power vacuum left the vehemently anti-Jewish preacher Ferrant Martínez, archdeacon of Écija, as the highest religious authority in Seville's archdiocese. Led by Martínez, a mob stormed the walled quarter of the city where the majority of Jews lived. The rioters destroyed property and synagogues and threatened the inhabitants of the aljama with conversion or death. Between seventy and eighty families converted, while as few as sixty families survived to form the remaining core of the Jewish community.[85] The surviving Jewish families were mostly impoverished and faced periodic attacks in the fifteenth century, notably in 1465 and again in 1473 and 1474.[86] Fernando and Isabel eventually decreed the expulsion of Jews from Andalusia in 1482 and from the entire Crown of Castile in 1492. Given the option to convert and remain in their native lands, some Jews chose exile while others accepted baptism and joined the existing population of New Christians.

While the influence of the Jewish community declined after the 1391 pogrom, the size and power of the converso population grew. Some prominent Jewish families, such as the Marmolejo, Sánchez de Sevilla, and Martínez de Medina, who had converted before the pogrom, successfully assimilated into the elite ranks of the city's Christian population.[87] The converso Francisco Fernández del Marmolejo served as senior treasurer for Pedro I in the 1360s.[88] Samuel Abravanel, who converted and changed his name to Juan Sánchez de Sevilla, supported Enrique de Trastamara's winning faction in the dynastic struggle against King Pedro.[89] Juan came to hold the offices of senior royal controller of

accounts (*contador mayor del rey*) and royal treasurer for Andalusia. He continued to possess these offices during the reign of Enrique III, and with the support
of his patron, the Count of Benavente, he sought the additional office of controller of royal revenues in 1391. In 1398 he became the lord of the villages of Chillas
and Gatos in the agriculturally rich Aljarafe district immediately west of Seville.
His son Alfonso Sánchez de Sevilla secured the office of veinticuatro of Sevilla,
and their descendants continued to remain active in the city's politics through
the fifteenth century. Other families of Jewish descent such as the Fernández
Cansino, Susán, Lugo, and Lando, also converted in the late fourteenth or early
fifteenth century, and likewise succeeded in obtaining public offices previously
denied to them as Jews, especially the offices of jurado, mayordomo, and fiel
ejecutor, and eventually even veinticuatro.[90] Some of the more successful converso families intermarried with local Old Christian elites in the course of the
fifteenth century.[91]

The religious beliefs of the converts and their descendants were diverse in
nature. While some genuinely embraced the Christian faith, others maintained
Jewish beliefs and practices in secret or even blended elements and customs of
the two faiths. Popular suspicions about the sincerity of converso faith and
resentment over the success of some converts led to growing tensions and ultimately contributed to the Catholic Monarchs' establishment of an Inquisition
tribunal in Seville in 1481.[92] The following year, in response to rumors concerning a conspiracy to assassinate the new inquisitors, a number of highly placed
conversos were arrested and even executed.[93] Among the many conversos convicted of "judaizing" heresy, the majority chose to abjure their errors and sought
to be reconciled with the church. Other conversos, who refused to renounce
their Jewish faith or who received second convictions of heresy, faced execution
at the stake. Contemporary chroniclers such as Hernando de Pulgar and Andrés
Bernaldez provide figures of between 300 and 700 executed in the archdiocese
of Seville in the first decade of the tribunal, with as many as 5,000 reconciled.[94]
Many fled the city to take refuge in smaller towns, especially those under seigneurial jurisdiction. During the high point of persecution in the 1480s and
1490s, many conversos lost their council positions due to charges of heresy (see
table 3).[95] Notably, the Inquisition removed the veinticuatros Diego Susán and
Pedro Fernández Cansino from their offices.[96] At least a dozen conversos were
also deprived of the office of jurado. In some instances, when converso jurados
were purged, other more assimilated and established conversos replaced them,
as when Pedro Secutor's office was transferred to Pedro Sánchez del Alcázar.[97]

Table 3 Jurados deprived of office on charges of heresy

Jurado charged with heresy	Office and parish	Office transferred to	Year
Juan Alemán	Jurado	Gonzelo Nuñez de Écija	1479
Pedro Díaz de Rafaya	Jurado of San Esteban	Suero de Gangas	1480
Tomás de Jaén	Jurado of San Juan and mayordomo of Seville	—	1482
Alemán Pocasangre	Jurado of Santa María	Fernando Portocarrero	1482
Pero Fernández Cansino	Jurado of Santa María	Fernando de Medina	1482
Pedro Secutor	Jurado and fiel ejecutor	Pedro Sánchez del Alcázar (converso)	1482
Luis de Sevilla	Jurado of San Vicente	Antón Bernal (converso)	1482
Pedro de Illescas	Jurado of Santiago	Alfonso Fernández Melgarejo; Francisco Pasete*	1483
Pedro de Illescas	Jurado of San Juan	Pedro de Villegas	1483
Juan de Sevilla	Jurado and mayordomo	—	1483
Fernan Gómez de Córdoba	Jurado of San Isidoro	Juan Rodríguez de Vallecillo	1485
Francisco de Olivares	Jurado of Santa María	Gonzalo de Mena	1486

Source: Carande and Carriazo, *Tumbo*, 3:156, 254; 3:442; 3:82, 97, 260; 3:299; 3:182, 189; 3:297; 3:526, 548; 3:260, 304; 3:264, 334, 380; 3:578; 4:99.

Note: Dashes indicate when the source did not specify the parish or recipient of the office.

*After Illescas was charged with heresy, the vecinos of the parish of Santiago elected Fernández Melgarejo, but Fernando and Isabel invalidated the election and provided the office to Pasete.

Between 1495 and 1497 church and royal officials made efforts to reconcile those conversos who had fled or committed minor offenses and their descendants. In the archdiocese of Seville, about 6,204 were spiritually reconciled and brought back to the church during these years. Of these, about 2,000 had been residents or citizens of the city itself.[98] By 1508 Fernando's regency government proposed to the descendants of those pardoned and reconciled by the Inquisition a means to regain lost or seized property. In exchange for a large monetary donation the monarch would recognize their rights to property and mollify prejudicial measures against them. The lists of contributors indicate the considerable number of prominent converso families still surviving in early sixteenth-century Seville and their identities.[99]

The social and political status of conversos in general remained precarious through the sixteenth century, as important local institutions established new prejudicial restrictions against them. Factions among the city's clergy introduced formal prohibitions against the acceptance of members with Jewish blood—so-called statutes of blood purity—for Seville's cathedral chapter in 1515 and similar ones for the University of Seville in 1537. But these restrictions, often circumvented in practice, were not rigorously enforced, and conversos continued to hold prominent positions in these institutions through the century.

While many converso families lost property and public political offices, others—especially those who evaded charges of heresy and prosecution—continued to possess these positions and engage actively in the affairs of the city. During the Comunero Revolt in 1520, local rebels targeted conversos and complained about their presence on the city's council. But none of these men lost their offices or control over their offices in the wake of the revolt.[100] As members of Seville's city council, those conversos who retained their offices and their family members began to enjoy the tax exemption that came into effect with the implementation of the blanca de la carne in 1515. Moreover, as the previous chapter describes for all Seville's councilmen, these conversos and their relatives came to be listed on the city's tax records as receiving the exemptions provided to hidalgos. Among the conversos who received exemptions from the tax on meat were the veinticuatros Alonso Gutiérrez de Madrid and Francisco del Alcázar, Francisco's relative Pedro del Alcázar, and the jurados Antón Bernal and Juan de Torres.[101] The Torres clan was particularly well represented among the recipients of the return, with four other members receiving refunds.[102] From the prominent Fernández Marmolejo family, Luis and Martín also enjoyed the exemption. Through their positions on the council, or long-term connections to it, these men assumed the identity of caballeros hijosdalgo that was applied to the councilmen, as did conversos who managed to obtain seats in subsequent decades. Significantly, the city clerks' tax records also provided these individuals and their families with tangible evidence of their status that could be used in disputes outside of Seville.

Although conversos did not easily fit the definition of hidalgo provided by the *Siete partidas*, few members of established and assimilated converso families from Seville faced litigation against Seville's city council. The few cases that left surviving records did not take place until the later decades of the century. Two of the rare examples of such lawsuits involved Juan Fernández Marmolejo in 1574 and Pedro Caso Marmolejo and his relatives in 1576.[103] The litigants in both cases successfully secured court recognition of their status, and the evidence suggests local support. Among the many witnesses who substantiated Juan Fernández Marmolejo's claims was the jurado Hernan Pérez.[104] Not surprisingly, those converso families who had come to public attention due to convictions for heresy and had lost their social standing in the city, such as the Súsan clan, did not attempt to claim hidalgo status in Seville. Conversos arriving and settling in Seville in the course of the sixteenth century did at times claim hidalguía, as did those families who gained wealth and prominence after the period of intense persecution in the 1480s and 1490s. The exact origin of the converso Illescas family is uncertain, but one prominent member of the family and citizen of Seville, the wealthy merchant Rodrigo de Illescas, sought hidalgo status with the council of Seville in 1567.[105] Similarly, other members of the family and citizens of Seville, Juan Nuñez de Illescas and Francisco Nuñez de Illescas, did the same in 1569.[106] As the following chapter addresses in greater detail, new settlers in Seville, whether they were New Christians or Old Christians, faced resistance and challenges to claims they made to hidalgo status regardless of their actual lineage. Before claims to hidalgo status could be made, new residents had to obtain citizenship. Those who obtained citizenship and who successfully presented their case at court could gain royal recognition of their status as hidalgos. While some of the claimants who were challenged came from converso families, this information did not necessarily come to light in the litigation.

Even when the surviving records of a lawsuit of hidalguía are complete, it is not always possible to determine from the evidence given by the two sides the true origin, occupation, or status of the litigants and their ancestors. This is especially true when the documents are fragmentary and only the evidence given by one side has been preserved. In fact, the final ejecutoria the court provided to the successful claimant conventionally included summaries of the victor's supporting probanzas but excised the opposing evidence presented by the municipality and prosecutor. From the surviving evidence, those individuals who made up discernable ethnic or occupational demographic groups are relatively few out of the total that litigated. To better place disputes over hidalgo status involving members of these groups in their social context, the chapter has sought to provide a history of these groups and their role in the political, economic, and social life of the city through the late Middle Ages and the sixteenth century. Although these social groups have been treated in isolation, they should not be viewed as hermetic communities. Members of some of these groups, most notably conversos and Basques, often followed endogamous marriage patterns. Nevertheless, there is ample evidence that members of these groups married into long-established Sevillano elite families, as well as evidence of intermarriage among these distinct groups. As is evident in chapter 5, those who proved successful in integrating into the city elite often married outside their particular occupational and ethnic group, either with established Sevillano families or with other recent settlers in the city who could provide advantageous alliances. Members of these groups and their descendants could have overlapping identities, such as the descendants of converted Jews who married Basque merchants, and Genoese financiers who married Burgalese merchants. Consequently, the following statistical conclusions about litigants should be understood in light of processes of integration and assimilation that were in play in sixteenth-century Seville.

The largest identifiable group of litigants for hidalguía in sixteenth-century Seville were natives or descendants of the natives of the Basque territories of Vizcaya and Guipúzcoa. Out of the 387 lawsuits that left some record at the chancery court in Granada, 28 involved litigants of unquestionable Basque origin or descent, with perhaps another half dozen of possible Basque identity, amounting to roughly 7 or 8 percent of the disputes.[107] Litigants of definitively Italian origin or descent generated 12 lawsuits that left evidence in the chancery court and amounted to about 3 percent of the total cases. Due to the difficulty of identifying converso litigants the handful of cases that can be identified involving known conversos from Seville are most likely not representative of those who actually sought hidalgo status, but would constitute perhaps 1 to 1.5 percent of the cases. While individuals belonging to these groups constituted a relatively small proportion of the total number of disputants, the prominent place that they played in public perceptions of cases of hidalguía in Seville and the Crown of Castile as a whole contributed significantly to the evolution of the discourse about status and privilege, especially the notion of status as racially grounded or derived from lineage. Nevertheless, considering these rough figures, 90 percent of the claims to hidalguía that the city council chose to contest, and which led to lawsuits, involved individuals or families for which the city had little or no knowledge of their ancestry or origin. How and why the city council of Seville challenged these claimants is addressed in the following chapter.

Seville in the early sixteenth century was in some significant ways distinct from other municipalities in the Crown of Castile in terms of its considerable population and economic dynamism, but these differences were primarily in scale and not in nature. Seville was the largest city in the Crown, had a dynamic and expanding economy, and served as the entrepôt for commerce and migration to and from the Indies. Despite the greater number of inhabitants and participants in its government, Seville had similar political structures as other Castilian municipalities and operated within the same legal and judicial systems. While Seville received more migrants and settlers, these new migrants faced the same legal challenges to claims to hidalgo status that they faced elsewhere and in the face of resistance turned to the same judicial remedies. The following chapter examines in greater detail the legal actions pursued by those who sought hidalgo status and explains how Castile's judicial system and the legal procedures for litigating hidalgo status shaped these conflicts.

4

ANATOMY OF A LAWSUIT OF HIDALGUÍA

In the chancery courtrooms of sixteenth-century Castile, litigants spoke about hidalguía as though it was a form of heritable and inalienable property.[1] Despite this language, both municipal councils and officials of the royal government regularly challenged individual and family possession of hidalgo status, possession that had often been recognized at an earlier time or in a different community. Municipal complaints made in the meetings of Castile's Cortes and the royal laws enacted in response to these complaints indicate that contestation in the form of legal disputes claiming and denying hidalguía had troubled the royal appellate courts since at least the late fourteenth century, but they became far more common in the sixteenth century.[2] Royal judges adjudicated tens of thousands of lawsuits and issued royal writs authorizing or denying hidalgo status in numbers that far surpassed the several hundred royal grants of hidalguía sold during the entire Habsburg period.[3] In the sixteenth century, citizens of Seville alone brought at least 387 complaints of hidalguía to court.[4] Since these suits impacted the collective fortunes of entire families, and even related families, the number of individuals with a potential stake in these conflicts was in the thousands. Rather than serving as an impartial mediator, the Crown, represented through the royal prosecutor, supported municipal resistance to these claims to limit the proliferation of privilege. From the late fifteenth century, royal governments, with the acquiescence of the major municipal councils, elaborated and regularized a system for adjudicating status that was inherently biased in favor of those with wealth and connections—including the newly rich—and one in which the governing substantive rules, as opposed to the procedural ones, were highly elastic. In practice, the Crown did not seek to defend old or existing hidalgo lineages and in fact tacitly sought to control the number of fiscal exemptions while maintaining the appearance of being the provider of justice and defender of legitimate privileges.

Irrespective of the substantive arguments the opposing sides made in these contests and even the evidence they presented, ultimate success depended heavily on whether the claimant had the means to initiate litigation and the will to pursue the lawsuit to its full completion. References to lawsuits of hidalguía frequently give the impression that only fraudulent claimants to the status of hidalgo litigated at court.[5] However, in his study of the Castilian nobility, Domínguez Ortiz recognized that individuals of authentic hidalgo descent often lacked the means or the will to initiate a lawsuit or having begun one failed to take it to its completion.[6] Just as some "genuine" hidalgos failed to maintain their status because they could not litigate, other claimants—both descendants of families who had previously been recognized as hidalgos and families of new wealth who wished to enjoy the privileges of hidalguía—actively pursued recognition or rerecognition.

By the 1593 meeting of the Cortes, municipal representatives explicitly addressed the expenses involved in providing evidence of hidalguía in the courts and how these efforts had become too difficult and costly for most hidalgos to complete.[7] Although litigants typically employed rhetoric that justified the enjoyment of privilege as the result of descent that carried with it heritable qualities, this did not keep individuals who did not descend from hidalgo lineages from attaining recognition of this status. Conversely, such claims did not easily convey the status held by their ancestors to those descended from previously recognized hidalgos. In the event municipal authorities chose to deny a claimant's hidalgo status, the ability to obtain its recognition, either for the first time or subsequent recognition in a different municipality, or as the representative of a new generation of the same family, did not depend exclusively—or perhaps even primarily—on the litigants' descent but rather on the ability to engage in litigation itself. The ability to litigate involved not only the means to pursue a long lawsuit but the ability to construct arguments for the recognition of status through the presentation of witnesses and written documents that appealed to existing, and at times seemingly opposing, rules and norms. A claimant's success also required the skill and fortune to counter the arguments made by opposing municipal councils and the royal prosecutor.

Although municipal councils did not always provide the same degree of resistance to all claims to hidalgo status, they held certain procedural advantages in these lawsuits. Due to the nature of tax collection in the cities and larger towns as it developed in sixteenth-century Andalusia, councils held the power to refuse to provide a claimant their privileges. In fact, the decision to litigate for recognition of hidalgo status was the last resort of someone who faced resistance from the local council or from a dominant faction on the council. When claimants submitted a complaint to the chancery court to force the provision of their privileges, municipal councils were free to use a barrage of general and formulaic charges to deny the claimant's possession of the status of hidalguía. Of even greater significance for the outcome of these disputes, the burden of proof rested on the party claiming hidalgo status, creating an extraordinary disadvantage for litigants claiming hidalgo status. Moreover, in the vast majority of lawsuits, a form of complicity existed between municipal councils and royal officials to deny claimants their recognition of status. They denied this status not through substantive rules but through initiating a dispute whose procedures required considerable economic means and the support of local authorities to successfully traverse.

In these lawsuits disputants on both sides used the term *hidalgo* to refer to a fixed social category even as they contested the exact meaning of the term. As an object of dispute, the term *hidalgo* itself became a legal claim in a greater effort to acquire or deny privilege. Litigants appealed to a diversity of existing rules and laws about the status of hidalgo that proved advantageous and convenient in order to achieve their ends. In these disputes a tension existed between whether nobility and hidalgo status was an inherent quality passed through one's lineage or the result of meritorious service and virtuous deeds. Determination of status was further complicated by the existence of laws that verified status through past enjoyment of privilege, particularly exemptions and immunities from the fiscal demands of royal and municipal authorities. In the course of the sixteenth century the parties opposing recognition of hidalguía, municipal councils and royal prosecutors at court, made a range of arguments that contributed to a dominant discourse that ultimately defined hidalguía as based on descent and lineage rather than merit or service.[8] Consequently, the efforts of municipal councils and royal officials to prevent the proliferation of privilege contributed to the instituting of a form of legal inequality based on the need to appeal to essential inheritable qualities rather than service as the ultimate authoritative basis for privilege. Despite this rhetorical shift, the rationales made to gain recognition of hidalgo status and accompanying privileges continued to interweave tales of noble descent with accounts of service to the Crown and commonwealth. Lawyers in these disputes appealed to an essentialist definition of hidalgo in the rhetoric of their arguments, especially referencing the language of blood purity that became more common in the second half of the sixteenth century, and thereby nominally strengthened the racial aspects of this social category.[9]

The surviving documents from litigation over hidalguía, especially from early in the sixteenth century, are often fragmentary and give only limited elements of the lawsuit. Even those cases that received a final ruling and were copied for preservation often omitted sections of the process and are incomplete. Moreover, the very nature of the lawsuits and how they were argued impede efforts to get genuine particular information about the claimant. Municipal councils and royal prosecutors used formulaic charges that received blanket denials from the opposing party. In surviving depositions witnesses often limited their answers to affirmations or denials of formulaic charges. To provide a window on lawsuits of hidalguía, this chapter uses the mostly complete record of the lawsuit of Pedro Sánchez Paneque to describe the procedures of litigation and the substance and nature of arguments for and against hidalgo status. Sánchez Paneque's case began in 1526 but followed procedures that governed such lawsuits through the sixteenth century.[10] The suit further illuminates the nature of these disputes by including the complete appeal arguments made by the opposing attorneys and thereby reveals competing ideas from early in the sixteenth century about how the status of hidalgo could be obtained, cultivated, and possibly lost. Although Sánchez Paneque's case was unusual, the procedures he had to employ and traverse were the established framework for all lawsuits of hidalguía in sixteenth-century Castile.

LEGAL PROCEDURE AND THE BURDEN OF PROOF

In a study of royal justice in early modern Castile, Jack Owens emphasizes the importance of legal procedures in the outcome of disputes. He warns that a common problem with historical studies based on trial records is their failure to give attention to the ways in which the procedures and legal constraints within which the disputants acted served to shape their actions.[11] In lawsuits of hidalguía, as in most litigation, the legal procedures that governed them influenced not only the likelihood of beginning litigation but also the litigants' chances of gaining recognition of their status. Like sixteenth-century civil lawsuits disputed at the chancery court, lawsuits of hidalguía consisted of a series of legal actions or stages. The formal process began with the presentation of a complaint (*demanda*) to the tribunal of the hijosdalgo at one of the two chancery courts. The judges of the tribunal then notified the opposing party about the complaint with a royal writ (*real provisión*). The opposing party, usually a municipal council, responded either by letter or through their representative at court, invariably denying the validity of the complaint. The court then gave a preliminary ruling (*sentencia interlocutoria*) that agreement between the parties was impossible and issued a summons to both parties to appear at court within a specified amount of time to provide evidence in support of their respective claims. The court conventionally dictated a deadline of fifteen to thirty days, but these deadlines were often extended to sixty or even ninety days.[12] Within this time the parties presented witnesses and written testimony. After the presentation of evidence, the judges of the tribunal of the hijosdalgo provided their ruling (*sentencia definitiva*) on the matter. The losing party had the right to make a preliminary appeal (*apelación en vista*) of the judges' ruling to the review of the president of the court and two other appellate judges (*oidores*). In the event of another unfavorable ruling, or a reversal of the ruling, the truly determined litigant could appeal the matter a second time to the same magistrates for reconsideration (*apelación en revista*). Further lengthening the litigation process, a royal order (*cédula*) in 1565 required all three judges of the tribunal of the hijosdalgo to decide unanimously to render a decision.[13] In the event that the judges disagreed on the ruling, the court assigned one of the appellate judges to review and decide the case with the original judges and the tribunal's clerk.

In the sixteenth century, the party claiming hidalgo status almost always initiated the lawsuit. Whether or not a council initiated a lawsuit depended on the manner of tax collection and the relative strength of the hidalgo to resist a municipal council's infringement of legal privileges attendant to his or her status. As the cities and major towns took greater control over local collection and administration of the servicio, the tendency for councils to initiate litigation declined significantly and in some municipalities almost never occurred. In a study of lawsuits involving citizens and municipalities of southern Extremadura between 1490 and 1609, municipal councils initiated only 54 of the 255 complaints examined.[14] Moreover, the municipalities made 23 of these complaints between 1501 and 1516, when the collection of direct taxes for the servicio was divided between tax farmers and municipal councils. Consequently, in most sixteenth-century suits the claimant to hidalgo status was the plaintiff and the council was the defendant accused of violating his or her liberties and privileges.

After 1515 all the lawsuits of hidalguía involving the citizens of Seville and its subject towns and villages began as complaints against the city council, since the city effectively controlled the means for allotting or denying the fiscal and political privileges tied to the status. The city's control of these privileges, particularly the tax on meat, forced individual citizens who did not get recognition from the council to call for royal intervention through the chancery courts. In the previous century, when Seville still collected the servicio as a direct property tax, a few of its most powerful citizens, especially members of the powerful Guzmán clan, at different moments challenged the city's traditional practice of requiring all citizens to pay the pecho regardless of their nobility. Due to the size and influence of the families involved and the military force they could bring to bear, the city council did not attempt to coerce them into paying but resorted to other means of collecting these monies, such as freezing the payments owed to these aristocrats from royal and municipal bonds.[15] In these late medieval conflicts Seville did not deny the status of hidalgo to these families; it simply upheld the principle that they too were responsible for contributing to the city's allotment of the servicio. By the second decade of the sixteenth century the city's even more effective control over the disbursement of economic privileges related to hidalgo status initiated a growing wave of litigation.

In early modern Castile the development of legal procedures for lawsuits of hidalguía and the language employed in these suits served to undermine the ability of families to maintain status they had previously enjoyed and created potential obstacles for new claims. The lawsuit Pedro Sánchez Paneque began in 1526 serves to illustrate the obstacles faced by litigants in these disputes. In the final appellate ruling for the case in 1536, Pedro lost the status and "liberties" that his family had held for the previous hundred years, with the judges' simple decision that he was a "good taxpayer."[16] The final ruling came after ten years of litigation, two earlier rulings against Pedro, and two appeals to overturn these rulings. Evidence that Pedro presented to the court revealed that members of the Sánchez Paneque family and their extended relatives had litigated successfully on multiple occasions in the past. In at least three separate instances, in 1420, in 1440, and again in 1478, members of the family had secured favorable verdicts from royal judges recognizing their status. But in Pedro's case the very evidence proving the family's possession of hidalgo status provided the city of Seville with information that the Sánchez Paneques were distant descendants of Jewish converts to the Christian faith, information the city subsequently used to challenge Pedro and his family's status of hidalgo.

As the previous chapter reviewed, in sixteenth-century Castile, municipal citizenship was an essential first step in suits of hidalguía. In Pedro's case, his family originated from the city of Écija, ninety kilometers east of Seville, where branches of the family had lived for more than a hundred years. While Pedro had been born in Écija and lived there long enough to attend the local grammar school, his family chose to resettle sometime in his youth. After the family arrived in Seville, Pedro married. Whether he married a citizen of the city is uncertain, but it would have facilitated his naturalization by shortening the wait to become a citizen. Whatever the situation, by the time the suit began Seville's own attorney acknowledged that Pedro had lived in the city as a citizen for fifteen years.

Both before and after their arrival in Seville, Pedro and his family engaged in various commercial enterprises and the farming of royal and municipal incomes and taxes in and around Seville. One witness also testified that Pedro had been involved in the Indies trade. Besides Pedro's commercial and financial activities, the family held and continued to hold significant landed properties in and around Écija. His grandfather and father owned the rich farmsteads (*cortijos*) of Pilar de Tejada and Isla Redona, the latter upstream from Écija on the banks of the River Genil, as well as the watermills of Alhonoz, also on the Genil.[17] Additionally, other members of the family had engaged in tax-collecting and tax-farming enterprises since the early fifteenth century. As will become evident in the next chapter, Seville's elite families and members of the city council engaged in similar commercial and even financial activities, and these occupations did not serve to exclude someone in the city from holding high political office or enjoying hidalgo status. Likewise, neither the city's charges, the deposition questions, or the responses of witnesses suggested that commercial activity was incompatible with hidalgo status. In I. A. A. Thompson's review of the letters granting hidalgo status sold by the royal government between 1552 and 1700, the economic occupation and activities of the petitioner were entirely ignored.[18]

As the head of a prosperous household, a citizen of the city, and the descendant of recognized hidalgos, Sánchez Paneque sought to obtain the refund on the city's tax on the consumption of meat. When his efforts elicited opposition from the city council, he presented a complaint before the judges of the hidalgos at the royal chancery court of Granada on July 16, 1526. In this complaint he claimed to be an hijodalgo and declared that the opposing party, the city council of Seville, obligated as it was to keep and recognize his rights and privileges, had—in violation of these rights—seized securities from him. Pedro insisted that the chancery judges order the city council to erase his name from the list of common taxpayers where they had placed him and return to him either the property they had seized or goods of equivalent value. Before the summons' deadline, the city's attorney appeared to deny his claims. Contradicting Pedro's statement, the city contended that he was not an hidalgo but instead a common taxpayer who had never been exempt from paying taxes in the city of Seville or in any other municipality where he had lived.

The council's decision to respond to this challenge denied Pedro an easy recognition of his family's privilege. Moreover, the first round of proceedings demonstrated the decided bias of Castile's legal structure against an easy recognition of privilege. After both sides had made their original claims at the royal appellate court in Granada, neither side returned to give supporting evidence within the given deadline. Consequently, on November 27, 1527, the judges ruled that Pedro had not proven his case while the council—without ever providing a scrap of evidence or a single witness—had completely proven its objections.[19] Because the burden of proof rested with Pedro, the council was the winner by default. Thus, a simple procedural rule that determined which party bore the burden of proof decided the outcome.

The position that the ruling monarch and his immediate representatives took in these disputes further highlights the existing structural resistance to privilege. From the late fourteenth century Castilian monarchs had placed a royal prosecutor at the chancery court in Valladolid to oversee cases in which the Crown had a stake and to defend the monarch's interests in these cases. By the early sixteenth century the chancery courts in Valladolid and Granada each had two fiscales, who were responsible for prosecuting lawsuits of hidalguía.[20] The records of these lawsuits always listed the royal prosecutor as a colitigant with the municipal council in its opposition to its own citizen's claims to the status of hidalgo and as defender of royal patrimony. Through these officials the monarchs of Castile nominally took part in tens of thousands of disputes in which the Crown denied the status and privileges of litigants. In addition to acting on the king's behalf, these officials ideally kept the Crown informed of hard cases and problems in the application of laws governing status in the king-dom. In contrast to the prosecutor's ceaseless participation in cases of hidal-guía, this official rarely intervened in either commercial or inheritance cases.[21]

Nevertheless, the royal judges' tendency to rule against these claimants was not absolute. The structure of sixteenth-century legal proceedings allowed a litigant with sufficient resolve and means to continue the dispute in later rounds of litigation. The city's decision to send a representative to the chancellery court denied Pedro an uncontested acknowledgement of his hidalguía in the first instance. Through this simple maneuver, the city had initiated a new round of litigation and had considerably increased the efforts that Pedro had to expend to win the dispute. He now appealed the ruling by submitting a petition of grievances claiming that this sentence was harmful and that it should be revoked because of the damages done to his rights. To present favorable evi-dence, Pedro now had to pay various clerks to take witness depositions, copy existing judicial rulings, and pay the travel expenses for himself, his legal repre-sentative, and his witnesses. These were additional expenses over and above the court costs owed to the tribunal and its various officials. The Crown published an official tariff (*arancel*) that detailed the court fees to be charged for drawing up a petition, copying a document, or filing a lawsuit. Richard Kagan has calcu-lated that in the 1570s the officially recorded fees for lawsuits settled at the chan-cillería of Valladolid ran between 2,500 and 5,000 maravedís. However, he recognized the actual fees were much higher, citing a visitation report that the cost of a lawsuit was approximately 24,000 maravedís.[22]

Success in lawsuits of hidalguía required the presentation of witnesses either to attest to or deny both a claimant's status as an hidalgo and their possession of privileges. In these lawsuits each side had to pay for the presentation of their own witness, including the expenses of transporting them to the court and lodging them during the trial or until they gave their statements. Age, infirmity, or sickness often impeded witnesses from making what was typically a long trip to the chancery court. In these cases the court dispatched a functionary (*dili-genciero*) to take depositions from citizens of the plaintiff's current and previ-ous municipality and in some cases even the municipality from which the litigant or the litigant's family originated. For example, in the lawsuit Francisco de Cifuentes had with Seville between 1579 and 1585, a functionary traveled to Valladolid and Burgos to depose a number of elderly witnesses who were citi-zens of Burgos and its subject towns. Among these witnesses, all of whom were listed as hidalgos, were Martín López Barahona, citizen of Burgos, more than eighty years old; Diego de Vidobro, citizen of Burgos, seventy-four years old; Juan Robles, citizen of Pedrosa, ninety years old; Antonio de Mixangos Cabrestero, citizen of Burgos, eighty-six years old; and Lope Rebollo de Ayala, citizen of Burgos, eighty years old.[23] The functionaries also made copies of any relevant municipal tax rolls if they existed and were available. The party that presented the initial complaint to the judges of the tribunal paid the expenses of the court official who made the trip. Deposing witnesses at times required long trips to multiple locations, especially for cases involving litigants whose ancestors originated from the Basque provinces, Asturias, and Cantabria, territories where the designation of hidalgo had traditionally been more widely applied and claimed.[24] In some lawsuits, especially later in the century when royal prosecutors took a more active role initiating and pressing litigation, the payment of these officials became an issue of dispute between claimants, municipalities, and the courts themselves.[25] In the event of an adverse sentence, the plaintiff was also charged with the court fees of the municipal council.

Due to the number of stages in the lawsuit, the time involved collecting evidence and witnesses' statements, travel back and forth from the court, and the tendency to appeal unfavorable rulings, the lawsuits often took many years, and the length of lawsuits of hidalguía appears to have grown in the course of the century. The case involving Fernando Díaz de Santa Cruz, discussed in chapter 2, began in 1515 and lasted until at least 1532.[26] Juan de la Rentería litigated for five years, from 1520 until 1525, before receiving a ruling on his complaint.[27] Similarly, Luis Calderón's case dragged on from 1528 to 1538, by which time his son Cosme de Orozco became a colitigant.[28] These cases from the early decades of the century are rare in receiving a final decision. Because many of the surviving sources are incomplete and consist only of initial complaints and notifications, it is difficult to determine an average length for these lawsuits. For the entire sixteenth century documents for lawsuits of hidalguía at the chancery court of Granada between the city of Seville and citizens of Seville survive for 387 cases. Out of these cases, 173 have surviving final rulings, but many of the final rulings lack preceding documents necessary to determine the length of the suit or the number of appeals.[29] Among those lawsuits that did not receive a final ruling, it is impossible to know if the cost and trouble of litigation deterred the plaintiff from continuing the suit or if these documents have been lost.

Whether the majority of plaintiffs in these early decades abandoned their lawsuits or not, as the century continued, completed lawsuits dragged on for extraordinary lengths of time (see table 4). For the 1560s the average length of

Table 4 Length of lawsuits of hidalguía between citizens of Seville and Seville's city council

	Number of lawsuits	Lawsuits with final rulings	Average length, in years, of lawsuits with final rulings	Median length, in years, of lawsuits with final rulings
1500–1509	2	1	—	—
1510–19	6	2	—	—
1520–29	18	5	6.40	7.0
1530–39	24	13	2.10	2.0
1540–49	23	10	11.75	7.5
1550–59	42	9	9.30	10.0
1560–69	65	28	9.50	6.0
1570–79	79	34	6.80	5.0
1580–89	90	43	6.10	4.0
1590–99	38	28	8.80	4.5
Total	387	173	—	—

Source: ARCG, H.

Note: Due to incomplete evidence concerning the length of the lawsuits in the first two decades and the limited number of lawsuits, the average and median columns have not been calculated.

suits that received a final sentence and generated an executive writ ordering the implementation of a judicial ruling was more than nine years.[30] Of the 65 lawsuits initiated during this decade, 28 received a final ruling. The average length of lawsuits initiated in the 1570s was just under seven years. In one of these cases, Pedro Hernández de Andrada, a citizen of both Seville and the town of Umbrete, first filed a complaint in 1573.[31] Although the suit received an initial sentence two years later, litigation continued with repeated appeals for another twenty-seven years, apparently coming to a conclusion in 1602 when the president of the court ruled definitively that Hernández was a pechero. Other citizens of Seville with lengthy suits include Francisco Pérez Romero and Pedro de Villacis, who both litigated for fourteen years.[32]

In Marie-Claude Gerbet and Janine Fayard's study of hidalgo lawsuits in Extremadura, the average case before 1520 lasted only a year and a half. For the period 1520 to 1539, the average jumped to a little more than six years. For the next twenty years, 1540–59, the average length of a case increased to ten years, and then declined to roughly seven years for the rest of the century.[33] Castilian municipalities in the sixteenth century made it increasingly expensive for their citizens to acquire recognition of status by effectively extending the length of these lawsuits. Long lawsuits required not only multiple presentations of witnesses but also the retention of legal counsel to draft frequent correspondence with the court. The need to retain an attorney gave certain advantages to large municipalities, which kept permanent salaried legal advocates at the chancery courts.[34] Similarly, prosperous seigneurial and merchant families involved in significant commercial and business enterprises retained legal representatives who could generate both the motions and evidence necessary for these suits.

Whether claimants to hidalguía ultimately proved successful in their litigation or not, the growing tendency of municipal councils to appeal adverse rulings demonstrates municipal resistance to the proliferation of privilege and the enjoyment of privilege by individuals and families outside the ruling elites of these towns and cities. In 1603, the lawsuit of Juan López de Mendoza, a citizen of Palomares—one of Seville's subject towns—seemed to come to an end when the court at the first appeal confirmed the initial ruling in his favor and charged the opposing town with the costs of his litigation.[35] Palomares challenged this ruling and succeeded in overturning it in the second appeal to the court, in which the court not only reversed its position and declared López a pechero but also sentenced him to paying the costs of all three rounds of litigation. Richard Kagan has demonstrated the dramatic increase in all types of litigation in the sixteenth century, along with the growing length of suits and the increased number of appeals.[36] The data collected on lawsuits involving towns in Extremadura show a significant increase in the number of rulings appealed in the course of the sixteenth century. Before 1520 litigants appealed roughly 25 percent of the extant lawsuits. For the period from 1560 to 1609, the total number of rulings appealed increased to a dramatic 50 percent, and rulings appealed twice constituted 20 percent of the lawsuits.[37]

The spotty preservation of court rulings makes it difficult to determine the degree of success of those who litigated for status. In all but two of the cases reviewed in the study of Extremadura, the municipality, not the claimant, appealed the original sentence. Moreover, in all but two of these lawsuits the municipality lost the case. The evidence for these figures comes exclusively from the archives of the chancery courts in Valladolid and Granada and does not include documents preserved in the municipal archives of the towns in Extremadura. A comparison of surviving documents in the municipal archive in Seville with those in the chancery archive in Granada suggests that the court itself, as opposed to the individual court clerks, sporadically preserved the rulings of lawsuits in which the council won the case. In 1530, at the end of a series of lawsuits in which the city council of Seville had successfully denied the claims of five of its citizens, the city's attorney solicited written copies of the rulings for the city's records. In these documents the chancery judges ruled against the hidalguía of Pedro Sánchez Paneque, Diego Jaimes, Juan Ortega de la Peña, Hernando de Medina, and Luis Calderón.[38] Despite the appearance of these men in the documents preserved by the city of Seville, the chancery archive in Granada possesses records concerning Luis Calderón and Diego Jaimes only. Calderón continued to appeal this adverse ruling until 1538.[39] By the time the final court sentence was issued, he had been litigating for ten years.

A litigant needed both sufficient means to engage in a long bout of litigation and the influence to present the necessary evidence to support his claim. Neither of these ends necessarily required descent from ancestors whom authorities recognized as hidalgos; rather, it required the means to fashion evidence of such descent. Chapter 6 addresses the malleability of evidence for the status of hidalgo and the relative ease with which evidence could be fabricated in terms of both witnesses' depositions and notarized written records.

THE FORM OF MUNICIPAL RESISTANCE AND OPPOSITIONS

Against the efforts of these litigants to claim hidalgo status, municipal councils asserted multiple legal oppositions. Significantly, these oppositions often served to obtain information that could be used to deny the plaintiff's claim to hidalguía.[40] The municipal councils' ability to employ a diverse barrage of objections against a claimant provided these authorities with a significant advantage in their resistance to the recognition of an individual's status.[41] In the official response that Seville's city council submitted to the chancery judges against Pedro Sánchez Paneque, the municipal attorney listed a wide range of reasons why Pedro either was not or should no longer be considered an hidalgo. These oppositions were standard and appear repeatedly with only minor variations in all denials of hidalgo status.

The nature of the oppositions further reveals both how the burden of proof rested on the claimant to status and the structural bias of the legal system against these individuals. From the start of the dispute the city responded with formulaic and general opposing claims to the complaint without particular details about Pedro Sánchez Paneque or supporting evidence for their claims. All parties involved in lawsuits (*pleitos*) of hidalguía, most notably the chancery judges who mediated them, understood that these claims were formulaic. Not only did the structure of litigation allow the municipal council this advantage, but it also allowed the council to modify their arguments against the litigant in light of information presented during the course of the litigation.

Initially, the city drew the language for its charges from the pages of old legal codes and laws enacted by past monarchs. At the first summons, in addition to the charge that Pedro was a pechero, the advocate claimed that he and his forefathers had never come to the muster calls of the hidalgos. Furthermore, the city claimed that the litigant, his father, and his grandfather had all asked for and been given public offices in the city and in other places but that these offices were of the sort held by pecheros. After Pedro's first appeal, the city added the claims that neither Pedro nor his father nor grandfather was of legitimate birth, but instead each was a bastard born from wicked sexual intercourse.[42] Having denied his legitimacy, the advocate made an abrupt shift in his argument to introduce a claim specific to Seville. He explained the introduction of the blanca de la carne fifteen years earlier and asserted that Pedro had never received this return while he lived in the city. He then added, in the alternative, that if Pedro had received the refund, this was due to some special connection he had and not because he was an hidalgo.

The accusations made against Pedro had less to do with those qualities that ought to pertain to an hidalgo and more to do with the legal justifications the city could mount to deny his claims. The city fashioned some of the charges against Sánchez Paneque from archaic or general laws and ordinances that no longer or had never been implemented or were in use in the city. Court officials and opposing municipal councils did not pose questions about the military service of claimants to hidalguía to see if they lived nobly and were therefore authentic hidalgos. They asked these questions as a way of appealing to existing laws and royal edicts—enacted during the late medieval period to address political needs and not to define nobility—to deny the claimant's right to this status. In the earliest extant lawsuit of hidalguía from 1395, Gonzalo de la Torre, a citizen of the village of Barajas near Madrid, sought recognition of his status because the village council had placed him on the tax lists and seized some of his goods.[43] In Gonzalo's case, the royal prosecutor made arguments about his absence from required military service similar to the objections the city of Seville made about Pedro Sánchez Paneque in 1526. Specifically, the prosecutor charged that he had not joined the campaign of Juan I against the king of Portugal in 1384, suggesting that failure to serve was detrimental to Gonzalo's hidalgo status. In response Gonzalo's witnesses testified that his father had served in the Calatayud campaign in 1362 and at the siege of Montiel in 1369, which brought about the deposition and death of King Pedro by his half brother Enrique de Trastamara. In opposition to the royal prosecutor's assertions about Gonzalo de la Torre's military service, the litigant himself argued that his failure to attend the royal summons should not cause him to lose his status.[44]

Gonzalo de la Torre's statement about his obligations as an hidalgo stand as an argument about which legal norms should hold primacy in determining status and ultimately whether the monarch held the right to make laws tying hidalguía to service. By 1395 recent royal statutes enacted in the Cortes of Castile and Léon—in contrast to and distinct from municipal charters—required military service to maintain caballero status. Only a year before Torres's suit, at the Cortes held in Zamora, the king had enacted a law that required all the men that he had knighted to maintain horse and arms and serve the king in wartime to enjoy tax exemption. Although the law from 1394 specified caballero and not hidalgo, laws enacted in subsequent decades conflated the two terms. At the Cortes of Valladolid in 1417 the government of Juan II confirmed the law made at the assembly in Zamora and added the clause that those who adhered to it should not pay taxes, except for those taxes that hijosdalgo pay.[45] More than a hundred years later, by the time Pedro Sánchez Paneque began his lawsuit, a series of monarchs had issued and confirmed similar laws and edicts demanding service or attendance at royal musters. In both the war of succession against her niece and during the conquest of the kingdom of Granada, Isabel I required through a series of edicts that all hidalgos join the royal musters. As punishment for those who failed to join the campaigns, she threatened to revoke their hidalgo status. Consequently, the accusation that the Sánchez Paneques had not attended the muster calls of the hidalgos had little to do with living nobly and more to do with discovering a legal basis for denying them tax exemptions.

Many of the charges made by the city's attorney and the royal prosecutor rested on norms they claimed to be universal, but which either were archaic or had never applied to the particular legal context of Seville. In fifteenth-century Seville no rules existed to limit pecheros from holding the majority of the city's public offices. While in practice the city's elite families controlled these positions, no ordinances required particular social rank or status. Access to office in fifteenth-century Seville depended on membership in and connections to powerful families and social networks and not on the ability to claim to be an hidalgo. Since all citizens in fifteenth-century Seville contributed to the royal servicio through a direct tax, the essential fiscal difference between hidalgos and pecheros was also absent. Likewise, the city neither held individual musters for hidalgos nor used the category of hidalgo to keep account of its military strength or its citizens' military obligations. In the documents recording Seville's military forces during the first quarter of the fifteenth century, city officials listed both citizens and residents in terms of their military function as knights, crossbowmen, or pikesmen.[46] In these lists the clerks occasionally recorded whether a caballero was a vassal of the king, a vassal of a lord, or a knight on account of royal favor or one's wealth. Nevertheless, all these men were required to appear in Seville's military musters and were considered members of its military forces as citizens of the city. In addition to these lists, the city kept records of the annual musters these men were required to attend. The failure to attend could result in the imposition of a fine, the amount of which depended on the person's military function, for example, fifty maravedís for a knight and forty for a crossbowman. In the fifteenth century, although attendance at the muster allowed for a public demonstration of a person's wealth and military occupation, it did not distinguish a person as a pechero or hidalgo.

The accusation that the Sánchez Paneques had not come to the musters called for hidalgos did not agree with the military practices of the city of Seville or for that matter with the practices of the city of Écija, during either the late fifteenth or early sixteenth century. The accusation appealed instead to an extraordinary edict issued by the Catholic Monarchs during the conquest of Granada as a means to force recalcitrant individuals to join the campaign. Not surprisingly, Pedro presented witnesses who attested to the fact that certain relatives had fought in these wars, specifically that his grandfather had sent a proxy to fight in the campaigns against the kingdom of Granada.[47]

Similarly, general Castilian legal norms on inheritance denied illegitimate children rights of inheritance, and various monarchs had issued specific edicts depriving such offspring the enjoyment of hereditary privileges.[48] Consequently, the first questions in the depositions from Pedro's witnesses sought to clear his family of these charges. The clerk asked if the litigant's grandfather, Juan Sánchez Paneque, had married Blanca Gonçález according to canon law and with the blessings of the church, had consummated the marriage, had lived with her in a matrimonial state, and in this state had conceived as their legitimate son Manuel Sánchez de Sevilla Paneque. These questions were repeated for the litigant's father, Manuel Sánchez, and his mother, Beatriz Sánchez. Like many of the charges leveled by the city, this accusation says less about the inher-

ent qualities of an hidalgo and more about the legal basis the city had for reject-
ing the litigant's claims.

Charges of illegitimate birth could serve to nullify the status of many who
claimed hidalgo status. However, one had to formally claim hidalguía to face
such challenges. Although Francisco Pizarro, the conqueror of Peru and one of
the most famous hidalgos of the sixteenth century, was born out of wedlock, the
issue never arose since he lived the majority of his life in the Americas, where
hidalgo status offered fewer tangible privileges, especially in the early decades
of colonization. Francisco was born the illegitimate son of the teenage Gonzalo
Pizarro, an hidalgo and native of the city of Trujillo, and the farm girl Francisca
González.[49] Although Francisco later used the Pizarro surname, he was raised
with relatives of his mother and not in his father's household. At the age of
twenty-four, before ever living independently as a citizen and head of his own
household—and consequently in a position to pay direct taxes—Francisco traveled to the Caribbean. He spent the next two decades in Panama and Nicaragua,
where he rose to be the most senior and experienced leader in Tierra Firme. He
successfully co-organized and led the expedition to Peru, which culminated
with the capture of the Incan capital of Cuzco. Until his death in 1541, he acted as
de facto governor of Peru in the king's name. Despite his questionable birth and
rebellious actions as governor, his descendants through his mestiza daughter,
Francisca, and his legitimate half brother Hernando enjoyed the status and privileges of hidalguía. Notably, Francisco's descendants enjoyed hidalgo status due
to the success members of the Pizarro family had in a lawsuit of hidalguía against
the city of Trujillo in the 1520s, while Francisco was in Panama.[50]

In cases of hidalguía, questions about the marital relationship between a
litigant's grandfather and grandmother and about his mother and father served
to establish whether there had been any violations of consanguinity, failures to
properly fulfill the requirements of marriage, or false claims of paternity, and
therefore grounds to dismiss the claim to hidalgo status. Furthermore, in the
context of early sixteenth-century Seville, these questions served to detect the
descendants of false converts whose ancestors had committed heresy by maintaining Jewish customs and failing to adopt Christian ceremonies, offenses
that would likewise be grounds for denying status. In the case of Juan Bautista
Espinosa Polanco from 1590, the prosecutor asserted that Juan was of illegitimate birth and the witnesses were asked if he or his ancestors "descended from
bastards, those corrected for errors, or the race of Muslims, Jews, or conversos,
or those reconciled by the Holy Office of the Inquisition."[51] Converts convicted

of heresy who confessed and were reconciled with the church were spiritually forgiven but faced significant material punishments, including the loss of a portion of their property and prohibition from holding certain public offices.[52] These punishments extended to the second generation of the male line. Viewed as a form of property, the status of hidalgo would also be forfeit for any who were discovered.

Consequently, the party opposing the recognition of status regularly used the accusation that the claimant was a bastard, whether or not there was any supporting evidence or information concerning the litigant's birth status; this objection became a standard question posed to witnesses. As such it could reveal damaging information, as in Ortuño de Avendaño's efforts in 1535 to gain recognition of his hidalgo status from the city of Seville. Among the city's evidence against Ortuño was testimony from his father's native town of Durango in Vizcaya provided two years earlier at the chancery court in Valladolid. The evidence revealed that Ortuño was a "natural child" born from a union between his young unmarried father and Mari Ortiz de Verayaga, a single women known to be his father's companion.[53] Likewise, in the 1582 case of Fernando Serrano de Santillan, citizen of both the town of Aznalcazar and the city of Seville, the opposing town's advocate asserted that the litigant's father was conceived while his grandfather was in holy orders so that even if Fernando descended from noble blood he should not be allowed the privileges accorded to hidalgos.[54]

The fact that the city made the alternate pleadings that Pedro Sánchez Paneque had never received a refund from the blanca and the claim that if he had it was due to some connection and not on account of being an hidalgo further indicates that the city knew very little or nothing about its opponent even in terms of its own tax history.[55] Obtaining information about an individual's tax history was a difficult and costly task. Domínguez Ortiz has pointed out that in practice many towns and villages lacked or failed to maintain municipal tax rolls, especially when they used communal properties to pay their contribution to the royal servicio.[56] Moreover, these records were typically in the property of the former clerk and not the municipality. The willingness of royal officials to accept not only unsubstantiated charges but charges that made contradictory claims about the litigant further supports the systemic bias against claimants to the status of hidalgo.

The city's seemingly more particular accusation—that in the event Pedro had not paid taxes it was due to some connection and not due to any specific privilege—resulted from the practice of religious and royal institutions and corporate entities extending the fiscal privileges they held to their retainers (*criados*). In particular, Castilian prelates and religious corporations provided tax immunity to those who served or had served them. Through the fifteenth century the cities and towns had repeatedly complained about this issue in the meetings of the Cortes. In the 1455 Cortes of Córdoba, the cities' representatives had pressed Enrique IV to curtail the practice whereby clerics, cathedral chapters, monasteries, and universities extended their own exemptions to their lay servants and retainers. The representatives of the cities viewed the extension of these exemptions as an abuse of corporate privileges. Similarly, Juan II had responded to complaints about these abuses with edicts prohibiting exemptions for those without privilege in at least four assemblies of the realm, the Cortes of Palencia in 1431, Zamora in 1432, Madrid in 1435, and Valladolid in 1447.[57] The fact that the issue was raised time and again indicates both the frequency of the practice and the Crown's inability to curtail the practice to the satisfaction of the Castilian municipalities. Royal institutions similarly provided such exemptions to their members, particularly the chancery courts themselves.[58] Graduates in law from the Universities of Salamanca, Valladolid, and Bologna enjoyed exemption from the servicio similar to that enjoyed by hidalgos in some municipalities. Likewise, judges at the chancery courts enjoyed the tax-exempt status of hidalgos. In Seville those who ran the royal mint and managed the royal palaces and arsenal also enjoyed a range of fiscal privileges and tax exemptions.

Moreover, the frequent assertion of influential connections or the extension of immunities to explain a person's enjoyment of tax exemption in cases of hidalguía highlights the diffuse border between privilege derived from status and exemptions accruing to an individual for other reasons that existed during the early modern period. This issue became more contentious in the sixteenth century due to the 1492 Pragmática de Córdoba, which set the manner for the courts to establish hidalguía through evidence of three generations of exemptions from taxation. Pedro Hernández de Andrada's lawsuit against both the city of Seville and the town of Umbrete illustrates how the precedent of exemption could lead to disputes over status or provide the basis for objections to hidalgo claims. The dispute began when Umbrete's officials seized property from Hernández in 1573 to pay the town's contribution to the servicio.[59] This action precipitated Hernández's complaint against Umbrete at the chancery court and the demand to be recognized as an "hidalgo of blood." Umbrete's attorney, Diego Martínez, responded by asserting that Hernández, his father, and grandfather were all pecheros, but if at some time the opposing party and his relations had been free from contributing to the servicio, it was for being armed knights and for being favored retainers in the entourage of the arch-bishop of Seville, who had previously been the Lord of Umbrete.[60] The town of Umbrete was situated only sixteen kilometers west of the city of Seville and had been under the jurisdiction of the archbishopric of Seville since the late thir-teenth century. After almost three centuries under ecclesiastical lordship, the town's status changed significantly in the years immediately before the dispute. As a means to raise badly needed revenues, Felipe II negotiated a concession from Pope Pius V in 1569 to alienate and sell ecclesiastical properties and juris-dictions belonging to bishops and cathedrals.[61] In the following years, as a result of sales, the archdiocese of Seville lost all of the towns over which it held lord-ship, except Umbrete, although in the case of Umbrete, it lost important rights of governance.[62] As part of the shift in administration following the sale of lord-ship, it appears that the town's council reformed Umbrete's collection of taxes, which in turn led to the dispute over hidalgo status. To be safe—and in the nature of general oppositions—the town's advocate added that the family also might not have paid the servicio because of the influence of municipal councils or powerful individuals, for being so poor that they had insufficient property to be taxed, or because their ancestors had been required to serve in the wars as people of means.[63]

Both royal officials and municipal councils employed laws enacted in the Cortes against the extension of privileges and against the inheritance rights of illegitimate children to restrict access to privilege and impede the proliferation of individuals who enjoyed these privileges. As a result, language drawn from these laws became fundamental components of the accusations that councils made in lawsuits of hidalguía during the sixteenth century.

In response to the city's objections to his claims, Pedro Sánchez Paneque submitted a diverse range of evidence, including the records of past lawsuits and the depositions of citizens of Seville and other municipalities in Andalusia. The documents he brought to court as evidence recorded six separate cases of litigation concerning the family's claims to hidalguía during a period of almost a hundred years (see fig. 6). Not all these cases were initiated to gain or deny tax exemption. In one case a cousin named Pedro Gonçález Paneque initiated a suit of hidalguía to avoid imprisonment for debt. In another incident a relative identified as Pedro Paneque appealed to his status as an hidalgo to escape judi-cial torture when accused of adultery with the wife of a jurado in the city of

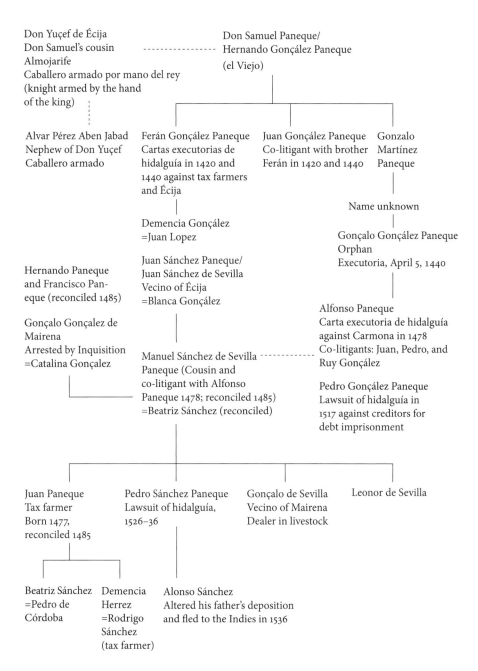

Fig. 6 Members of the Gonçález Paneque/Sánchez Paneque families and their litigation for hidalgo status. Direct lines of descent are represented by solid lines; dashed lines represent kinship relations that are indirect or unspecified in the documents.

Écija. The family's opponents in these legal contests varied and included tax farmers in the city of Écija in 1420, the city council of Écija in 1440, the town of Carmona in 1478, a councilman of Écija in 1517, former business partners and creditors from Burgos the same year in Écija, and finally the city council of Seville in 1526. In response to this litigation, the royal councils of two different monarchs, Juan II and Isabel I, provided executive writs ordering municipal councils and royal officials to recognize the family's status and the privileges tied to this status. Unsurprisingly, Pedro Sánchez Paneque provided notarized copies of these documents as supporting evidence in his suit.[64]

Nevertheless, the possession of supporting royal documents did not shield those who claimed hidalgo status from having to initiate subsequent litigation, and it did not guarantee victory in future lawsuits of hidalguía. Despite the family's possession of royal documents recognizing their status, Pedro Sánchez Paneque still had to present a full complement of evidence in his suit with the city of Seville. Pedro provided depositions taken in 1527 and 1528 from citizens of Seville who had previously been residents of Écija or held offices in that city and were thereby able to testify to the family's public reputation and status. Included with the royal letters were related documents, including depositions from citizens of Écija in 1420. Both sets of depositions expressed public knowledge of the family's rights and honors as hidalgos and their long history of exemption from paying taxes in the municipality of Écija.

Despite earlier success, the process of litigation placed Pedro in a disadvantageous situation. The very authoritative documents testifying to the family's status as hidalgos, which the litigation had required him to present, revealed information about the family that Seville's attorney and the royal prosecutor subsequently used to deny his status. Although the earliest judicial ruling from 1420 recognized Juan González Paneque's possession of hidalguía, the accompanying depositions revealed the family's Jewish ancestry. In the case of the Paneques, at least three generations of the family had received royal recognition and local acceptance of their hidalgo status despite having Jewish ancestors. Until the presentation of this evidence, neither the city nor the royal prosecutor had made any charges against Paneque that suggested that he was a converso or related to convicted "Judaizing" heretics or that they had information about these facts.

The witnesses' responses in this earlier dispute indicate that during the fifteenth century the citizens of Écija had applied the term *hijodalgo* to all persons with hereditary privileges, regardless of their status either as recent converts to

Christianity or as Jews. The witnesses stated that they had known Juan's father, Don Samuel Paneque, who after his conversion was called Hernando González Paneque.[65] Another witness identified Juan as the great-grandson of Don Yuçef, the influential fourteenth-century Jewish courtier. This Yuçef served as the overseer of customs dues in Andalusia (*almojarife mayor*) during the reign of Alfonso XI.[66] Given the timing, it is likely that Samuel/Hernando converted during the terrible anti-Jewish pogrom of 1391. The depositions recorded that Don Samuel was in fact an hijodalgo before his conversion and that the entire Jewish community of the town recognized him as such.[67] Multiple witnesses stated that he was an hidalgo by lineage (*fijodalgo de linaje*) and that among the Jews and among the Christians he was so recognized.

In a similar case of elite Jewish families in Seville in the years before the pogrom, another Samuel—Samuel Abravanel—converted and changed his name to Juan Sánchez de Sevilla.[68] Juan Sánchez came from an illustrious and wealthy Jewish family, which had supported Enrique de Trastamara's winning faction in the civil war against Pedro I. As reviewed in the previous chapter, Juan came to hold a number of important fiscal offices for the Crown. In these offices he would have been well acquainted with González Paneque of Écija and his relatives, who engaged in tax farming throughout the region. Juan's son Alfonso Sánchez de Sevilla became a veinticuatro of Sevilla, and their descendants remained active in the city's politics until the end of the fifteenth century, when members of the family faced charges of Judaizing heresy. The witnesses that testified on behalf of Pedro Sánchez Paneque noted that his grandfather, a vecino of Écija, was known variably as Juan Sánchez Paneque and Juan Sánchez de Sevilla. Given the conspicuous use of the surname Sánchez by Pedro's grandfather and the family's shift in residency to Seville, it is likely that the family was related to or descended from the converso Sánchez de Sevilla clan prior to its fall from prominence. Pedro's connection to the Sánchez de Sevilla clan could also have been through his mother, Beatriz Sánchez.

In the 1420 lawsuit of Juan González Paneque against the city of Écija, the presiding magistrate, after a review of the evidence, ruled in his favor, and royal secretaries issued a writ in the name of Juan II supporting this ruling. In the early fifteenth century, not only the citizens of Écija but the Crown's magistrate and the king himself all appear to have found the convergence of Jewish blood—and even faith—with the title of hijodalgo to be unproblematic. Nevertheless, Pedro's legal representative found the coincidence of these factors to be a significant obstacle in the chancery court of the early sixteenth century, especially when it became linked to conviction for the crime of heresy.

The Paneque family won their first two cases of litigation for status during the reign of Juan II and the royal government headed by Álvaro de Luna. Benzion Netanyahu argues that Álvaro de Luna actively promoted conversos to important royal offices as a means of developing a loyal corps of officials.[69] Moreover, he claims that Luna actively supported both Jews and conversos. Whether the support of conversos was an active royal policy or not, in the fifteenth century conversos held important offices in the royal government and at the local levels in municipal governments.[70] In contrast to his ancestor, Pedro Sánchez Paneque litigated in a different religious climate and in the shadow of the implementation and continued operation of Inquisition tribunals that actively sought to identify and discipline false converts.

THE MEANING OF HIDALGUÍA

Pedro Sánchez Paneque's case effectively reveals how sixteenth-century disputants strove to impose their own definition of hidalgo and their own claims about how one arrived at this status. Moreover, it illustrates the growing emphasis placed on the meaning of hidalgo status as exclusively blood based and originating with one's descent. Most suits of hidalguía provide tediously formulaic complaints and objections, employ similar questions to witnesses, and rarely contain the arguments made by legal representatives. Sánchez Paneque's case is both unique and illuminating for the complete inclusion of the appeal arguments provided by the attorneys. In the course of litigation, the disputants' efforts to define hidalguía itself became an object of contestation. The opposing litigants appealed to two distinct discourses in their competing efforts to define an hidalgo: one discourse emphasized the performance of service to the Crown and the república, and the other, possession of an essential heritable quality or qualities. When sixteenth- and seventeenth-century treatise writers debated the criteria for nobility, some emphasized service and the authority of monarchs to employ their sovereign power to create or at least authorize nobility, and others emphasized lineage and qualities tied to it.[71] This debate is equally evident in the arguments made by opposing attorneys.

Arriving at the issue of the Sánchez Paneque family's Jewish ancestors, the disputants began a more explicit contest to define the status of hidalgo. In the arguments made in the second and last appeal, Pedro's legal counsel went as far as to claim that the prejudice arising from this knowledge had cost his client a favorable ruling. While still claiming that his client possessed hidalguía and tax exemption, the attorney explicitly associated hidalguía with nobility and argued that converts could obtain such nobility. The understanding of nobility the attorney applied to his client combined both essential inherited qualities and an eminence resulting from virtuous actions. Importantly, he denied that inherited qualities of this nobility were tied to particular races and consequently to blood descent. To make this argument, the lawyer appealed to discourses articulated by medieval church and royal authorities that argued for the ability of converts to acquire all the rights and privileges of their fellow Christians. The *Siete partidas* established that converts "can have all the offices and honors which other Christians have."[72] The attorney asserted that even if his client "should be descended from Jews on his father's side, he, his father, and his grandfather had all been very good Christians and noble people."[73]

Additionally, he stated that no one can possibly doubt that this right of nobility can be earned and proven by immemorial prescription (*prescripción*). Sixteenth-century civil law jurists understood prescripción as the acquisition of rights or property from possession over multiple generations. With this last assertion Pedro's attorney claimed that the possession of this right for a lengthy period of time—at least three generations—undeniably provided the holder of privilege with hidalguía for perpetuity. The advocate stated that "the reason the ruling should be revoked is because even though the family's beginning was depraved, by converting, as [the litigant's] ancestors converted of their own free will to our holy Catholic faith, they and their descendants should have been and were capable of nobility, and they were able to prove their nobility by the above said immemorial prescripción or by the legal efforts of the father and grandfather in accord with the laws of these kingdoms."[74] Laws enacted at the Cortes meetings of Toro in 1398 and Tordesillas in 1403 established that one could substantiate hidalgo status through possession of exemption for three generations. Isabel and Fernando reaffirmed these laws in a pragmática issued in Córdoba in 1492.[75] To substantiate his claim that conversos could acquire the privileges of hidalguía, the attorney appealed to a principle articulated in decrees of the church and laws of Castile that he left unspecified, but it included canons of the council of Constance and statutes enacted by Isabel and Fernando. According to the decrees of church and Crown, the attorney argued that the Sánchez Paneques rightfully deserved all the offices and privileges open to other Christians.[76]

Through a review of the family's history and Castilian custom, Pedro's advocate further attempted to deny the claim that hidalguía and former Jewish blood and faith were incompatible. Having addressed the issue of his descent, the lawyer made a forceful claim about the nature of hidalguía, derived from observations of monarchical practices rather than from a reading of royal legal texts: "It cannot be doubted that all the nobility of hidalguía, at the beginning, had its origin in the grant of royal privilege, [and] the prescripción of time immemorial had the force of royal privilege."[77] By this claim he sought to state the legitimacy of both the grant of royal privilege and prescripción, since he confidently asserted his client had shown possession of both. On the one hand, he held evidence of the Crown's recognition of his hidalguía through royal judicial rulings, and on the other he had given evidence that his family had held this privilege for at least three generations and thereby satisfied the terms of prescripción.

In response to these arguments Seville's lawyer revised the city's basis for denying Pedro his hidalguía. Challenged on the nature of hidalguía itself, the city finally discarded the use of formulaic charges, directly addressed Pedro's claims, and sought to employ the claimant's evidence to its advantage. The city's attorney articulated precise—and apparently novel—distinctions between privilege and prescripción, created or employed new categories of privilege based on descent, and authoritatively made claims about the meaning of the witnesses' depositions, earlier judicial rulings, and royal letters.

The attorney pointed out that although some of the witnesses said that Pedro's ancestors were free from paying taxes because they were held to be hidalgos, the litigant did not possess the other qualities that the laws and ordinances of these kingdoms demanded should converge for someone to be held as an hidalgo. He left these qualities unstated, but in light of the evidence the city now produced, these qualities included Catholic orthodoxy and Old Christian blood. While in the depositions some of the witnesses had stated merely that the family held tax exemption, which hidalgos also possessed, some had specifically said that the community had esteemed the family as hidalgos and treated them as such. Consequently, the advocate's argument sought to undermine the traditional authority of community recognition in favor of the possession of certain essential and undefined qualities. The city's advocate simultaneously sought to establish a precise distinction between those who held mere privilege and those who held hidalguía and to lump Pedro among the former: "[The witnesses] meant that [the Sánchez Paneques] had privileges from past kings, but that is not the same as saying that one is an hidalgo by blood."[78] With the use of this phrase, the city's lawyer placed greater emphasis on a racial and hereditary element inherent in hidalguía, which stood in stark contrast to the formulation typical of the late medieval period. Jurists and royal scribes through the fifteenth century had almost exclusively employed the phrase "hijodalgo of known house" (hijodalgo de solar conocido). The use of this formulation in earlier documents typifies the period's concern with community standing.[79]

Since Pedro had substantiated his claim through an appeal to both the grant of royal privilege and to prescripción, the city attempted to use these dual appeals as a means to deny their respective worth as sources of legitimate possession of hidalguía. The procurador argued not only that privilege and prescripción were different but that they were mutually exclusive. Using Pedro's evidence, the city created its own version of the family's past. In his argument the attorney acknowledged that perhaps past kings had provided this family of pecheros with certain liberties and freedoms, but this was not because the family descended from hidalgos. He then gave the proposition that whoever was trying to attain privilege by legal means cannot be called hidalgo by blood, because privilege and prescripción are different and they cannot coincide to acquire hidalguía or any other lordship: "If the ancestors of the opposing side were free by privilege they are not afterward able to acquire it by prescripción. That is, once free and liberated from the servitude in which one was born, or in which one falls, one is not able to be more liberated."[80] These statements assume a clear distinction between hereditary privileges and privileges that end in the grantee's lifetime. The lawyer's statements implied that even if earlier members of the family had possessed privilege, these privileges were not hereditary and therefore could not serve as means to legitimate Pedro's current claim to hidalguía and tax exemption. Incidentally, it also denied Pedro—as the plaintiff in the suit—the ability to plead in the alternative, as the council had done.

Although the city's attorney addressed a number of issues in his final arguments, the evidence he brought to court in response to this last appeal focused exclusively on demonstrating Pedro's Jewish ancestry and the family's guilt as false converts in the 1480s. The first piece of evidence consisted of the account book of the 1518 *composición*, a forced loan Andalusian conversos paid to the Crown. The document recorded the precise amounts that two members of the family had contributed.[81] The city also presented a record from Seville's Inquisition tribunal documenting the public penance (*auto de fe*) for convicted heretics held on September 14, 1485, at the town of Constantina in the territory of Seville. Among those named were Manuel Sánchez Paneque and Juan Paneque. The inquisitors ruled that they had committed the crimes of heresy and apostasy and were sentenced to the loss of all their material property. The document recorded that these men abjured their crimes and errors and confessed the Catholic faith, so the church absolved and reconciled them.

Both the advocate's claim that Pedro did not possess the necessary qualities and his choice of evidence implied that the essential qualities of hidalgos and Jews—including Jewish converts and their descendants—were mutually exclusive. The judges' ultimate ruling does not specify whether the president of the court and the oidores rejected Pedro's claim on the basis of his ancestry or on the religious offenses of his father and grandfather. Notably, more than twenty-six years later in 1552, Carlos I prohibited the "sale of hidalguía to anybody guilty of public infamy, to sons of clerics, descendants of unpardoned comuneros, or to anyone with any trace of heretical or Jewish blood."[82] Nevertheless, the officials of the court, including the judges themselves, who were supposed to be hidalgos, came from diverse backgrounds. A 1559 review (*vista*) of the chancery court in Granada detailed not only that there were advocates at the court who were conversos but that some of them were the descendants of condemned heretics. At least one of the converso lawyers, Lic. Lope de León, even served as a judge at the court.[83]

PUBLIC REPUTATION AS AUTHORITATIVE EVIDENCE

The challenges involved in the reproduction and preservation of written documents during this period made it difficult for disputants to provide textual evidence of the possession of hidalguía. The frequent lack of documents, due to the expense involved in producing and the difficulty in preserving them, often left claimants, and their multiple family members and descendants in future generations, without tangible proof to present at court. In a sample of cases involving citizens and municipalities of southern Extremadura, litigants produced a document in only 43 out of 255 lawsuits, or 16.8 percent of the cases. Moreover, almost all so-called grants or patents of hidalguía were usually issued in the form of writs ordering the recognition of status after a ruling in previous litigation. Of the forty-three documents presented in the lawsuits from Extremadura, thirty-nine of them were ejecutorias, two were written documentation of earlier litigation, and only two were letters granting hidalguía.[84] This evidence strongly suggests that royal grants of the status of hidalgo were not the usual path by which individuals acquired the status but that they served as a means to buttress existing status or pretensions to status in a community. Community opinion and reputation (*publica voz y fama*) was what mattered in most cases.[85] Moreover, the rarity of formal written grants as opposed to the greater number of judicial writs recognizing status suggests that grants were given in the form of judicial rulings and were sought primarily when a person's status was challenged. Although the Crown may have claimed the right to grant status, government officials found it easier to justify the confirmation of status in the form of a royal writ ordering the implementation of a judicial ruling rather than the straight provision of status. In contrast, litigants sought documents that testified to existing status, because it offered them additional arguments for their enjoyment of privilege based on previous possession.

As the case of Pedro Sánchez Paneque illustrates, the possession of documents, or typically copies of documents, testifying to earlier recognition of status or a grant of status did not ensure that a litigant would win his case. Both city councils and the royal prosecutors employed arguments to cast doubt on the authenticity of earlier documents, question whether they deserved to have been given in the first place, or deny their continued validity. Municipal attorneys also commonly accused litigants of providing altered or forged documents. Sánchez's own lawsuit ended with an official investigation to discover which court clerk had assisted his son in a last-minute attempt to change deposition answers that had revealed the family's converso background. The difficulties involved in the production and preservation of documents and the ambivalent worth of the documents as authoritative evidence of status required the additional support of community opinion and estimation.

The most conventional and ubiquitous type of proof that both claimants and the opposing parties presented was the testimony of witnesses. Not only did these witnesses give information about the community's assessment of the claimant's status, they also gave information on his possession of privilege, most notably his payment of taxes. Positive proof that an individual held some sort of exemption from taxation allowed claimants to use the enjoyment of privilege as the basis for substantiating one's authoritative right to privilege. Witness depositions suggest that the two issues sometimes became confused in the community's opinion and estimation of the litigant, and the actual enjoyment of privilege—for lack of supporting documentation—could serve as the basis for the right to privilege.

Community confusion between the enjoyment of privilege and the right to privilege made it necessary for the city to make the dual charges that Pedro was not an hidalgo and that he had always paid his taxes. The two charges also addressed the difficulty officials faced when trying to assess who should hold privilege in a society where local standing vied for authority with written documents, especially when written documents, either court rulings or municipal tax records, could not be produced. In Pedro's case the court clerk asked the witnesses if they knew whether the litigant was a "well-known hijodalgo from his father and grandfather and therefore deserving of remuneration of 500 *suel-dos* according to the ancient charter of Castile."[86] The clerk also asked if the family members, in the places where they had lived, had been in this state "or in a similar or quasi state" (vel casi de omes de hijosdalgo). The court clerk subsequently asked the witness whether or not the litigant and his family had contributed in either royal or council taxes or any other tributes that pecheros of these places paid and that hijosdalgo did not. Last in this series of questions the witnesses declared whether municipal authorities had ever placed any of the family on the lists of taxpayers.[87]

The formulation of these questions and their responses demonstrates how the court officials and the disputants recognized the need to appeal to both the authority of royal documents and the authority of public reputation in the presentation of their evidence. The witnesses' testimony, resulting from these specific questions, minutely focused on the physical existence of a document and on the actual transaction of the tax collection. Furthermore, they linked both document and nonpayment specifically to the possession of hidalguía. Seventy-year-old Juan de Hoyo claimed that he had seen the privilege in person, but owing to his inability to read, had heard it read aloud. Likewise, Antón Nuñez Paneque claimed that Pedro's father, Manuel, had never paid the pecho in Écija, because of a privilege that the family had on record with the city council. The silk weaver, Antón Rodríguez Carmona, provided a more graphic account. As a neighbor of Manuel Sánchez in the parish of San Juan in Écija many years earlier, he had seen how the tax collectors had come to his own house and those of other pecheros in his neighborhood, but when they had arrived at Paneque's house they had walked on by without entering or demanding the pecho. He stated that the officials exempted the house because Manuel was from the lineage of the Paneques, who were publicly held to be hidalgos.[88] Diego López de Lorca, a former notary, citizen of Écija, and hidalgo himself, provided similar testimony. He stated that roughly twenty years earlier he had accompanied some tax collectors on their rounds. "When they arrived at Manuel's house one of these men asked why it was that they weren't going in, and the other man responded that Manuel was exempt and didn't owe the pecho on account of being an hidalgo."[89]

The last questions put to the witnesses sought to substantiate this possession of privilege by showing his family's participation in activities appropriate to hidalgos, such as holding the proper offices, attending the musters of hidalgos, and going to war with the king. Antón Rodríguez Carmona testified that for the muster of the hidalgos made for the war against Granada, the litigant's father, Manuel Sánchez, as an hidalgo, had sent a proxy to serve in the war in his place. The inspector of Seville's slaughterhouse, Juan Ruiz Toquero, originally a citizen of Écija, had heard that the Paneques were held to be hidalgos in Écija because they had some sort of privilege that their grandparents had earned in the war. In addition to the services that the family would have provided as hidalgos, the witnesses mentioned the family's possession of other privileges that accrued to hidalgos. Toquero for instance had heard that some of these Paneques had been freed from paying certain debts because of this privilege.[90] An inherent problem in all legal disputes is the reliability and truthfulness of the witnesses, and this was a regular issue in lawsuits of hidalguía and one addressed in chapter 6, which explores the malleability of evidence and possibilities for fraudulent testimony and documents. Whether Pedro's witnesses gave honest answers or not, the city of Seville never provided evidence that he, his father, or his grandfather had previously paid taxes in any of the municipalities where they had lived.

Migration to a different community, changes in tax regimes, and political rivalries and feuds within a community placed the recognition of status in jeopardy and provided royal and town officials the opportunity to deny families their privileges. In sixteenth-century Castile, individuals or families could move easily from one municipality to another, but the privileges they possessed could not. The litigation the Sánchez Paneque family had to endure highlights the troubles encountered by hidalgos who tried to move to other communities. In 1478, Pedro's grandfather had succeeded in gaining the royal chancery's authorization of his hidalguía in a dispute with the city council of Carmona, a town where the family had not previously gained public recognition of their status. In 1536, Pedro did not manage the same feat against the city council of Seville.

Both the manner in which municipal lawyers formulated their accusations against claimants to hidalguía and the support they received from royal magistrates gave them a favorable advantage in these legal contests. Additionally, the laws they appealed to and the language they employed in their arguments contributed to a dominant definition of hidalguía as hereditary or racial nobility. In the final appeal, both Sánchez Paneque and the city's lawyers sought to emphasize the noble nature of the hidalgo to advance their opposing claims. Nevertheless, the one emphasized meritorious nobility arising from service to the monarch and possession over multiple generations and the other a blood-based essence incompatible with Jewish ancestry. Although the plaintiff lost his claim either on account of his Jewish ancestry or his family's crimes of heresy, the city's opposition to Sánchez Paneque's claim did not begin with this knowledge. Instead, the city began with a number of general accusations that led to particular knowledge about the litigant and ultimately served as the basis to deny his claim.

The final ruling of the president and judges at the chancery court denied Pedro recognition of his hidalguía. Despite this sentence the court did not order him to pay the opposing side's final court costs, a typical penalty assessed on the loser in a lawsuit and one originally assessed on Pedro. Through this gesture, the judges acknowledged that Paneque's claim had not been an act of frivolous litigation. Nevertheless, they could not accede to his claim. In an age when monarchs aggressively sought to increase state income, the interests of royal and municipal revenues could not allow an easy recognition of privilege.

5

SOCIAL NETWORKS AND PRIVILEGE

On September 7, 1583, the royal prosecutor Diego de Amezaga filed a complaint with the judges of the tribunal of hidalgos at the chancery court in Granada.[1] In this complaint the prosecutor charged that the city council of Seville was providing a number of its highest-ranking officials and some of its leading citizens with undeserved economic privileges. Specifically naming six men, he claimed that despite the fact that they were common taxpayers and the descendants of pecheros, the city treated them as hidalgos and allowed them to receive the refund from the excise tax used to pay the city's servicio. Among the six men were the four veinticuatros Juan de Cuevas Melgarejo, Hernando de Almansa, his brother Melchor de Almansa, and Bartolomé de Mesa.[2] Having denounced these men, he requested that the king, through the judges of the court, grant him a royal order against the city and include in it a copy of the edict of Enrique IV. The order and the legal basis for his complaint were necessary so that these men would render the taxes appropriate to their social status and so that Seville's judicial magistrates would place them on the taxpayer rolls and strike their names from the registers where they were listed as hidalgos. The tribunal's judges reviewed the charges the same day in public audience and ordered that the court provide Amezaga with the order he requested and the copy of the law.

Through his request for royal writs from the chancery court, the royal prosecutor sought to use the law enacted by Enrique IV at the Cortes of Ocaña in 1469 as a precedent for denying anyone without hidalgo ancestry the privileges of tax exemption in Seville. The Cortes in 1469 had produced this law in response to a particular political problem brought on by a dynastic struggle and civil war. The law itself referred to a limited set of individuals and stated that the king revoked and nullified the grants of hidalguía he had provided to those men who came to his defense after September 1465. Nevertheless, in the *Ordenanzas reales*, the jurist Alfonso Díaz de Montalvo's 1485 redaction of royal legislation, the presentation of this law included the clause that "all those who were pecheros or who descended from pecheros should not enjoy the privileges, exemptions, or offices of hidalgos."[3] Neither Amezaga nor the royal judges made any explicit reference to the language or substance of the law and simply invoked it as the authoritative basis for the writs against Seville's citizens.

With this initial court order the royal prosecutor began what would be a three-year campaign against dozens of Seville's citizens. During the following weeks Amezaga filed seven more complaints against other officials and citizens of the city of Seville repeating identical charges. In total he denounced as fraudulently receiving the refund eighteen councilmen and fifty-eight prominent citizens, including a judge of Seville's audiencia, a judge of the regional militia, the constable of the city walls, and the city council's chief clerk (see table 5).

By the end of the month the city council of Seville received notice of these writs. On September 28 the members of the council met together in the city hall in the presence of the asistente, Juan Hurtado de Mendoza Guzmán y Rojas, the Count of Orgaz. The asistente, referred to as corregidor in other municipalities, served as a proxy for the king in the settlement of disputes in the city and since 1478 had held important voting powers on the city council equal to roughly a third of the present veinticuatros.[4] At the meeting the attending councilmen deliberated on the city's course of action and ultimately crafted a response that denied the claims of the prosecutor and delegated power of attorney to the councilman Gonçalo de Saavedra and the parish representative Pedro de Fuentes—both of whom were already resident at the court in Granada—to contest these charges. Although the council clerk did not record the exact vote, the council reached this decision with the support of at least two-thirds of those present, since a broad consensus among the councilmen would have been necessary in the event the asistente had voted against the decision to oppose the prosecutor's charges.

After being notified of the city's refusal to comply with the writs and its decision to contest the charges, the royal prosecutors Amezaga and Dr. Heredia sent a detailed list of arguments to the chancery court, arguing why the judges should not hear the city's objections. Four days later, on October 15, Dr. Villalta, as attorney for the city of Seville, wrote to Antonio de Torres at the court of

Table 5 Citizens of Seville charged as fraudulent hidalgos by the royal prosecutor, 1583–1585

Surname	First name	Year charged	Offices/Titles	Connections to council and other families	Other litigation
Alcázar	Felipe del	1583	Veinticuatro	Guzmán, Caballero, Illescas, León	1585
Alcázar	Melchor del	1583	Veinticuatro	—	1585
Alcázar	Don Francisco del	1583	Señor de la Palma	—	—
Alcázar	Don Francisco del	1583	Señor de Gelo	—	1593
Alcázar	Don Fernando	1583	Judge of the militia	—	—
Alcázar	Luis del	1583	—	—	—
Suárez de León	Gonzalo	1583	—	Felipe and Melchor del Alcázar's younger brother	—
Alcocer	Baltazar	1583	Commander of the city walls	—	—
Alcocer	Gaspar	1583	—	—	—
Alcocer	Diego (and sons)	1583	—	—	—
Almansa	Hernando de	1583	Veinticuatro	—	1587–91
Almansa	Melchor de	1583	Veinticuatro	—	—
Argote de Molina	Gonzalo	1583	Jurado, veinticuatro, and provost of the regional militia	Daughter of the marquis of Lanzarote's husband; Saavedra	—
Baena	García de	1583	Veinticuatro	Related to jurado Melchor de Baena	1586
Contador	Diego	1583	—	García de Baena's brother	—
Contador	Hernando	1583	—	García de Baena's brother	—
Caballero de Cabrera	Diego (and sons)	1583	Veinticuatro	Alcázar, Illescas, León	—
Caballero de Illescas	Pedro	1583	Veinticuatro	Alcázar, Cabrera, León	—
Caballero de Illescas	Alvaro (and sons)	1583	—	Pedro Caballero de Illescas	—
Céspedes	Don Pedro de	1583 1584	Señor de Carrión and veinticuatro	Marmolejo, Guzmán, Corzo	—
Céspedes	Juan de	1583 1584	Either Pedro de Céspedes's uncle or his second cousin	—	—
Quadros	María de	1585	Mayorazgo of Torres de Quadros	Alonso de Céspedes's daughter; Pedro and Juan Céspedes's cousin	—
Céspedes y Figueroa	Don Pedro de	1583	Veinticuatro	Pedro de Céspedes's first cousin	—

(continued)

Table 5   (continued)

Surname	First name	Year charged	Offices/Titles	Connections to council and other families	Other litigation
Cuevas Melgarejo	Juan de	1583 1585	Veinticuatro	—	—
León	García de	1583	Veinticuatro	Alcázares	1567
León	Juan de	1583	Veinticuatro	Alcázares	—
León Garavita	Pedro de	1583	—	García and Juan de León	—
Segura de León	Diego de	1583	—	García and Juan de León	—
Nuñez de Silva	Baltazar	1583	Veinticuatro	—	—
Nuñez Pérez	Diego	1583	Veinticuatro	—	—
Pérez	Marcos	1583	—	Diego Nuñez Pérez	—
Ruiz Torre Grose	Pero	1583	Veinticuatro	—	—
Villareal	Pedro de	1583	Veinticuatro	—	—
Alvo/Dalvo	Don Fernando de	1583	—	Illescas, Caballeros	—
Cabrera	Don Pedro de	1583	—	—	—
Cardenas	Don Alonso de	1583	—	Juan de Céspedes's brother	—
Cavala y Raba	Juan	1583	—	—	—
Cornejo	Don Rodrigo	—	—	—	—
Corzo Vicentelo	Juan Antonio	1583 1584	—	Portugal, Counts of Gelves	—
Escobar Melgarejo	Francisco de	—	—	—	—
Esquivel	Don Gonzalo de	1583	—	—	—
Esquivel	Juan de	1583 1585	—	—	1572 1602
Fuente	Don Gonzalo de la	1583	—	—	1580s 1590
Goyas	Miguel de	1583	—	—	—
Hernández de Esquivel	Gonzalo	1583 1585	—	Juan de Esquivel's brother	—
Juran	Alvaro	1585	—	—	—
[Lorves?]	Doña Isabel de	1585	—	—	—
María	Juan de	1583	—	—	—
Mesa	Bartolomé de	1583	Veinticuatro	—	1586–96
Mexía de Guzmán	Don Fernando	1583	Related to the veinticuatro Hernán Mexía de Guzmán	Cabrera, Soria, Vergara, Guzmán	—
Monsalve	Juan de	1585	—	—	—
Pineda	Don Hernando	1585	—	Related to Pedro Pineda	—

Surname	First name	Year charged	Offices/Titles	Connections to council and other families	Other litigation
Nebreda	Don Alonso de	1585	—	Inés Nebreda married Gonzalo de Céspedes	—
Nuñez de Xeres	Francisco	1583	—	—	—
Ordonel Confitero	Diego	1585	—	—	—
Pacheco de Carase	Juan	1583	—	—	—
Pinto	Alonso	1585	—	—	1584–89
Ponce	Luis	1585	—	—	—
Ponce de la Barrera	Rodrigo	1585	—	—	—
Ponce de León	Don Alvaro	1585	—	—	—
Puñosa de Montetel	Antonio del	1585	—	—	—
Ramírez de Cartagena	Pedro	1585	—	—	—
Ríos	Don Alonso de los	1583 1585	Lieutenant of the chief constable of Seville	—	—
Rodríguez de Herrera	Pedro	1583	Judge of Seville's royal appellate court	—	1580
Ruiz de Montoya	Gaspar	1583	Veinticuatro	—	—
Ruiz Cabeza de Vaca	Hernan	1585	—	—	—
Salinas	Rodrigo	1583	Chief clerk of the city council	—	1608
Suárez de Galdo	Gaspar	1583	—	—	—
Suherr[dro]	Don Andres	1585	—	—	—
Torre Fatiga	Diego de la	1583	—	Francisco de la Torre, factor for Ponce de León	1580s
Urquica	Antonio	1583	—	—	—
Urquica	—	1583	—	—	—
Ugarte	Francisco de	1583 1585	—	—	—
Vallejo	Lorenzo	1583	—	—	—

Source: AMS, sec. 1, carp. 146, doc. 192.

Note: In general, family names in this table are given in alphabetical order; members of the same family are grouped together, even though some individuals had different surnames (thus Gonzalo Suárez de Leon, for instance, appears with his brothers, Felipe and Melchor del Alcázar). Dashes indicate when information was unavailable or did not apply to the individual.

Granada, countering the prosecutor's arguments and presenting the city's reasons to dismiss the writs. Over a year later, on November 5, 1584, the judges of the court provided their ruling on the city's objections. They declared that after examining the eight charges submitted by His Majesty's prosecutor and reviewing the writs ordered by the court itself and the responses of the city of Seville, they revoked their earlier writs and declared them void. Although the judges did not provide an explanation for their decision, they ruled that they did not have the authority to provide the royal prosecutor the writs (*provisiones*) and with them the law of Enrique IV.

Through the sixteenth century Seville's city council did not consistently or conscientiously apply either royal or municipal rules governing hidalguía and its attendant privileges. In actual practice municipal authorities deliberately allowed many of their own officials and magistrates and their family members the privileges and consequently the status of hidalgo. Through these actions the council extended both privileges and status to individuals and families from diverse backgrounds, who entered the city's ruling class by means of political and economic alliances, marital unions, and royal and municipal service. This informal provision of privileges was largely hidden from public view and effected through the actions of the council officers, particularly the jurados and mayordomos. The unusual initiative by the chancery prosecutor brought to light the city council's illicit provision of privilege that was largely outside the oversight of the Crown.

During the first half of the sixteenth century the royal government had largely left the policing of status to the local municipal governments and had acted against claims to hidalgo status primarily in a supporting role at the chancery courts. But since the 1560s the Crown had made irregular initiatives to influence the recognition of status in the city of Seville. These efforts culminated in the 1580s, when royal prosecutors and their subordinates sought to limit the number of people with legal privileges by enforcing the city's own ordinances and applying laws concerning status enacted in late fifteenth-century meetings of the Cortes. While these officials acted in a manner consistent with a royal policy intended to protect the Crown's patrimony, they also acted in pursuit of their own private economic interests. The efforts of royal officials to impose these norms clashed with the desire of Seville's municipal government and local factions to regulate and determine the status and privileges of the citizens in their own community.

In this contest and in previous ones Seville's municipal council proved largely successful at defending its prerogatives and its practice of extending social privileges to those families and individuals within the ruling elite and those that joined this elite. Thus, in Seville and many other sixteenth-century Castilian municipalities, existing local political and social networks and relationships played a greater role in determining an individual's ability to gain recognition of the status of hidalgo than a person's actual descent or what existing laws said about the connection between status and descent.

INFORMAL ACCESS TO PRIVILEGE

Individual and family interests supported by and realized through powerful social networks often mediated or impeded the application of laws governing status and significantly influenced their implementation. The important networks for establishing status in this context included marriage alliances between families, business partnerships, political patronage between members of the city council, and relations between city council officials and royal officials at court.[5] In sixteenth-century Seville these networks even developed through artistic and cultural associations, which gathered around the city's scholars, jurists, poets, and artists, many of whom were members of prominent families. Individuals and families who previously lacked privilege or the status that authorized privilege typically came to acquire them through the support of these social networks and not through litigation, which was in many ways a last resort. As the means by which individuals and families constructed and improved their status, these networks allowed assimilated families to evade laws intended to restrict outsiders from the enjoyment of privilege. Only when such networks broke down did these individuals and families become susceptible to efforts by local or royal authorities to limit the number of people with privileges and in turn have to resort to litigation to prove their status. Despite what could be intense rivalries between families in the city and even outright conflict, members of these dominant families in the sixteenth century rarely broke ranks to reject the status of other families in their milieu.[6]

Early modern European historians in general and scholars of Spain in particular have long recognized the ability of individuals and families of wealth to enter what they designate as an urban patricate or urban aristocracy.[7] They typically describe the process in terms of new and old elites. In the case of early modern Seville the use of such classifications obscures the process of social mobility and the claims to status that actually occurred. The process of mobility often involved the incorporation and assimilation of individuals and families, most graphically evident in the adoption of old elite family names by those who married into these families.

Despite the momentary victory that the judges' ruling gave the city council in November 1584, the royal prosecutor, Diego de Amezaga, aggressively advanced similar charges almost immediately after this ruling. Within months of the decision, Amezaga filed new denunciations against Juan Antonio Corzo; Pedro de Céspedes, a councilman of Seville; and Juan de Céspedes, his brother, all three citizens of Seville. The former two also held significant lordships (*señorios*) near Seville. The new charges met with continued opposition from the city council, which on April 11, 1585, again designated power of attorney to one of its most important officers, this time to the councilman and representative to the Cortes Don Cristóbal de Mexía. These charges did not prove to be an isolated act. In the following two years Amezaga submitted at least five more separate complaints, each naming multiple persons. These denunciations listed men the prosecutor had targeted the year before as well as new individuals. Among these new names, he also listed women from some of the city's prominent families, including Doña María de Quadros, the widow of Pedro Sánchez Alrio; and Doña Isabel de Virves, the widow of Rodrigo Varo de Andrada.

The men and women denounced by Amezaga all enjoyed two main privileges: access to political office—or the ability to control the transfer of political office to a family member—and exemption from a tax on a basic commodity.[8] The majority of them enjoyed these privileges through the acquiescence of the local authorities and not through formal litigation. In other words, they had gained them through successful assimilation into the elite governing class of the city. Although some of the individuals and families targeted by Amezaga did not descend from hidalgos, they were themselves politically and economically prominent or connected to important regional seigneurial families through ties of marriage and business. Because the city council was composed of representatives from both established families and newly prominent ones, it collectively chose to support the accused citizens in their dispute with the royal prosecutor.

Class and group distinctions in sixteenth-century Seville were not absolute. Scholars have recognized not only the alliances and patronage between older established lineages and newly rich ones but also the fact that noble families were involved directly and indirectly in commercial activities, and some of the city's merchants and financiers successfully ennobled their families.[9] In this context, statements about one's background or status were often rhetorical claims substantiated by powerful social networks. Amezaga explicitly acknowledged in his first denunciation in 1583 that he was charging prominent individuals. Pointedly, he argued that their very eminence in the community had precipitated the abuse of the royal patrimony: "The abovementioned being councilmen, officials of the city, and rich and powerful men with connections and dealings with other officials of the city council attempt to enjoy the status of hidalgo and to never pay the royal taxes that the other common taxpayers of the city pay to the king."[10] Amezaga's description failed to mention other important characteristics of these men and women. The prosecutor leveled his complaints against known merchants, financiers, descendants of Jewish converts, and foreigners from other parts of Castile and from outside Spain. As members of these groups, the accused individuals would have faced potential, but not insurmountable, cultural and legal barriers to advancement in status. On the other hand, Amezaga also denounced on charges of fraudulently posing as hidalgos men with seigneurial titles, individuals connected by marriage to powerful aristocratic families, and royal officials. In actual fact, these groups were often mixed and not hermetically distinct. Likewise, Amezaga denounced both councilmen who had recently bought their offices and those from the main families of the city who had held these offices for generations (see table 5).[11] In its responses to the court, Seville's council supported all those denounced by Amezaga, regardless of the individual's actual background. In this contest the city government disputed the efforts of royal authorities to determine social status, while local nobles supported the social transformation of their merchant colleagues and family members, and Old Christians accepted the assimilation of New Christians. Furthermore, the council's actions in defense of its members of Jewish descent undermine simple expectations about late sixteenth-century prejudices against conversos and antagonism between Old and New Christians.[12]

Despite knowledge of the ancestry and occupations of those charged by Amezaga, the city responded to these accusations with the blanket claim that they did in fact descend from lineages of hidalgos. In Don Cristóbal de Mexía's response to the court's order that the city include Corzo and the two Céspedeses on their registers of taxpayers and apportion them part of the royal subsidy,

Mexía stated that they were hijosdalgo notorio, that their fathers and grand-fathers were also of this status, and that the city had provided them and their fathers and grandfathers refunds from the excise tax on meat that it tradition-ally provided to the hijosdalgo notorios of the city. In his review he explained that it did not matter whether they were publicly recognized hidalgos or hidal-gos who had received a royal grant of their status or hidalgos who had their status authorized by judicial writ.[13]

The Alcázares: Aristocratic New Christians

In terms of the number of family members charged, the prosecutor's denuncia-tions fell heaviest on the Alcázares, one of Seville's most prominent families and one with long and unbroken connections to the city council and a succession of royal governments.[14] Members of the family had filled council offices for more than 150 years, beginning as early as the 1430s, when Pedro González del Alcá-zar held multiple positions in the city government as veinticuatro, fiel ejecutor, and even the city's procurador to the Cortes.[15] Despite the Alcázares' long standing among the city's elite, the family was potentially vulnerable to charges that they were not legitimate hidalgos due to their descent from Jewish converts to Christianity and their connections and alliances with other converso fami-lies, which continued during the high point of Inquisition prosecution in Seville from the 1480s through the early decades of the sixteenth century.

Despite occasional problems with Inquisition officials, the family's active service to the city and Crown and its connections to other important families helped its members retain positions on the council without interruption over multiple generations and under changing sovereigns. The councilman Pedro del Alcázar fought in the conquest of the kingdom of Granada, serving during the siege of Alhama. His conspicuous participation in the war led King Fer-nando to personally knight him. Pedro also took part in the suppression of the Muslim revolt that broke out in the city of Granada in 1500 and spread to the surrounding rural communities. Perhaps more ingratiating to the royal govern-ment were Pedro's activities as collector of the customs dues for Seville and the monarchy's share of ecclesiastical tithes. His connections with the Crown alle-viated—in some measure—potential coercion and penalties from the Inquisi-tion. On one occasion, when Pedro's sister-in-law Juana Rodríguez had property confiscated on charges of being a false convert, he successfully secured the transfer of her property to his brother Francisco Ruiz del Alcázar. The return of the property did not come without cost and required a donation of 300,000 maravedís for the Granada campaign. Moreover, in 1493 the Crown interceded to block Pedro's arrest when he could not pay outstanding debts on account of the confiscation of his own property.[16] Pedro del Alcázar weathered these troubles and later played a major role in the negotiation of the cash payments from Seville's reconciled conversos for the return of confiscated property. He was one of three New Christians empowered to collect sums owed by others and he himself contributed 800 ducados. Through these turbulent years both he and his sons and nephews continued to serve the Crown as tax collectors and tax farmers and even as directors of the royal mint. In 1504, Pedro's son Francisco held the position of jurado and later took his father's seat on the city council as a veinticuatro. The Alcázares' success contrasts sharply with the fates of many converso jurados who lost their offices in the 1480s (see table 3). Pedro even obtained the office of jurado for the parish of San Juan in 1483, during a veritable converso purge. In addition to their connections to the Crown, the Alcázares maintained close ties with the Duke of Medina Sidonia and the Guzmán faction in the city.

While maintaining a presence on the city council and links to the Crown, the Alcázares succeeded in expanding their wealth and developing economic connections with other elite families in the city. Like a number of these families, the Alcázares invested in commercial developments connected to the growing trade with the Indies. Some of the oldest and most powerful of the regional aristocracy based in Seville, including branches of the Ponce de León and Guzmán families, had a history of involvement in Atlantic shipping and commerce that preceded the beginning of the Indies trade. These families and other old noble lineages such as the Fernández de Melgarejo and Medina families typically involved themselves indirectly in maritime commerce through ownership of vessels, though, as in the case of the Ponce de León, they also engaged in wholesale trade in merchandise and slaves. Like these regional magnates, the Alcázares also entered the ship-owning business as early as 1508, when Francisco del Alcázar held a third stake in the ship *San Salvador* with Cristóbal Rodríguez and Alonso de la Barrera. Francisco mixed family and business interests when he married Leonor de Prado, a member of another established Sevillian lineage. Members of Leonor's immediate family, especially the veinticuatro Luis de Prado and his nephew Gómez, were heavily involved in sea loans and the provision of capital and goods to Indies merchants. For the year 1525 they supplied the funds to outfit 24 percent of the ships that left Seville for the Indies.[17] Not surprisingly, two of Francisco's sons with Leonor, Pedro and Luis, became heavily involved in Indies enterprises, both investing in trade and Luis even serving as the receiver general for the customs dues of the Indies. Luis del Alcázar later came to hold the office of veinticuatro, which he passed to his own son Melchor when he died in 1551.

By the time Amezaga leveled his charges in 1583, the Alcázar family had a long history as influential members of the city council. Pedro's grandson, the councilman Melchor del Alcázar, was widely recognized as an effective and sensible administrator and member of Seville's city government.[18] The famous native of Seville and painter Francisco Pacheco wrote that Melchor's "capacity and prudence were so great, that His Majesty instructed the asistentes he was sending [to Seville] to be governed by him, and he ordered him to assist them."[19] Melchor also served as a treasurer of Seville's royal mint and as the deputy warden of the royal palaces in the city. Nevertheless, local esteem did not keep Melchor from being among the individuals targeted by Amezaga. The royal prosecutor's writs to the city in 1583 also listed Melchor's brothers, the poet Baltázar del Alcázar and Gonzalo Suárez de León; his cousin, Gaspar; and his second cousins, Francisco and Fernando.

The Alcázares established marriage alliances with other families, who were heavily involved in the Indies trade, had possible converso background, and either held or came to acquire seats on the council, including the interrelated Caballeros, Illescas, and Leónes and the branches produced by these unions. Melchor del Alcázar's brother, the licenciado Gonzalo Suárez de León, married Andrea Ponce, the daughter of Pedro Caballero, who was involved in the shipment of wine to the Americas. Pedro's brother Diego managed business interests for many years in the Caribbean, held important fiscal offices on the island of Hispaniola, served as a factor for the house of trade in Seville, and eventually obtained the position of veinticuatro in Seville, which allegedly cost him a million maravedís. The Caballeros in turn were linked to the Illescas through the marriage of Pedro and Diego's sister, Leonor Caballero, to the merchant Rodrigo de Illescas. Rodrigo's own father had served as a councilman in the 1480s and had succeeded in marrying a woman related to the family of the Marquis of Cádiz.[20] The match between Rodrigo and Leonor produced the influential brothers Pedro, Diego, and Álvaro Caballero de Illescas, all of whom were charged by the royal prosecutor as falsely claiming hidalgo status. At the time of Amezaga's complaints, both Pedro and Diego held seats on the council, and Álvaro would join the council by the early 1590s, when he served as collector of the customs dues.

The Caballero de Illescas family, like the Alcázares, had conversos among their ancestors, and like the Alcázares they also participated in commerce with the Indies. Their maternal uncles, Diego and Alonso Caballero in particular, had amassed fortunes in the trade of commodities and slaves to the Americas during the early decades of the century. Diego Caballero de Illescas even appears to have spent some years in Peru in his youth, representing the business interests of his father's brother Alonso de Illescas. The Alcázar family also had close ties and marriage connections with the León de Garavitas, another converso family engaged in commercial activities.[21] Members of this family included the councilmen García and Juan de León, and their brother, Pedro de León Garavita. Like the Caballero de Illescas brothers, all three were denounced as pecheros by the royal prosecutor.

Señores and Señorios
While conversos and merchants appear to be obvious targets, Amezaga did not limit his denunciations to New Christian families. He accused a wide range of individuals of considerable local reputation and standing. In the writs to the city Amezaga himself provided the honorific title of Don to twelve of the men he claimed were pecheros. Although the appropriation of the title Don became more common in the seventeenth century, in the late 1500s it continued to be used to refer to men whose families held señorios. Four of these men, Don Gonçalo de Esquivel, Don Gonzalo de la Fuente, Don Álvaro Ponce de León, and Don Francisco del Alcázar, came from principal Sevillian families of the fifteenth and sixteenth centuries. Rafael Sánchez Saus included these four families in his study of twenty-five aristocratic lineages in late medieval Seville. Three others, Don Pedro de Céspedes, Don Hernando de Pineda, and Don Alonso de los Ríos, came from well-established families that rose to significant prominence in the course of the sixteenth century.

Diego de Amezaga's actions and writs reveal how royal officials accepted that these men could possess titles of lordship over a community, while simultaneously denying that they had the qualities or status of a noble. In the ideal social hierarchies fashioned by treatise authors in late medieval and early modern Castile, lords and titled aristocrats held a position significantly higher than mere hidalgos. The logic of these hierarchies suggests that lords should have possessed the right to enjoy the privileges held by men and women of hidalgo status. Nevertheless, the royal prosecutor's willingness to deny privileges to titled lords demonstrates the scale and nature of resistance to privilege and the absence of a strict hierarchy.

In particular, the purchase of señorios contributed to the instability of clear hierarchies and to the possibilities for social mobility. Scholars of the French nobility have described comparable social mobility by commoners who acquired or purchased noble (*franc*) fiefs.[22] During the sixteenth century the Habsburg monarchs imitated their Trastamara predecessors and alienated seigneurial jurisdiction over communities from royal and church domain to provide them to loyal supporters. Often described as grants of towns and villages, such royal actions turned their recipients not simply into landlords but into lords of subjects (*señores de vassallos*). After the first Trastamara monarch, Enrique II, usurped the throne from his half-brother, Pedro, in 1369, he began the innovation of providing these lordships as permanent grants rather than as grants for the recipient's lifetime, in order to secure his tenuous hold on the throne.[23] Enrique and his successors also began to favor their most significant and powerful supporters with the honorific titles of duke, count, and marquis to accompany these lordships. Unlike the Trastamara of the late medieval period, who gave grants of jurisdictional lordship and authority to regional aristocrats and court favorites in return for service and loyalty, the Habsburgs provided this lordship for a simple cash payment.[24] Henry Kamen goes as far as to describe the second half of the sixteenth century as an open market for the purchase of lordships.[25]

While material success and even marriage into old elite families secured local standing, and at times even the ability to acquire lordships, it did not necessarily protect these men and women from efforts to deny them legal privileges. This social mobility did, however, have the paradoxical effect of placing agents of the royal government in somewhat opposing roles, both providing lordly titles and simultaneously denying hidalgo status to the same individuals. Among the men charged, the examples of Don Francisco del Alcázar and Don Pedro de Céspedes illustrate how different Crown officials could participate in the process of making someone a lord at one moment only to have other officials deny them noble privileges at a later time. Francisco del Alcázar and Pedro de Céspedes further demonstrate the process of family advancement, from gaining public office to the acquisition of lordship. For both families service to the royal government, possession of municipal council seats, and successful alignment with powerful local families secured their advancement into the local aristocracy.

Francisco del Alcázar, the grandfather of the Francisco del Alcázar denounced by Amezaga, had an impressive career in the city government, holding the offices of jurado, fiel ejecutor, veinticuatro, and even alcalde mayor. Besides his public duties, Francisco distinguished himself in financial and commercial activities, collecting the alcabalas, investing in shipping loans, and sending goods to the Indies. The attainment of lordship began when Francisco bought the jurisdiction and incomes of the town of La Palma and the castle of Alpízar in 1519 from Don Diego Colón, the son of Christopher Columbus, for 11,700,000 maravedís. By 1531 he succeeded in gaining royal recognition of the entailment (*mayorazgo*) of these properties and the right to bequeath this endowment on his oldest son, Pedro.[26] The act of entailment turned his newly acquired jurisdiction into the hereditary lordship of La Palma. Francisco later did the same for the village of Gelo and the estates of Puñano and Collera. In Alcázar's acquisition of lordship, the extent of his dealings with the royal government involved the monarch's legal permission and favor to establish an entailed property.

In other instances, the monarchy itself publicized and sold señorios, especially during the second half of the sixteenth century, when demands on the royal treasury grew to fantastic levels. The extraordinary expenditures involved in fighting the revolt in the Netherlands and defending the Mediterranean coasts from increased attacks by Muslim pirates in the early 1570s led Felipe's government to aggressively market the sale of various communities belonging to the military orders over which the king held jurisdiction. In 1574, Gonzalo de Céspedes, councilman of Seville and participant in the Indies trade, placed a bid for the town of Carrión de los Ajos, previously under the jurisdiction of the military Order of Calatrava. After a complex process of appraising the worth of the town, reviewing the bid, and transferring jurisdiction, Gonzalo officially became lord of the town of Carrión on November 26, 1576. As lord, he took ownership of the order's real property, including a couple of buildings, a few fields, a brick-and-tile kiln, a bakery, and income from one-fifth of the olive oil produced in the town and two-thirds of the tithe. Céspedes's seigneurial rights also included the prerogative to select the town's officials from a list provided by its council, the authority to nominate the local priest, and the legal jurisdiction for the town, which he immediately delegated to the existing municipal council.[27] Becoming a lord gave him privileges in a relationship with a specific community, but it did not provide universal legal privileges based on status, such as exemption from taxation, freedom from judicial torture, or immunity from debtor's prison. Conversely, at no time in the process of the sale did Crown officials raise the question of Céspedes's social status or his right to become a señor, since no rule prohibited his purchase and his acquisition of the lordship effectively conveyed the status of señor.

The Céspedes family originally settled in Seville in the last decade of the fifteenth century. Juan de Céspedes had been raised in the house of the constable of Castile and royal favorite Don Álvaro de Luna and subsequently became a knight in the Order of Santiago. After Luna's fall from power and execution for treason, Juan astutely gave his support to Alonso de Cárdenas in the struggle for the mastership of Santiago and was rewarded with the encomienda of Monestero in Extremadura. From the family's base in Extremadura, two of Juan's sons, Alonso and Pedro, eventually established themselves in Seville. Despite being newcomers to Seville, the Céspedeses quickly entered the upper strata of the city and intermarried with its elite (see fig. 7). As a graduate in civil and canon law from the University of Salamanca, Alonso de Céspedes acquired the position of judge of the audiencia of Seville, and in 1519 the parish of Santa María la Blanca elected him their representative to the city council.[28] He succeeded in marrying into one of the Guzmán clans, first to Doña Ana de Guzmán y Gallegos, the daughter of Gutierre de Gallegos and Doña Beatriz de Guzmán, and after her death to Doña Juana de Cárdenas y Guzmán, the granddaughter of the third Count of Niebla. Before his death in 1537 he had acquired the office of councilman, which he left to his son Juan. Amezaga denounced both Juan and his half sister Doña María de Guzmán, who was also known as María de Quadros due to her inheritance of the mayorazgo of Torres de Quadros from her mother. Alonso's brother Pedro also arrived in Seville in the 1490s. Pedro eventually married the daughter of Gonzalo Díaz Marmolejo, a councilman of the city, and passed this office on to his own son Juan. Alonso's and Pedro's respective heirs continued to hold council positions in Seville and intermarried with the most prominent families in the city, such as the Pineda and Figueroa. Both branches of the family succeeded in establishing entailed estates and eventually gained exemption from the city's tax on meat. They managed the second feat through the connections they held on the city council and through marriage alliances, not through a formal litigation for status.

When Francisco del Alcázar and Gonzalo de Céspedes acquired their seigneurial titles, royal officials involved in the transaction either ignored or proved indifferent to the purchaser's social origins or the implications that possession of lordship held for the purchaser's social status. But this lack of concern regarding

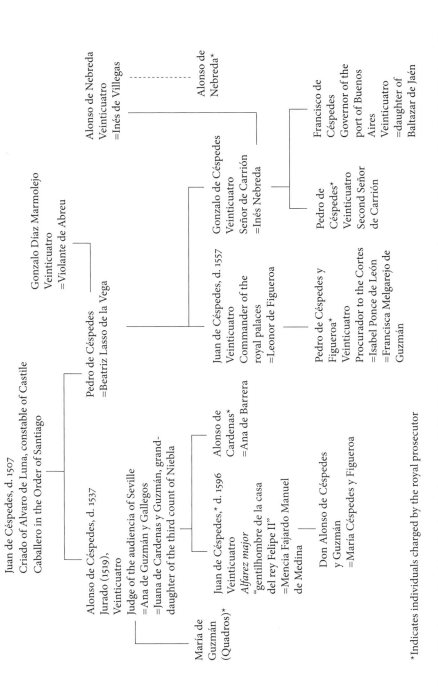

Fig. 7 Members of the Céspedes family charged with falsely claiming hidalgo status and their connections to other elite families in Seville. Direct lines of descent are represented by solid lines; dashed lines represent kinship relations that are indirect or unspecified in the documents. *Note:* Asterisks denote individuals charged as fraudulent hidalgos by the royal prosecutor.

social status, either by royal officials or the purchaser himself, was not always the case. Either at his own initiative or at the demand of royal officials, the merchant Juan Antonio Corzo sought formal royal recognition of hidalgo status before his purchase of the lordship of the towns of Cantillana, Brenes, and Villaverde in 1575. Situated along the Guadalquivir River, upstream from Seville and previously in the possession of the archbishopric of Seville, the towns were significant municipalities, not mere villages or hamlets.[29] Prior to the sale Corzo went through the formalities of presenting evidence to verify his hidalguía.[30] As his name suggests, Corzo descended from a family that originated from the island of Corsica and had settled and become naturalized as citizens of Seville. At the time of the sale the king—or more accurately, a royal clerk—provided Corzo with the merced of a privilege of hidalguía, despite his well-known foreign origin. This privilege provided royal authorization for status the family had already tacitly secured through informal acceptance by Seville's council. The Corzo family had enjoyed the privilege of the blanca de la carne for at least the previous four decades, and the records of the return from 1542 specifically cited that Juan Antonio's father, Antón Corzo, received them "for being an hijodalgo notorio."[31]

The Corzos were far from inconspicuous in Seville, and Diego Ortiz de Zúñiga recorded how Corzo's extraordinary wealth and admirable enterprises had been famous in the city. During Felipe II's visit to Seville in 1570 he had lodged in the home of Juan Antonio Corzo.[32] The family's prominence continued in subsequent generations. After Sir Francis Drake's sack of Cádiz in 1596, Juan Antonio's son Juan Vicentelo Corzo served as a captain of a permanent force created from the city's militia to respond to pirate attacks.[33] Moreover, his daughter Bernardina Vicentelo married Jorge Alberto de Portugal, the third Count of Gelves. The count was a descendant of Christopher Columbus through his paternal grandmother, Isabel Colón, who was herself the granddaughter of the explorer and admiral. Significantly, Carlos I had created this title in 1529 when the Count of Ureña sold the lordship of Gelves to Jorge's grandfather. In the documents providing Juan Antonio and his wife permission to entail their estate for their eldest son and to stipulate the dowry for their daughter's marriage to the count, royal officials similarly ignored any impediments or consequences that a foreigner's or merchant's status would have on such legal actions.[34]

To evade the royal prosecutor's writs demanding that Seville strike Corzo from the tax rolls of the hidalgos and litigate against him, the council ironically placed responsibility for his status on the Crown by reminding the judges of this earlier grant and what His Majesty had declared. Moreover, on the basis of this grant of hidalguía the council's attorney pointed out that the city had recognized his fiscal exemptions and refunded him the sums from the excise tax on meat. He also declared that "for these reasons the city has no obligation to pursue the lawsuit with Juan Antonio Corzo. If the lord licentiate Diego de Amezaga, His Majesty's prosecutor, wants to pursue the case, the investigation and litigation should not be at the cost of the city of Seville."[35]

A Servant of the Crown and a Man of Letters: Gonzalo Argote de Molina
One of the more seemingly unlikely individuals to be charged as fraudulently claiming hidalgo status by the royal prosecutor was the man of letters and historian Gonzalo Argote de Molina. Gonzalo's career and the strategies he followed to enter local elite society and to maintain his position in it further reveal how elite networks facilitated the tangible enjoyment of legal privileges ostensibly based on rigid rules of descent. Modern scholars know Gonzalo primarily on account of his efforts as an editor and publisher of literary and historical works and as author in his own right of a history of the nobility of Andalusia and a treatise on hunting.[36] He also served both his city and the Crown in a range of offices and commissions and actively engaged in the Atlantic commerce and colonization of the sixteenth century.

Although Gonzalo's family did not originate in Seville, he was born in the city in 1548. His father, Francisco de Molina, held the office of jurado, which he passed to Gonzalo in 1568.[37] By the sixteenth century these offices had ceased to be elected and, like the offices of the veinticuatros, were essentially hereditary property, which could be transferred to heirs or sold with royal authorization. Since 1515 city ordinances confirmed by the Crown also required the status of hidalgo to hold either council office. Allegations that the council had failed to oversee these rules had produced complaints and halfhearted royal admonishments, most notably in 1562 and 1581, but no serious censure.[38] Gonzalo's grandfather Gomez Zatico de Argote was not a jurado in Seville, and it seems that Gonzalo's father, Francisco, obtained his office through marriage to Isabel Ortiz Mexia.

The same year the twenty-year-old Gonzalo succeeded his father as a jurado, he took part in the pacification of the Morisco revolt in the Alpujarras. According to later reports, Gonzalo not only served at his own cost but also paid for the expenses of thirty mounted fighters for the conflict.[39] This was not his first or last experience of war or service to the Crown. He had already served as a page to Don Fadrique de Caravajal in the defense of the fortress at Peñon de

Velez in North Africa at the age of thirteen. More significant, he also fought in the naval victory at Lepanto in 1571. His involvement in these conflicts provided Gonzalo with the necessary experience and connections to request the positions of provost and judge of the regional militia of the territory of Seville, for which he obtained royal appointment in 1578.[40] Gonzalo held these offices until 1585, and again after 1589 when he had to apprehend bandits operating in the mountains around Jerez de la Frontera.[41]

Gonzalo's political service and exercise of arms complimented his economic activities in the growing Atlantic trade. By 1582 Gonzalo had entered into various business dealings with the Marquis of Lanzarote, Augustín de Herrera Rojas y Saavedra, who possessed a number of lordships in the Canary Islands. Their business initially involved the lease of a ship belonging to Gonzalo and progressed to his management and sale of cattle from the Canary Islands on behalf of the marquis.[42] In the paternal line, the marquis descended from the Saavedras, an influential and powerful Sevillano family that had a long history in Andalusia, both in the city of Seville and serving on the frontier with Granada.[43] Augustín's particular branch of the Saavedra clan had been involved in colonization in the Canaries for three generations while continuing to hold high political positions on Seville's city council, including the offices of veinticuatro and alcalde mayor.[44] Notably, Seville's city council appointed the marquis's kin, the veinticuatro Gonzalo de Saavedra, as one of its two representatives to the chancery court to contest the prosecutor's charges in 1583.[45]

Gonzalo and Augustín's business dealings eventually led to Gonzalo's betrothal to the marquis's illegitimate daughter, Constanza, who—at the time—stood to be the heiress of his title and property. Although legitimately married, Augustín's only offspring were two daughters he had with his mistress, the wife of Genoese merchant Teodoro de Espelta. Gonzalo celebrated his wedding to Constanza on May 3, 1586, in the Canary Islands. Three months after the wedding the captain general of the Ottoman fleet in Algeria attacked the island of Lanzarote with the intention of capturing Don Augustín, who had a history of raiding the Mediterranean and Atlantic coasts of Morocco.[46] In the initial foray on July 30, the Muslim forces captured a number of prisoners, including the marquis's wife and daughter, but Gonzalo succeeded in holding the main town's fortress against the attackers. The fighting quickly ended in a stalemate, and Gonzalo arranged the ransom of twenty-two captives for the sum of 10,000 ducados in coin, jewels, and goods. The surviving treaty identified Gonzalo as Count of Lanzarote, provost of the regional militia of Andalusia, and veinticuatro of the city of Seville. While Gonzalo appears to have obtained his father-in-law's office of veinticuatro as part of the dowry, the treaty's designation of him as Count of Lanzarote was premature.

While Gonzalo continued to possess the office of veinticuatro until his death, he never inherited the lordship of Lanzarote. Constanza died a few years later without producing any children, and Don Agustín had a legitimate son from a second marriage. Even before Constanza's death, relations had soured between Gonzalo and his father-in-law, with lawsuits over the property owed to the new couple. Her death, lack of an heir, and bitter financial disputes definitively ended Gonzalo's claims to inherit the marquis's title and estate. Despite these disputes, Gonzalo continued to engage in enterprises in the Canaries and appears to have maintained properties there. As late as 1595, he took part in the islands' defense against English raids led by Sir Francis Drake and died there in 1596.

Gonzalo's other business enterprises further reveal his integration into Seville's networks of elite families. In 1585 he concluded a lawsuit with a former commercial partner, Juan Antonio Corzo.[47] In the course of Gonzalo's dispute with Corzo, he had placed a number of valuable paintings as surety in the hands of the veinticuatro Melchor del Alcázar, who served as mediator for their dispute. As we have seen, both the Corzo and the Alcázar families possessed lordships around Seville and exercised considerable influence on the city council and with other prominent men in the city. As the provost of the regional militia, Gonzalo was well acquainted with one of Melchor's relatives, Don Fernando del Alcázar. Fernando was a judge for the militia and was another of Seville's citizens charged as fraudulently enjoying hidalgo status.

Gonzalo knew Melchor del Alcázar not only through the council but also through Seville's cultural associations and circles. Gonzalo began to develop a reputation as a man of letters in 1575 with his edition of Juan Manuel's fourteenth-century collection of exemplary tales. In 1582 he published González Clavijos's history of the Central Asian ruler Tamerlane and his own *Libro de Montería*. As a noted scholar and writer, Gonzalo actively attended the informal academy of Juan de Mal Lara, which included an extensive group of Seville's humanists, writers, artists, and scholars. Notable among the attendees were the Latinist Francisco Pacheco, uncle of the famous artist; the poet Baltázar del Alcázar; Baltázar's brother, the councilman Melchor del Alcázar; and the artist Pablo de Céspedes. Gonzalo's treatises and histories also brought him to the attention of the Crown. Pacheco later wrote that Felipe II honored Gonzalo for his literary accomplishments with the title of royal chronicler and criado. Felipe's favor most likely helped Gonzalo obtain not only the royal license for the publication of the *Nobleza de Andaluzia* but also the royal grant of access to all municipal archives that allowed for the research of the work.

Gonzalo's completed volumes of the *Nobleza de Andaluzia* provide a history of the kingdom of Jáen from ancient times but focus primarily on the historical origins and genealogies of the region's noble families from the thirteenth to the fifteenth century. The foreword of the work also served as a vehicle for asserting the author's own noble lineage. Although Gonzalo Argote de Molina claimed noble descent, the evidence to support his claims comes from either his own writings or from the painter Francisco Pacheco's *Libro de descripción de verdaderos retratos de ilustres y memorables varones* (True portraits of illustrious and remarkable men). Pacheco's unique work mixed brief biographical sketches of notable intellectual, artistic, and political figures of Seville with their portraits. His biographical sketch of Gonzalo's notable deeds mostly repeated information from the foreword to *Nobleza de Andaluzia* and the epitaph that Gonzalo wrote for himself shortly before his death in 1596. In the epitaph Gonzalo claimed descent from Hernán Martínez de Argote, the first Lord of Lucena and Espejo, both towns on the old frontier between the city of Córdoba and the Muslim kingdom of Granada. Pacheco further identified Hernán Martínez as one of the thirteenth-century conquerors of Córdoba, who even received his coat of arms from the sainted king Fernando III. Despite these grand claims, Gonzalo—in his history of the nobility of Andalusia—did not trace Hernán Martínez's three-hundred-year old lineage to the sixteenth century. Unlike the attention he provided for other families, he left his own descent undocumented. This lack of information is in stark contrast to the full description and drawings he provided of the coats of arms for the Argote, Molina, and Zatico, all patronymics used either by Gonzalo, his father, or his grandfather. Pacheco described Gonzalo as coming from a family of "much nobility and wealth" and stated that this nobility was thoroughly proven in a lawsuit adjudicated in 1580 by the royal council.[48] No records of this litigation survive. The fact that the decision came from the royal court—an unusual and extraordinary jurisdiction for such a matter—rather than from the chancery court's tribunal of hijosdalgo suggests favors on Gonzalo's behalf. Significantly, the royal council's ruling came after two years of opposition to Gonzalo's royal appointment to the office of provost of the militia from members of the hermandad's own council.

Like many members of Seville's elite in the early modern period, Gonzalo sought to advance his social and political position. These efforts included marriage into established lineages, service to the Crown, acquisition of local and regional political offices, participation in potentially lucrative business ventures, and even scholarly pursuits. Through these efforts Gonzalo successfully integrated himself into the local networks of power and influence in the city of Seville. In Gonzalo's case his family, particularly his father, had begun the process of assimilation and integration that he successfully continued. Francisco obtained the lower office of jurado through royal service and marriage and left his son with considerable wealth to continue in similar occupations. While Gonzalo ultimately failed to obtain a seigneurial title, he was sufficiently embedded in the city's network of elite families to enjoy both the legal privileges afforded hidalgos and the city council's protection when his status came to be challenged.

THE NATURE OF COMMUNITY AND COUNCIL SOLIDARITY

Whether or not Gonzalo's noble lineage was fabricated or genuine, the status of some of the other men denounced by the royal prosecutor was certainly questionable.[49] Among the seventy-six individuals charged by the prosecutor were members of families of Jewish descent, such as the Alcázar, Caballero, and León, as well as merchants, financiers, and foreigners from other parts of Castile and from outside Spain, such as Juan Antonio Corzo. Some of these men with questionable lineages and others with seemingly more legitimate claims, such as Gonzalo, held seigneurial titles, had intermarried with the ruling elite families in the city, held positions on the city council, or served as royal officials. Regardless of their descent, the council responded with blanket support for all those accused of fraudulently posing as hidalgos. This was perhaps unsurprising, since four of the veinticuatros attending the meetings that received the prosecutor's writs were among the indicted or soon to be indicted. Solidarity among the members of the council continued through the subsequent three years of litigation that led the chancery court to rule in favor of Seville's concejo in its dispute with the royal prosecutor.

In the face of a royal challenge to the ability and authority of Seville's ruling families to decide on the privileges of their own community and membership in their elite, these families closed ranks and vigorously denied the charges and attempted to stymie the efforts of royal officials. While the city categorically denied the royal prosecutor's charges on multiple occasions, it responded in a differentiated manner to the individuals charged. City officials repeated the claim that none of those charged were pecheros, but the council did not support all these men and women in the same way.

Despite the converso backgrounds and business enterprises of some of those men, their longtime connections with the city council ensured their continued protection. The city actively shielded men such as Alonso de Céspedes and Juan Antonio Corzo, who had important ties and business dealings with prominent families despite the fact they did not have deep roots in the city. Neither these men nor their family members lost the privileges they held in Seville. There is no evidence that the royal officials at the chancery court succeeded in forcing Seville's city council to deprive its councilmen of their exemptions or to begin litigation against them on an individual basis. On July 3, 1584, the city's treasurer, Pedro López Gavilan, recorded paying Alonso de Céspedes's brother, Juan, also denounced by Amezaga, the refund for the previous seven years ending December 1583. López's account books show that the city continued to pay refunds to a number of Seville's citizens denounced by Amezaga and the family members of these citizens.[50] In addition to Juan de Céspedes, the city paid the refund to Bartolomé de Mesa, the widow of Juan de Esquivel, and members of the Almansa, Baena, León, Pineda, Ponce de León, and Ramirez de Cartagena families. The surviving documents of the refund for the year 1583 are incomplete and consequently make it difficult to determine if all the individuals accused received the refund.[51] Moreover, many of the recipients of the refund did not collect every year and often waited for their return to accumulate.

Since the city did not try to tax these men or seize their property, only a handful of them began formal litigation to gain recognition of their status, and these few appear to have entered into litigation because of complaints made against them by other municipalities and not by the city of Seville. The citizen Gonzalo de la Fuente never faced the city of Seville in litigation but had a dispute concerning his hidalgo status with the town of Ayamonte in 1590.[52] Likewise, the Sevillano Alonso Pinto de León went through a five-year lawsuit with the town of Manzanilla between 1584 and 1589 over his hidalguía.[53] Although Seville's council refused to act against certain connected members of its community, the local connections of these individuals did not secure them from challenges to their privileges outside of Seville.

Despite the city's obvious resistance to the chancery court's efforts to impose the status of pechero on the men charged by Amezaga, the clerks of the chancery court continued to maintain a fictive partnership with the city in the formulaic descriptions of these lawsuits. When Crown officials referred to those cases involving citizens of Seville who had been forced to litigate, they described the lawsuits as between the individual on the one side and the royal prosecutor and council of Seville on the other. The formulaic nature of this feigned alliance is evident in the addresses of royal letters to the city and in court orders that the city pay for the expenses of investigating the individuals.

Such a case involved the denounced councilmen and brothers Hernando and Melchor de Almansa. The prosecutors' continued efforts to deprive the Almansas of their hidalgo status despite the council's protests forced the Almansas to continue their litigation. Although the chancery clerks listed the city of Seville as litigating against the two brothers, a review of the documents reveals that the role of the city was nominal at best and the result of repeated efforts by the court to coerce its participation. Writing to the city about the lawsuit, the court clerk noted that "as the city knew or should know" there was a pending case between these two men and the city.[54] Moreover, the letter ordered the city to pay the expenses incurred by the court functionary Juan de Barahona, whom the court had sent to the town of Almansa to collect information and depositions. The city had refused to pay for the thirty-two days, at 300 maravedís a day, that Barahona had spent on this task. Expecting resistance, the court issued Barahona a letter providing him the power to seize city income or property and to sell or auction the property to cover his salary and expenses.

Despite Amezaga's repeated attempts to force the city to apply the court rulings, the council remained obstinate in its resistance. In early 1586 Amezaga complained to the judges in Granada that the city was acting criminally and that it had replied impertinently, saying it wouldn't implement the order. Amezaga therefore ended his report with the request that the court add to the writ an additional statement that monetary penalties should be imposed against the officials present in the city council if they again failed to comply with the court's orders. On May 23, 1586, Seville's council received another writ on the matter and agreed to obey it. Nevertheless, they continued to insist that these men held the status of hidalgo. They responded that in regard to the first part of the writ those mentioned were considered to be hidalgos; for this reason the refund of the blanca was returned to them, and with this action they executed the legal precept of the law of Enrique IV. Despite the council's compliance, it asked for a second letter from the court iterating these demands. The council informed the court that for the meantime it had ordered the city's treasurers to not refund the tax until the cases concerning these individuals' hidalguías should be justly determined or His Majesty should order otherwise. Additionally, they demanded that the costs that the city had expended in the course of this litigation should be imposed on the prosecutor.

The city's resistance to the demands of royal officials took multiple forms. The city continued to stall the execution of repeated royal writs against Corzo and the Céspedes family by requesting additional orders. The court ultimately sent a second, a third, and finally a fourth letter on the matter. In the face of these demands, and defiantly ignoring royal threats to impose monetary penalties against the councilmen present at the time of notification, the city refused to budge.

Not only did the council refuse to execute the writs sent by the chancery, but it also denied any responsibility in the process of investigating the individuals charged with being false hidalgos. When an individual initiated a lawsuit of hidalguía with a municipal council, the burden of providing proof of status normally rested on the claimant.[55] In this case royal officers intervened in the city's affairs, and the council replied by affirming the status of the individuals whom Amezaga denounced. The city council's support for these individuals and the fact that the royal prosecutor had begun the suits reversed normal procedures for investigating and paying for the investigation of people who claimed to be hidalgos. The royal officials who ordered the investigation consequently tried to force the city to pay the investigators. In the case of the Céspedeses, the city responded that under the circumstances neither those charged nor the city itself were obliged to pay the costs. As a means to avoid responsibility for the investigation, the city's attorney questioned whether the law Amezaga had inserted in the writ applied to the Céspedeses and claimed that his denunciation was insufficient to force an investigation. He added, "If some other party besides the prosecutor denounced the Céspedeses, then, in accord with the laws of these kingdoms, the pursuit of the case should be accessed to them and not to the city of Seville."[56] In any event, the city claimed that it was not obliged to pay these costs. In a letter to the court, Seville's council specifically addressed the matter to the president and the chief justices and asserted that the chancery should not try to compel the city on the matter.

A Rupture in Community Solidarity: The Espinosas

In the city of Seville's dispute with the royal prosecutor, the members of the city council maintained solidarity and supported their colleagues, whom the Crown charged as falsely claiming the status of hidalgo, regardless of their colleagues' ancestry. The officials of the city chose to defend their fellow councilmen despite factional animosities and personal disputes because they wished to maintain local control over claims to status and minimize the role of the royal government in this matter. Nevertheless, conflicts occasionally did arise between members of the council and between these councilmen and the clients and relatives of other councilmen, which ruptured local solidarity. At these moments the web of local networks unraveled as disputants appealed to royal institutions to pursue their individual advantage.

Unlike most conflicts over the status of hidalgo, Alonso de Espinosa's dispute began with his arrest in 1578. An unfortunate turn of events with a former business associate, Enrique de Guzmán, the second Count of Olivares, forced Alonso to have to litigate to gain recognition of the status of hidalgo. Although the exact nature of the financial arrangements between the two men is uncertain, the count claimed that Espinosa owed him the staggering sum of 36,000,000 maravedís.[57] At the count's promptings authorities in the city of Valladolid, where Espinosa had traveled for business, arrested the citizen of Seville when he proved unable or unwilling to settle the debt. Alonso insisted that his arrest was illegal because he was an hidalgo and thereby possessed immunity from imprisonment for debt. Consequently, he filed a lawsuit charging violation of his status. Within weeks the chancery court in Valladolid provisionally recognized his status and ordered his release. Alonso's brother and financial partner, Juan Bautista, likewise suffered a brief imprisonment in Seville. The count promptly challenged the Espinosas' claim to the status of hidalgo, and the judges of the court ordered the two sides to give their respective evidence for and against Alonso de Espinosa's nobility. Despite the fact that Espinosa's principal dispute was with the count, a lawsuit over hidalguía necessarily required the participation of the litigant's municipality. Consequently, the venue for the dispute moved to the chancery court in Granada, where Alonso was listed as contesting his status with the city of Seville and a number of towns in Seville's jurisdiction. As in all suits of hidalguía the royal prosecutor joined the party opposing recognition of status.

The documents concerning the dispute preserved by the city of Seville fail to record the source of the debt, but it appears to have been connected with royal incomes, a situation which placed Espinosa in an even more precarious situation. The counts of Olivares began as a cadet branch of the house of Medina Sidonia. Carlos I provided the title to Pedro de Guzmán in 1535 in reward for various services and fidelity, including the suppression of comunero rebels in Seville and participation in Habsburg military ventures in Italy, Germany, and North Africa. At the time of Espinosa's arrest, Enrique de Guzmán, the second count, was a member of the royal council, held the office of chief controller of accounts (*contador mayor de cuentas*) for Castile, and had recently served as ambassador to Rome.[58] In the count's capacity as the lord of the villages of Lora, Alcolea, Cantillana, Brenes, and Villaverde, all in Seville's Aljarafe and Ribera districts, he paid the alcabalas owed by these municipalities. In a document included in the case record, Enrique de Guzmán arranged to pay these dues from annuities generated by property of his entailed estate, and it appears that these funds were on deposit with the Espinosa bank or under the Espinosas' management.[59]

Whatever the precise nature of the count's relationship with the Espinosas, the resulting dispute between the two sides over the breakdown of their financial arrangement or the failure to make good on a major loan evolved into a contest over privilege that drew in a number of participants beyond the principal disputants. These additional participants included members of the city council, other local aristocrats, and municipal officials of Seville's subject towns. The evidence provided by the count's witnesses reveals that the ability to enjoy the privileges of hidalgo status in practice fluctuated according to place, local connections, and the intervention of powerful patrons.

Until the time of his arrest in 1578 Alonso had largely avoided formal litigation in court but had managed to gain recognition as an hidalgo in a number of Castilian towns, including some in the territory of the city of Seville. But this information did not become evident until the presentation of opposing evidence. The Count of Olivares sent his steward to arrange evidence against the Espinosas in the form of witnesses and copies of tax lists from a number of different municipalities, including Salteras, Castrilleja de la Cuesta, Gerena, Pueblo de Cazalla, and Alcalá de Guadaira. Although the count's agent succeeded in obtaining evidence and testimony that the Espinosas paid their taxes in some of these towns, most notably Cazalla and Seville itself, the steward failed to produce evidence for the other towns despite considerable efforts.[60] In these other towns Alonso had achieved partial recognition of status through local acquiescence rather than through a formal lawsuit. He pursued his goals of social advancement and the enjoyment of legal privileges through informal avenues that included the acquisition of landed property, marriage with influential local families, and the support of powerful patrons and business partners, for whom he provided a range of economic and financial services.

The court documents listed Alonso as a citizen of Seville, where he was a prominent resident of the city. Born in Medina de Rioseco in 1537, he came to Seville in the early 1560s to work for the family bank and help manage the diverse business ventures established in the city by his father, Pedro de Espinosa, and his uncle Alonso de Espinosa the elder. Pedro and Alonso had long and ultimately successful careers as bankers and merchants, amassing significant fortunes. At the time of Alonso the elder's death in 1560, his property was valued at a staggering 400,000 ducados (150,000,000 maravedís). Although less successful than his brother and partner, Pedro's worth at his death in 1558 was roughly 200,000 ducados (75,000,000 maravedís).[61] Alonso the elder died unmarried, and his will left the majority of his property to his nephews, the sons of his brother Pedro. Consequently, in 1560 Alonso de Espinosa the younger became the head of the family and the principal manager of the family bank and businesses.

From the surviving documents it appears that Alonso never claimed to be an hidalgo in the city of Seville prior to his arrest, but he and his siblings made this claim in some of Seville's subject towns and in other municipalities in Andalusia.[62] To advance the prosperity and reputation of the family, Alonso de Espinosa followed traditional strategies of diversifying his investments and establishing advantageous marriage alliances. These strategies were also all important avenues for advancing and establishing claims to hidalguía. In pursuit of these ends Alonso benefited from the efforts of his father and uncle. Alonso the elder had acquired significant assets in the form of juros and large farms in the territory of towns surrounding Seville, including Salteras, Alcalá de Guadaira, and Pilas. In Pilas he owned extensive olive orchards and mills for processing the oil. His father, Pedro, had acquired the monopoly on the production of soap in the archbishopric of Seville and consequently oversaw the construction of numerous factories.

In 1571, after a decade of running the family businesses, Alonso married the Sevillana Inés de Guzmán, daughter of Don Luis de Guzmán, who was the younger brother of Francisco de Guzmán, Lord of the Algava. Either through this marriage alliance or through his financial and commercial dealings, Alonso also became familiar with the major branches of the Guzmán family and the heads of these families, including the Duke of Medina Sidonia, Alonso Pérez de Guzmán; and the Count of Olivares, Don Enrique de Guzmán.[63] He arranged for his younger sister, Gracia, to marry into the prominent Ortiz de Zúñiga family. Another sister, Leonor de Espinosa, wed a distant cousin, Francisco de

Espinosa, who had acquired the lordships of Robladillo and Cuestahermosa. Of greater consequence for his immediate descendants, Alonso's eldest daughter, Mariana de Guzmán, entered the ranks of the titled aristocrats when she married Don Pedro Pacheco y Chacón, first Marquis of Castrofuerte.[64]

To maximize the value and profitability of family properties, Alonso de Espinosa and his siblings sought to acquire recognition of their possession of the status of hidalgo. The success and failures the Espinosas had in securing recognition of hidalgo status became evident in the testimony of witnesses gathered by the Count of Olivares. In 1578, the count's steward, Juan Márquez, assembled more than thirty witnesses from three distinct municipalities to provide evidence concerning the status of the Espinosa family. From the city of Seville the councilmen Pedro Caballero de Illescas and Luis Sánchez de Albo, former councilman Alonso de Medina, and parish representative Alonso de Soria provided testimony against Espinosa's claim. As veinticuatros or jurados, all four were themselves recognized as hidalgos. Despite serving as an authoritative witness in the case against the Espinosas' claim to hidalguía, Caballero de Illescas a few years later found himself denounced as a pechero by the royal prosecutor Diego de Amezaga. Some of these witnesses mentioned the Espinosas' business dealings and the bank they had in the city, but they did not suggest that such activities were incompatible with the status of hidalgo. Instead, they simply claimed that the Espinosas come "from the race and lineage [*casta e linaje*] of pecheros." A number of the witnesses also reported that the Espinosas had never received the refund on the blanca. They did not mention, however, that the Espinosas had contested the city's refusal to provide the refund for almost two decades. Alonso Espinosa and his brothers had begun a suit in 1561, and members of the family had pressed the case in subsequent years, providing a range of evidence including depositions from an earlier lawsuit adjudicated at the chancery court of Valladolid. In the previous suit the depositions of witnesses from Medina de Rioseco testified that the related Cabrera family had held hidalgo status and enjoyed tax exemptions.[65]

Although the Espinosas had gained recognition of their status in other municipalities in the Crown of Castile, they continued to face resistance from the city of Seville and some of its subject towns. The chief clerk from the town of Utrera, thirty kilometers southeast of Seville, testified that certain Espinosas had paid taxes on property they held in Utrera since at least 1574 for the allotment of dues for the servicio. For the year 1577 the sum had amounted to 30,000 maravedís. Nevertheless, the clerk admitted, perhaps under pressure, that he didn't know for sure if the persons who paid these amounts were in fact the same Espinosas. As evidence from later lawsuits reveal, not only were they the same Espinosas, but they continued their efforts to gain recognition in Utrera until at least 1609.[66]

The ability to enjoy the privileges of hidalguía depended in part on the intervention of powerful patrons. Martín de Morón, citizen of the town of Cazalla and receiver of the town's royal subsidies, described the Espinosas' efforts to avoid paying taxes on their property in Cazalla, a town under the jurisdiction of the city of Seville and in the hills to its north. The council of Cazalla had apportioned part of the taxes it paid to the Crown on the Espinosas for a mill the family owned on the river next to the community. Municipal officials assessed the annual amount the Espinosas owed on the incomes of the mill at 2,400 maravedís. Some years earlier the Espinosas and their factors at the mill had argued that they did not owe this tax because the Espinosas were hidalgos. The town officials had responded by forcibly collecting the tax from the Espinosas' agents. Morón stated that after that one incident these men paid each year without any further objections.

The deposition of Juan Díaz Roldán, municipal council clerk for Cazalla, revealed that the Espinosas' efforts did not end after the first altercation with the town officials. Díaz Roldán testified that in 1572 or 1573 he had heard from Juan de Soto, the commander of the town's fortifications, that the Duke of Medina Sidonia had tried to exert his influence on behalf of Espinosa. The duke was head of the principal branch of the Guzmán family and a relative of the Count of Olivares. According to Díaz Roldán, the duke had told Soto that it would please him greatly if the Espinosas were removed from the register of pecheros subject to paying the subsidy, because they were hijosdalgo. He further requested that the town not try to apportion this tax to the Espinosas in the future. The same day the duke spoke with the commander, he appeared at the meeting of Cazalla's council, made the same request, and submitted various testimonies that the Espinosas did not pay taxes in other localities. He claimed that the councils of these other towns did not attempt to tax the Espinosas because of their status as hidalgos. Despite these efforts, the town council refused to remove the Espinosa family from the list of taxpayers. Two years after the duke's solicitation, Alonso's brother Juan Bautista came to the town and insisted that the council end their taxation of the Espinosas' property. He brought with him letters from the Duke of Medina Sidonia and other important persons testifying to the justice of the family's claims. During his visit he provided the town councilman Alonso Sánchez Candeleda with a loan of 300 ducados and lavishly entertained another councilman named Diego de León. According to the witnesses, Juan Bautista did all of this with the sole end of enlisting their support to remove the Espinosas from the tax lists. Nevertheless, none of the council members wished to do so, and they continued to collect the dues on the mill from the Espinosas.

The machinations of the Duke of Medina Sidonia on behalf of the Espinosas, and the apparent success that the family had in gaining exemption from taxes in some municipalities, although not Cazalla or Seville, reveal the slow and piecemeal nature of the process toward the public acceptance of hidalgo status and enjoyment of accompanying privileges. The failure of the Espinosas' Seville-based bank in 1578 brought a sharp though not final interruption to this process. Considering the timing of the count's efforts to collect the 36,000,000 maravedís, it seems certain that he had deposited either private or public funds with the Espinosa bank. Despite the count's active and unusual role in what formally constituted a lawsuit between Espinosa and his municipal council, the case dragged on for decades. The case produced voluminous paperwork from both sides in copies of padrones and depositions of witnesses testifying both to the Espinosas' reputation as pecheros and to their and their other family members' possession of hidalguía. The suit came to a final conclusion in 1615, after the deaths of the original litigants, when Juan Bautista's natural son Alonso de Espinosa Pimienta received a ruling from the chancery judges declaring the family to be hijosdalgo.[67]

Even if the court had ruled against the Espinosas, this sentence would not have definitively ended the family's chances of enjoying legal privileges based on hidalgo status, because what proved most effective in maintaining and acquiring hidalgo status were informal lines of influence and power. In 1626, Alonso's eldest son, Francisco Andrés de Espinosa y Guzmán, concluded an agreement with the Count-Duke of Olivares, bringing to an end the litigation over the debt. This same son succeeded in becoming a knight of the military Order of Santiago, which in the seventeenth century strictly required noble or hidalgo descent.

The lawsuit with the count brought to light the efforts of the Espinosas and their patrons to attain the status of hidalgo and the resistance these efforts provoked. Initially, the family sought to establish their status by gaining local acceptance through informal channels and coaxing and cajoling municipal officials. Only to escape imprisonment did Alonso claim that municipal and royal authorities had violated his privileges as an hidalgo. The subsequent litigation revealed the informal networks that proved essential for the enjoyment of privilege.

In contrast to the rupture of local solidarity evident in the case of the Espinosas, the efforts of the royal prosecutors to denounce dozens of prominent citizens as frauds elicited a united front from Seville's concejo. The city council resisted the demands of the prosecutor and chancery judges because they attacked and undermined the very social networks that structured political and economic relationships in the city. To deprive the individuals charged by the royal prosecutor of their privileges would have been tantamount to declaring as illegitimate the privileges of the other members of Seville's ruling elite. Social networks including marriage alliances, business partnerships, and political patronage both between members of the city council and between council officials and royal officials at court brought together the interests of families from diverse backgrounds and contributed to their mutual identification and support and in some cases their biological union. In sixteenth-century Seville contingent factors related to powerful social networks shaped both the ability to appeal to rules about privilege and status and the success in implementing judicial rulings on these appeals. These factors included solidarity and conflict within municipal councils, fluctuations in royal policy, and the individual interests of Crown officials and had little to do with the content of the law or how applicable the law might be to the situation or individual.

6

JUSTICE AND MALFEASANCE AT THE TRIBUNAL
OF THE HIDALGOS

In disputes over hidalgo status and the provision of accompanying privileges, the Castilian judiciary played a central role as the representatives of royal justice. In the name of the king the judges at Castile's two chancery courts were responsible for mediating disputes between municipal councils and their own citizens. While the chancery court was a royal institution staffed with personnel appointed by the royal council, it operated as a semi-independent judicial body.[1] This autonomy was also true in the courts' regulation of status. Furthermore, the Crown's delegation of its authority to the judiciary allowed municipalities to resist unwelcome court rulings that they viewed as unjust through the traditional appeal "we obey, but we do not comply" (*obedezcemos pero no cumplimos*) without directly challenging the king or the royal council.[2] The officers of the court exercised different functions, particularly the alcaldes and fiscales, and consequently had different concerns and duties. Unlike the judges, the prosecutors were explicitly appointed as defenders of royal interests and royal patrimony. They and their subalterns could also act as promoters of royal policy. But in the event that their actions or initiatives generated resistance and opposition, the chancery court's autonomy provided insulation from direct complaints against the king and a forum to resolve these complaints.

When the chancery judges ruled in favor of the city of Seville and against the royal prosecutors Diego de Amezaga and Dr. Heredia in 1585, they upheld the tacit tradition of municipal and royal consensus and cooperation in the determination of hidalguía, a consensus that the prosecutors had seemingly violated with their unilateral efforts. Responding to obstinate council resistance to the prosecutors' denunciations, the chancery judges reversed their earlier rulings, ordering the city to deny en masse prominent citizens of Seville—including members of the city council—their status as hidalgos, their enjoyment of the blanca, and potentially their possession of council office. As it turned out, the court's ruling did not stop the royal prosecutors from continuing to pursue individual cases against some of the men they had denounced, though they proved largely, if not completely, unsuccessful in their efforts. In the final sentence in favor of Seville, as in most chancery court rulings, the judges did not explain their decision. Nevertheless, a review of the arguments made by the city's attorney and the royal prosecutors sheds light on why the prosecutors' efforts to implement what they claimed to be royal policy and the proper norms of society ultimately failed. The factors that affected the outcome of the case arose from the particular political relationship between the Crown and Seville's influential city government. Moreover, the case displays the nature and limits of royal government in the late sixteenth century. At the chancery court the Crown provided a forum for disputes, in which it rendered verdicts on the legitimate status of claimants. But the royal government could not easily prevent a major municipality from recognizing its own citizens as hidalgos and providing them with accompanying privileges. The city council's defense of its own control over local matters, including the determination of status, and the subsequent support the council gave to its citizens' claims to being hidalgos ultimately served to deflect the application of general laws concerning status.

Just as the history and nature of the relationship between city and Crown mediated the application of royal policy and the provision of justice, the private interests of royal officials and the possibilities open to these officials to exploit and even subvert the legal system for their own benefit served to undermine the implementation of royal law. The second part of the chapter details the range and possibilities for malfeasance in the judicial system of sixteenth-century Castile and how such malfeasance influenced the initiation of lawsuits of hidalguía, their outcome, and the provision of justice in disputes over status.

MUNICIPAL COUNCIL AND CROWN RELATIONS: "OBEDEZCEMOS PERO NO CUMPLIMOS"

In matters involving the determination of hidalguía and implementation of laws governing privilege, royal authorities generally delegated oversight and policing of status in the first instance to local municipal councils. Although the most conventional contests over the status of hidalgo occurred between municipal councils and their own citizens, as earlier chapters related, royal judicial officials became involved in these disputes when they were appealed to the chancery courts. Beginning as early as 1582, royal prosecutors, contrary to past practice, actively initiated lawsuits against citizens of Seville they claimed to be falsely enjoying legal privileges. The efforts of royal prosecutors and chancery judges to apply royal law on status led to a significant dispute between the Crown and local authorities over who had the de facto power to recognize and bestow privilege. These disputes highlight the constraints on the royal government's ability to impose its will in the face of concerted resistance from city and town councils. When municipalities chose to resist the efforts of royal officials to impose inconvenient laws and execute royal orders that infringed on local prerogatives, they could force these officials to acquiesce to their control of municipal life. In 1584, the city council of Seville proved victorious in the legal contest initiated by the royal prosecutors Amezaga and Heredia, by effectively appealing to opposing legal principles and norms concerning the city's autonomy and rights in the oversight of local hidalgo status and privileges.

The chancery judges ruled in the city's favor, but as was often customary in the sixteenth century, they provided no rationale for their decision.[3] Multiple legal regimes existed and disputants appealed to the laws and principles of these regimes according to the nature of the suit to claim the juridical superiority of their cause. In cases appealed to the chancery court, the ability of litigants to draw from multiple sources of law and precedent also provided leeway for the judges interpreting the laws and deciding the cases. In this system chancery judges, who were beholden to the Crown for their offices and future advancement, held a natural bias to rule in favor of immediate Crown interests and the protection of royal patrimony.

Nevertheless, in cases involving the interests of the Crown, royal judges did not invariably rule in the monarch's favor. Through the sixteenth century Habsburg kings maintained and encouraged an impartial, if not completely independent, judiciary. Litigants by the thousands, especially city and town councils, brought their disputes to the royal appellate courts in search of justice. Often their cases involved complaints against Crown officials and royal policy and, like the council of Seville in the case initiated by the prosecutor Amezaga, succeeded in gaining a favorable ruling. To make a ruling, judges in sixteenth-century Castile followed the conventions held among legal experts about how to assess, apply, and interpret existing rules. These conventions in turn resulted from the education of the judges, shared values about justice, and an understanding of authority and the use of power. The Habsburg monarchs required that judges at the appellate courts be *letrados*, university graduates with five or six years studying canon and civil law and either a degree of licentiate (*licenciado*) or doctor.[4] Despite these educational requirements and accepted conventions concerning the law, judges could still disagree on the validity or superiority of contrary norms that applied to the same case. This was especially true in a legal system constituted from multiple legal regimes, without a clear designated hierarchy among the existing norms. Consequently, this system gave considerable freedom to judges to apply their own interpretation of the law, based on the particular moral and political conceptions they embraced or the contingencies they faced.

In contrast to rulings of sixteenth-century judges, which often lacked any written opinion, the arguments of litigants and their lawyers present the range of norms that judges considered in the process of formulating their decisions. The litigants operated within certain parameters dictated by the language available in the existing laws and customs of the kingdom. The ability of litigants to accuse the opposing side of failure to comply with the law did not require a consistent presentation of the legal rules that had been violated; it required only that sufficient arguments had been given to support one ruling over another. In the dispute initiated by the royal prosecutor, both sides gave multiple arguments for their respective causes and appealed to several laws and norms simultaneously. Referencing different norms and concerns, they crafted arguments that sometimes presented facts in an apparently inconsistent fashion. Nevertheless, the arguments presented by the attorneys reveal the nature of the dispute and the language the disputants needed to employ to resolve it.

The prime issue in this conflict involved a clash between municipal prerogatives and the prosecutor's effort to apply royal law. Although this was the main point of conflict, at least two levels of dispute existed. To successfully argue the position of their clients, the attorneys had to use existing legal rhetoric to present the actions of the city government, of royal officials, and of individual citizens and the consequences of their actions. This rhetoric included statements about how these actions impinged on the interests of the royal patrimony, the good of the kingdom and commonwealth, and the well-being of the local community and how these actions agreed with or violated authoritative rules and norms.[5]

The royal prosecutors justified their actions to the chancery judges by claiming that the maintenance of government incomes and the welfare of the city's disadvantaged citizens required the application of and adherence to the laws previously enacted in the Cortes of Castile. Their claim assumed that these laws were just and universally applicable in the Crown of Castile. After the city's initial denial of the charges and attempt to dismiss the writs, the prosecutors Amezaga and Heredia began their attack on the city's opposition by appealing to technicalities. Then they quickly shifted to central issues of conflict and highlighted the city's history of resistance to royal orders. The prosecutors claimed that in the past the city publicly had announced that it would obey and implement similar royal writs and orders against other citizens of Seville but had failed to do so.[6] They cited the laws enacted by Enrique IV and requested that the judges render a finding supporting their application in this instance. They ended their petition to the oidores with the charge that the city council engaged in practices that harmed both the royal patrimony and welfare of the taxpayers of Seville. The councilmen did so by allowing citizens in the city to acquire positions reserved for hidalgos. Acquisition of such positions provided tax exemption to the individual and reduced the tax base of the city. In this way some of the city's richest citizens would gain exemptions from taxation and the burden of their dues would fall on their neighbors. Therefore the two royal officials asked the court to disregard the city's objections and impose on the city the penalties that it had incurred in accord with the law of the kingdom.

In these arguments the prosecutors described municipal resistance to royal demands similar to past contests between Castile's towns and cities and the royal government in general and relations between the city of Seville and Crown officials in particular. Amezaga and Heredia claimed that the city had a history of resisting royal orders by refusing to implement them. Specifically, the prosecutors said that this included the city's refusal to execute similar earlier orders to place particular citizens on the lists of taxpayers. They explained how the city council had responded with the statement "we obey, but we do not comply," which municipalities regularly used to counter royal orders and legislation that they did not wish to recognize. In this case, Seville's claim to implement the royal order loyally also played upon its traditional loyalty to the monarchy, expressed in the city's motto (see fig. 8).

By the 1580s this legal formula had a long history of use in Castilian political disputes. The historian of Spanish legal history Manuel García-Gallo argues that the formula was a response to the problem of unjust laws, defined as royal

Fig. 8   Relief sculpture of Seville's motto, "no8do," a rebus signifying "No me ha dejado" ([Seville] has not abandoned me). According to legend, Alfonso X uttered this phrase in praise of Seville's loyalty to him during the rebellion by his son Sancho IV. Photo: author.

edits or dispositions that ran contrary to general legal norms.[7] García-Gallo asserts that in the late medieval and early modern periods it was widely accepted and agreed that any law or statute enacted by the monarch that was contrary to the existing bodies of law or was harmful consequently lacked legal force and did not require compliance. In such a case the law was nominally obeyed, in the sense that deference to royal order was shown, but the law was not implemented. According to García-Gallo and other scholars of Castilian law, the refusal to implement the law or royal order did not nullify it. Instead, local officials simply deferred implementation until the king could ratify or revoke the order or law.[8] More recently, Benjamín González Alonso has argued that the formula evolved from a means to maintain municipal rights in the face of the development of royal law in the thirteenth and fourteenth centuries into a means to conserve royal law enacted in the Cortes that came to be violated by the edicts, orders, and special privileges and favors issued by monarchs and their officials in the fifteenth and sixteenth centuries.[9]

While municipal councils at times made claims about the justness of an order in the way that García-Gallo and González Alonso describe, the principal point of the dispute rested on competing claims about the authority of existing legal principles. In the particular dispute between Seville's city council and the chancery prosecutor, the city's committed decision "to obey but not comply" with the royal writs ultimately forced the royal judges to reevaluate the situation and their original writs. After doing so, they tacitly acknowledged the existence of other authoritative principles and issued a favorable ruling for the city.

Parallel to these direct acts of resistance to royal authority, the city also had a history of surreptitiously ignoring or selectively implementing its own royally authorized ordinances when they proved inconvenient, such as laws limiting the enjoyment of hidalgo status, which began the dispute. In these instances Seville's council government simply chose not to enforce or apply certain laws when they went against the interests of the city's principal families and their allies and retainers. In matters concerning legal privileges, this included the active violation of laws restricting access to public office, specifically the laws issued by Juana I in 1515 requiring the status of hidalgo to hold any of the main positions in the city council. Both city council and royal government selectively applied the laws for their own benefit and accused each other of failure to enforce laws at convenient moments. In the case of Juana's law on public offices in Seville, the royal government chose to demand compliance from the city council on two separate occasions in the years 1562 and 1581.[10] In both instances letters from the Crown complained that the city violated the law and provided the offices of veinticuatro and jurado to men of pechero status. The Crown issued the first order for Seville to comply with the old law in the 1560s, a time when Felipe II's government had initiated efforts to force other Castilian city councils to implement similar, but locally unique, laws regarding status and access to public office.

In the case of the city of Toledo, Felipe demanded the implementation of fifteenth-century statutes of blood purity for the members of the city council in 1566 and again in 1569. Unlike Seville's veinticuatros, the Toledo city councilmen in the late sixteenth century were split into two benches, one for pecheros and one for hidalgos. The royal order required that those men on the noble bench be *hidalgos de sangre* and those on the commoners' bench be Old Christians of pure blood.[11] Six of Toledo's converso regidores wrote to the Crown protesting the order. In the long term none of the conversos on the council lost their office. Apparently, this statute, as with similar previous ones, did not apply to current officeholders. Only when one of the protestors died in 1567 did the Crown abolish his office and effectively end his family's possession of it. That same year the Crown sold another five offices of regidor in the city of Toledo and at least one of the buyers was a converso. During Felipe's reign the number of councilmen was not reduced, but the number on the commoner's bench diminished. In 1581, there were a total of thirty-six regidores, twenty-five nobles and eleven pecheros. In 1594, there were thirty-eight regidores, twenty-eight nobles and ten pecheros.[12] Considering how the royal order was ultimately implemented, it appears that Felipe II's government was less interested in either eliminating conversos or reducing the number of regidores than in generating income for the royal treasury. The Crown made similar efforts to require hidalgo status for half of the regidores on the town councils of Medina del Campo and Medina de Rioseco.[13] In both cases, after extended litigation, the municipal councils avoided the imposition of these new rules by providing cash payments to the royal treasury.

In both Seville and Toledo the Crown's efforts to require the implementation of the laws served as a means for the royal government to introduce new measures to control the verification of status during the transfer of office from the incumbent to his heir or designated successor. Felipe's order to the city council of Seville introduced an innovation to the law originally confirmed by Juana in 1515. The new ordinance specified that any successor to an office had to present evidence of his hidalgo status to the asistente, who would then provide the candidate with a written confirmation. The candidate would then have to present this certification to officials at the royal court, presumably to the council of Castile or its smaller cabinet, the Cámara de Castilla, a committee that James Boyden has described as a veritable "patronage bureau."[14]

In these instances the municipal councils of Seville and Toledo did not readily or willingly comply with the royal edicts. To achieve implementation of a particular ordinance, council and Crown had to agree to the legitimacy of that law. Consequently, in the royal letters addressing the status requirements for public office in Seville, the authors repeated two claims about the law: that the law originated from local requests and that it served to alleviate a harmful situation. In the 1562 letter Felipe began by reviewing the letters and provisiones issued by his grandmother Juana in 1515. The king's secretary, Francisco de Eraso, then gave a copy of the queen's letters and provisiones, each of which emphasized that the monarch issued the ordinance at the request of the city.[15] Considering the language used in the letter, it might be more appropriate to say that Juana's council confirmed or ratified an ordinance presented by the city council. In 1562, Felipe's letter likewise claimed that the city had petitioned him to examine Juana's *provisiones* and to provide an authoritative declaration on them. Whether the request came from the council, a faction within it, or worried citizens, the king took advantage of the request to try and introduce new procedures to verify hidalguía during the transfer of office. Upon receiving the king's letter, the council agreed to obey it and stated that they would execute it according to the king's demands.

The author of the king's letter to the council and the royal official managing the negotiation with Seville's council was Francisco de Eraso, who began his royal service as a secretary for Carlos I and became an important administrator in the first decade of Felipe II's reign. Moreover, he was an ally of the king's favorite, Ruy Gómez de Silva, who dominated the councils of state and finance in the early 1560s.[16] Eraso himself was the secretary of the Cámara de Castilla from 1561 until 1570.[17] In this position he played a central role in the management of royal mercedes, including the authorization of mayorazgos, naturalizations, pardons, the legitimizing of "natural" offspring, and, of course, the sanctioning and granting of hidalguía.[18]

Despite the council's apparent acquiescence to the royal order, the city did not apply the old ordinances or the new procedures, or at least it did not apply them in a regular or consistent manner. Almost twenty years later, in 1581, Felipe II again wrote to the council on this issue and provided copies of the earlier letters. Crown officials had attempted to apply these laws, and Seville's council, either in earnest or as a means of delay, had questioned whether they were genuine. Consequently, municipal and royal officials had to verify the authenticity of the law. This involved a formal comparison of the original provisión from Juana authorizing the ordinances—or a copy of the original— held by the royal government with the one in the city archive.[19]

The letters from Felipe to the council of Seville in 1562 and again in 1581, both of which ordered the city to implement laws restricting public office to hidalgos, describe a history of the city's selective application of these laws. In the 1562 letter, after explaining the procedures that he wanted the city to follow in the transfer of office, the king demanded that the offices be given only to hidalgos and that the councilmen follow these rules, "notwithstanding that until now, these letters and writs may not have been used or kept."[20] Consequently, the letters also provide evidence of selective efforts on the part of the royal government to gain adherence to these laws. Since at least the fifteenth century, the transfer and confirmation of a council seat in Seville required the formal recognition of the Crown. Consequently, the royal officials who certified and documented the sale and transfer of public offices since 1515 likewise disregarded these rules and were complicit in the failure to oversee status requirements for office.

Felipe's efforts to apply laws restricting access to public office according to status had similar outcomes in the cities of Seville and Toledo. Like the orders sent to Seville, those directed to Toledo's council required that the determination of social and ethnic status occur after the initial officeholder died and the municipal office was transferred to his heir or sold to another person. Toledo's council responded by doing nothing, and the order was suspended in April 1566. The Crown justified the order as a means to avoid "differences, litigation, and passions" that had caused much "uneasiness and anxiety."[21] Linda Martz speculates that the order was a stratagem for extorting money from officeholders. Under the dictates of the royal order, new councilmen would have had to have their nobility confirmed either by the Crown or the chancery courts or pay more in bribes to have their lineage certified locally.[22] Considering how these efforts corresponded with the Crown's initiatives to sell so-called patents of hidalguía, the demands to implement these laws seem intended to increase the sales, which were relatively few in number and would continue to elicit limited interest.[23] The efforts to implement these laws were part of larger royal policy with both political and economic ends. The royal government sought to assert its control over claims to status by giving local royal officials, such as the asistente, a greater role in determining status.

Amezaga and Heredia cited specific acts of Seville's resistance in their arguments, but they did not address the political culture of resistance to royal intervention in local affairs and the defense of municipal prerogatives founded on unique municipal charters and subsequent corporate privileges. In contrast to the royal prosecutors, the city's attorney, Dr. Villalta, emphasized the unique circumstances and status of the city and cited the special privileges the royal government had previously granted it and should continue to allow it. To justify the city's control over the designation of status, Villalta also expressed his arguments in terms of the good of the community, its citizens, and the royal government. However, he argued that the local government was in the best position to provide for the matters of the community. Consequently, Villalta's arguments stressed the role of Seville's city council in policing privileges and the dangers that would arise from royal interference in this role: "Although the provisiones should be able to be given for other places they should not be given for the city of Seville because there are so many foreigners and the city has royal writs so that such foreigners can't acquire possession of the status of hidalgo or [gain exemption from paying] the dues on the excise tax even if they should reside in the city for a long time."[24] The authority of the writs originally issued to Amezaga derived from the law made by Enrique IV, which the prosecutors claimed applied to all of the Crown of Castile. To deny the basis for the prosecutor's actions the city tried to show that such laws should not be applied to the city of Seville because of unique circumstances. To convince the royal judges of the city council's concern with the matter, the attorney remarked specifically on the economic dangers involved: "If [the writs] should be allowed, foreigners would be able to litigate with the city of Seville concerning their status of hidalgo, and there wouldn't be enough revenues from the city properties to pay the expenses for all the lawsuits."[25] In other words, the attorney argued that the royal prosecutor's use of writs, backed by general law enacted in the Cortes, to determine a person's status would only increase the number of disputes and deplete the city's resources. He repeated this point a few lines later, saying that to give the prosecutors these writs would initiate two hundred some lawsuits for his client, the city of Seville, without any of these actions producing an advantage for the royal patrimony or for the city.

Despite Villalta's argument for municipal control over issues of privilege and status, he still maintained that the city had followed and continued to follow royal laws concerning these matters. He contradicted the prosecutors' claims and argued that the city had allowed privileges only to those who warranted them. He repeated that the people who received the refund from the excise tax were hijosdalgo notorios or hijosdalgo from royal writs and letters of privilege or from some other manner: "In this matter the city takes such great care and diligence that no one can claim otherwise, because it is common knowledge that the city has always observed what is to the service of your highness and the benefit of the city."[26]

As part of his argument, Villalta emphasized the city's autonomy from royal interference and claimed that royal officials like Amezaga had violated this autonomy with the introduction of innovative practices. The city's last objection to the writs presented by the prosecutor addressed the change they might initiate in the procedures and practices of recognizing someone's status in the city. Villalta pointed out that this had already begun to happen and with bad effect. According to the attorney, the city had refused to provide the refund to some men who were not hidalgos and yet claimed to be. He stated that these men then gathered evidence and testimony and submitted their claims to the chancery court rather than pursue the matter in any other way. According to the attorney, these men essentially sought to circumvent the authority of the council by appealing to the royal court as a third party. As further evidence of the prosecutors' efforts to undermine the autonomy and prerogatives of the city, Villalta reported that they attempted to make a general list of Seville's citizens. The attorney strongly asserted that they should not be allowed to do so.

In the presentation of the city's case, Villalta did not attempt to provide a logically consistent representation of practices in Seville. Instead, he sought to provide a number of authoritative arguments. For instance, in these diverse arguments the attorney made a number of claims about the city's treatment of foreigners that did not agree. As we saw earlier, he claimed that the city had special privileges to prevent foreigners from gaining the status of hidalgo. Nevertheless, after arguing why the judges should revoke the writs, Villalta sought to explain the city's failure to comply with the most recent orders from the court: "The city's officials did not [complete] the recently presented writs even after the council ordered them implemented, because the people listed were foreigners and not known." In a strange reversal of logic concerning "foreigners," the attorney claimed that the city had not placed these men on the tax lists because their status was unknown and needed investigation. Similarly, despite the attorney's claims and the fact that the active involvement of the prosecutor in local matters may have been unusual, citizens of Seville had appealed to royal mediation in their efforts to gain recognition of status for more than seventy years. In the end, the manner of litigation allowed both the city and the judges deciding the case flexibility in developing and interpreting legal arguments. Whether on the merit of these arguments or due to other influences and pressures, the judges ruled in favor of the city council of Seville.

During their deliberation of legal disputes, royal judges had to take into account the short- and long-term interests of the Crown and how their decisions might affect future relations between royal and local authorities. Consequently, previous relations and transactions between the city of Seville and the royal government had important consequences for the city's autonomy from the royal government in matters involving the determination of privilege. In his arguments the attorney made the notable claim that the city possessed royal writs that prevented foreigners from acquiring the status of hidalgo. He did not elaborate on this writ or provide a copy of it. Only a year earlier, in April 1582, the city had presented Felipe II the sum of 50,000 ducados (18,750,000 maravedís) so that he would not sell the status of hidalgo to any citizen or resident of the city or territory of Seville. According to the agreement, the dire needs of the Crown for more income than the government raised from ordinary sources had forced the king to sell the status of hidalgo to interested buyers. For the city and territory of Seville he had given the commission for this duty to the Count of Villar, the asistente in 1579 and 1580.[27] The count had proceeded to sell titles of hidalguía to both citizens of the city and foreign residents who desired the status. Although modern historians often refer to these transactions as sales, the actual documents went to great lengths to mask the fact that the recipient was purchasing status.[28]

To stop these transactions the city had to provide the government with the sums it hoped to acquire and a justification for ending these practices. Consequently, much of the agreement listed the dangers to the royal patrimony, to the king's service, and to the good of the city that would come from continuing and fulfilling the sale of hidalguía:

> To concede the said privileges in this manner would bring the greatest harm to the royal patrimony and result in many inconveniences to his majesty's service and the good and public welfare of the city, especially to the poor and the people of less means and recourse. Those rich men, who acquired these privileges in this way and all their descendants forever, would come to be a great number, and the subsidies and taxes they [ought to have] paid would overburden the poor. As such a Christian and pious prince, his majesty should not allow such a thing to take place.[29]

Whether moved by these pleas or the offer of a cash payment, Felipe agreed to end the sales and set a price for his compliance.

To halt the sale of hidalguía the city had to acquire possession of a special legal privilege. For the payment of 50,000 ducados, the king not only ended the sale of status but also provided the city with a royal favor. The merced ended any future sales, it terminated those being processed by royal officials, and it nullified ones that had already been given. The clauses of the city's privilege set limits on the future actions of the king and his successors. Not only did Felipe agree not to sell any titles in the future, but he bound his heirs to adhere to these stipulations. In more than one place the document stated the king's pledge not to sell the title of hidalguía, but also not to bestow it for any service or item of equivalent worth, no matter how great the needs of the monarchy might be in the future. Furthermore, the document stated that the merced should stand even if the king should desire to return to the city the payment he had received. The drafters of the document fully acknowledged that this grant of privilege to the city might violate the individual privileges of others. The document deprived the king and his descendants of the right to "give or ennoble with the said privileges of hidalguía persons that in other places should have served them in such a way that they deserved to be honored and ennobled."[30] In other words, if the city of Seville refused to recognize as an hidalgo someone whom authorities elsewhere had recognized, not even the Crown had the authority to bestow this status on the person.[31]

From the perspective of the city council, the sale of status by the asistente infringed on the council's local control over who could be considered an hidalgo. In this sense it was the inversion of the prosecutors' later denunciation against "false" hidalgos. Control over status held immediate economic and political ramifications for the city's income and access to local public offices. Rather than addressing these issues in their plea to the Crown, the city government focused on the harm that would be done to the poor of the city, and for a promise to pay 50,000 ducados received a royal merced. Only a few years later, when Crown prosecutors applied royal law to citizens and councilmen of the city, the city argued that it had obtained formal concessions from the royal government that it would abstain from matters concerning hidalguía in Seville and its territories. Whether or not the royal judges took this transaction into account four years later, they ruled in favor of the city council.

THE USE AND ABUSE OF CHANCERY OFFICE

Individuals and families who sought to acquire privilege made use of diverse means to achieve this end, including the intervention of powerful patrons and the presentation of gifts and favors to local authorities. In these efforts claimants to status targeted chancery officials as well as local authorities. Moreover, these officials treated such income and gifts as part of their official remuneration and often actively sought out such compensation to the detriment of justice, at times in the recognition of legitimate hidalgo status and the enjoyment of attendant privileges. Consequently, the possibility of gaining improper or illicit favors from court officials in the expediting of lawsuits or in even more questionable actions, such as the fabrication of evidence or beneficial court rulings, also influenced the dynamics of claims to hidalgo status.

The royal prosecutor at the chancery court of Granada, as the official responsible for the protection of Crown interests and the implementation of royal policy, held a key position in the network of individuals with whom claimants to status had to ingratiate themselves. At the same time that the prosecutor Diego de Amezaga applied the laws of the kingdom to limit the proliferation of privilege—in accord with what appeared to be the policy of Felipe's government—he also made use of his office as a source of personal benefit. The two purposes did not necessarily contradict each other. The ordinances of the royal courts themselves dictated the amounts that prosecutors and clerks should receive for their services. Individuals sought to acquire positions in the civil service through purchase, sometimes even bidding for offices, with the expectation that the office should provide a return on the original investment.[32] The very possibility of increasing one's income provided the prosecutors with the incentive to pursue the application of the law. Moreover, both the practice of judicial officers and government oversight did not always draw a clear distinction between the honest execution of public duties and self-serving actions.[33] This is not to say that the Crown of Castile lacked a means to review the activities of its officials or to assess charges of corruption or that early modern Castilians lacked a notion of public corruption. Royal and council magistrates regularly made inquests and reviews of office (*visitas*) during the sixteenth century.[34] At times, these reviews revealed abuse of office and graft, and the royal council occasionally meted out penalties on those involved.[35] Considering the trouble Amezaga sparked for powerful persons in the city of Seville, who had important connections at court, it is not surprising that he himself eventually came under scrutiny.[36]

In the spring of 1590 Cristóbal de León, doctor of law and secretary in His Majesty's council, began a review of allegations of malfeasance made against the royal prosecutor Amezaga. His finished memo summarized forty-two separate counts of abuse of the prosecutor's office, dating back eight years, including solicitation of bribes, extortion, leveling false charges, and failure to protect the royal patrimony.[37] Despite what seemed like overwhelming evidence of official vice, the case against Amezaga had developed slowly and the verdict against him remained uncertain. The investigation of Amezaga and the functionaries who worked under him reveal how the public duties and individual interests of Crown officials intersected. The investigation also reveals how officials and litigants circumvented and undermined laws regarding the status and privilege of hidalgos both inside and outside of the royal courts.

Only a year before the prosecutor initiated the wave of writs and denunciations against citizens of Seville in 1583, complaints had arrived at the chancery court alleging Amezaga's misuse of his office and its benefits (*cosechas*). As prosecutor at the chancery court in Granada, he was one of several officers responsible for protecting the interests of the Crown in the southern half of the kingdom. Attached to the tribunal of hidalgos, he specifically held the position of litigating against those who claimed to be hidalgos, investigating their claims, and thereby maintaining the incomes of the royal patrimony. Nevertheless, during his time as prosecutor, from roughly 1580 until at least 1590, numerous allegations were made against Amezaga, especially concerning his failure to provide justice in suits of hidalguía and his subversion of justice for his own material ends.[38]

One of the earliest complaints originated from citizens of the town of Baeza in October 1582. Diego Martínez Lechuga, on behalf of the town's clerks, claimed that Amezaga had failed to pursue a complaint they had begun against the public notary Ventura Pretel, whom the clerks claimed was not truly an hidalgo.[39] As part of the process of initiating the investigation, the clerks had provided Amezaga with information and the necessary sureties for his services, and the prosecutor had sworn to file their complaint. Martínez stated that Amezaga never did so, even though various writs from the court's judges required him to act on the matter. Moreover, he alleged that the prosecutor had not submitted the complaint because of gifts and a quantity of jewels he had received from Pretel.[40] León's review of the evidence found that Diego Martínez, on behalf of the clerks of Baeza, had traveled to Granada to complain about the matter before the judges of the hidalgos. Martínez further complained that Pretel had succeeded in being listed as an hidalgo through the favors and schemes of Baeza's councilmen and had kept his status through the malfeasance of the prosecutor. Amezaga's misuse of office did not stop there. When the prosecutor discovered that Martínez had been making complaints against him, he ordered Martínez arrested without the necessary writ and had him brought to Granada, where he kept him imprisoned until the chancery judges finally ordered his release.

This was not the only instance in which Amezaga abused his powers to order the arrest or release of prisoners. As fiscal of the tribunal of hidalgos, Amezaga held the authority to punish those who provided false witnesses or fraudulent testimony and evidence in suits of hidalguía. Such punishment could be both severe and didactic in nature. A surviving account concerning the chancery court of Valladolid in 1515 describes how royal officials made an example of twenty-eight individuals who had either presented bogus witnesses and evidence to testify to their status as hidalgos or who had given false testimony. The court officials knocked out the teeth of the men who had perjured and sentenced them to the galleys, and they publicly whipped the would-be hidalgos who had presented these witnesses, after first hanging around their necks their fraudulent letters and documents.[41] In Amezaga's case, the witnesses related how on one occasion he was returning to Granada with forty prisoners convicted of offenses of perjury and giving false testimony, and—as noted by León—subject to corporal punishment and fines to the royal treasury.[42] En route to the court, rather than imposing due punishment upon these prisoners, he freed them in return for gifts and promises of future gifts and, unsurprisingly, failed to file official record of the arrests.

In their complaint to the chancery court, the clerks of Baeza made an argument almost identical to the one Amezaga made a year later in his own denunciations of citizens in Seville. They claimed that Ventura Pretel and his brother, the licenciado Pretel, were common taxpayers and descendants of such and through favors they had with the justices and councilmen of the city of Baeza and the connivance of these men they had been made hidalgos without being of this status. Like Seville's veinticuatros, the councilmen of Baeza acted for themselves as well as for relatives and clients. The investigation of Amezaga, carried out under the direction of Dr. León, revealed allegations that the councilman of Baeza Miguel de Cámara also provided the prosecutor with gifts to secure his own recognition as an hidalgo. In exchange for a horse, Amezaga used his connections at court to secure Cámara additional time to present evidence of his family's possession of hidalguía.[43] Although Cristóbal de León did not include in his report any allegations that Cámara's claim to being an hidalgo was fraudulent, he did say that the councilman had provided little proof of his status and could not have given more without Amezaga's assistance.

Like the allegations of malfeasance against Amezaga in the cases of Ventura Pretel and Miguel de Cámara, many of the counts against Amezaga involved illicit favors to those attempting to obtain or maintain the status of hidalgo. Such favors ranged from minor procedural infractions to flagrant fraud and disregard for duty such as extending deadlines for submitting evidence, failing to pursue investigations, providing perfunctory review of evidence, or rushing a favorable judicial ruling. The citizens who initiated these lawsuits came from most of the major cities and towns of Andalusia, including Seville, Úbeda, Jaén, Jerez de la Frontera, Córdoba, Carmona, and Écija. In these instances the prosecutor received a wide range of gifts, including horses, bolts of cloth, gold chains, and an array of agricultural commodities. The carter Alonso Canuto testified that he had delivered some barrels of olives and pickled fish, a chest of cloth, and fine scarlet fabric about thirty to forty varas in length to Amezaga on behalf of Bartolomé de Hoces.[44] A city councilman of Seville, Hoces had a lawsuit concerning his hidalguía pending at the chancery court. Through the assistance of Amezaga, the councilman obtained a verdict from the court confirming his possession of hidalguía without providing the proper paperwork or following the proper legal proceedings.[45] Revealing of official attitudes concerning such favors, the royal investigator made no comment on the propriety of the prosecutor's gift but concluded that Amezaga had not followed correct procedures and had concluded the lawsuit prematurely. Only a year later, in 1583, when the city council of Seville responded to the royal prosecutor's writs with categorical denial of the charges, Bartolomé de Hoces was one of the eight councilmen listed as representing the council in the city's initial written rejection of Amezaga's writs. It seems that Hoces had decided not to leave the question of his own status to an uncertain outcome and took the initiative to avoid potentially embarrassing and lengthy lawsuits. Although Dr. León's review did not produce any more information concerning Hoces, it is possible that he and other councilmen in Seville had been extorted to have their names kept out of the prosecutors' public denunciations.

Other citizens of Seville, like Hoces, sought to gain favorable treatment from Amezaga through gifts and services.[46] Pedro de León de Ayala and Miguel Gerónimo de León, citizens of Sevilla with lawsuits at the tribunal of the hidalgos against prosecutor Amezaga, also managed to gain a favorable executive writ concerning their status of hidalgo.[47] According to witnesses, Pedro de León gave the prosecutor's assistant, Pedro de Oleaga, a gold chain to pass on to Amezaga. This Pedro de León may be the same Pedro de León listed in the writ Amezaga sent to the city in September 1583, which also listed the councilmen García and Juan de León. Whether or not this was the same man, Amezaga did not list anyone with the last name of León in his denunciations after the court's ruling in November 1584, although he persisted in his efforts against other men whom he had previously denounced, such as the fabulously wealthy Juan Antonio Corzo.

Amezaga directed many of his charges against council members and their families, but he also directed them at ordinary citizens and in a few rare instances other royal officials. His actions against other royal officials may have been motivated by personal enmity or a desire to secure influence over these men. Among these officials, the prosecutor charged Pedro Rodríguez de Herrera, the royal judge of Seville's own audiencia, as a fraudulent hidalgo. Despite the charge, Rodríguez never began a lawsuit at the chancery court to deny Amezaga's charges. Only a few years earlier the judge had succeeded in gaining local approval of his status without recourse to royal intervention.[48] In November 1581 Rodríguez had petitioned the city to recognize his status as an hidalgo and refund him the taxes he had paid on his consumption of meat. In the depositions he presented the council and its lawyers, Rodríguez claimed that his family status as hidalgos went back at least as far as his great-grandfather, who came from Salamanca and fought in the conquest of Granada. Since the late fifteenth century the Rodríguez family had lived in various municipalities in Andalusia, including the city of Córdoba and the town of Guadix, but Pedro had lived in the city of Seville for only a short time. Nevertheless, after reviewing his evidence and the testimony of his witnesses, the city's attorneys recommended that the council accept the claim. At the council meeting of December 2, 1581, the council heard the opinion of its legal counsel and voted on the matter. The council chose to accept Rodríguez's status and ordered that his name be added to the list of the city's hidalgos.[49]

Alonso de Herrera, citizen of Jerez de la Frontera, also had a lawsuit of hidalguía pending at the chancery court. Herrera showed Antón Suárez, his solicitor, a list of goods worth 40,000 maravedís that he had provided Amezaga. Suárez testified that Herrera then told him that "by these means the business was concluded with brevity while others wasted their time in Granada and have no inkling how to reach a deal."[50] Herrera received a favorable ruling from the judges, who declared him an hidalgo in possession and property. The town of Jerez appealed the ruling, but the appeal failed because the prosecutor chose not to pursue the matter further. León wrote that the suit also went through a second appeal and thereby received three separate rulings—the original, en vista, and en revista—in a mere seventy-four days without the prosecutor having done any due diligence or investigation of the matter.

While some of the gifts may have been provided to simply shorten and ease lengthy proceedings and thereby bring about rapid recognition of legitimate claims, some of the litigants who obtained assistance from Amezaga had more dubious claims and their success brought public grumbling and scandal. In fact, León's evaluation of the prosecutor's improprieties focused on those moments that brought public attention, either due to gross disregard for duties or through the provision of status to scandalously bogus claimants. One witness stated that he had heard from a court summoner how Pedro de Vargas, a jurado of Seville, had obtained recognition of his hidalguía through the gift of a horse and other valuables. The verdict had amazed him, because Vargas's ancestors were neither hidalgos or even Old Christians.[51] Expressing similar concerns, a councilman of Écija named Luis de Eraso complained about a local licenciado who had obtained an executive writ in support of his hidalguía with Amezaga's assistance and how it had produced considerable comments and gossip in the city. In another incident the prosecutor ignored and suppressed the depositions of nine witnesses taken by one of the court associates. The prosecutor's suppression of the evidence had likewise brought considerable local grumbling and comment.

Perhaps the most egregious act allegedly perpetrated by the prosecutor that provoked disturbance at the court also suggested his collusion with some of the tribunal's judges. In the ruling on Miguel de Cámara's status of hidalgo, the judges of the tribunal were divided in their decisions, with the licenciado Luis de Mercado in dissent against the two other judges. Both of the judges who gave positive rulings were later suspended from their offices for unspecified reasons.[52] Despite these suspicious circumstances, the judges who subsequently reviewed the suit reaffirmed Cámara's hidalguía. Dr. León noted that their decision not only produced scandal but also defrauded the royal patrimony.

Investigation of the prosecutor Amezaga began as early as 1585 and continued until the beginning of a formal suit against him in 1590.[53] His investigation provides a window into the auditing process. During this investigation Amezaga continued to hold office and prosecute lawsuits of hidalguía, and it is unclear whether or not he ever received a formal sanction or penalties for his actions. Aurelio Espinosa has vigorously argued that in the wake of the Comunero Revolt, Carlos I established a judicial meritocracy firmly grounded on a system of regular visitations and audits of the royal courts. Under the system elaborated by Carlos and his key minister, the bishop Juan de Tavera, the council of Castile, particularly the graduates of law that staffed the Cámara de Castilla, oversaw the audits or visitations of the courts in the royal judiciary, including the audiencias and chancillerías. In the 1522 audit of chancery officials, the types of problems included factional strife, a growing number of unsettled cases, delays, bribes, and inappropriate purchases and investments. However, six of eight judges who received poor evaluations in the 1522 audit continued to hold their positions, because their offenses were not deemed to be serious. The visitation described prosecutor Ribera, one of the officials who was cited, as delaying prosecutions and receiving money from individuals accused of offenses. Ribera's punishment was unstated, but he did not advance to a higher position and appears to have faded out of royal service by 1528.[54] In other words, he did not leave royal service for another six years and whether he was pushed out or left of his own volition is unknown.

One of the causes of official misconduct, particularly the tendency to engage in graft, involved the system for compensating royal officials. It is difficult to determine the salaries of judicial officers, because they often were not fixed or regularized, and for the first half of the sixteenth century do not survive in chancery records. But it is clear from the chancery ordenanzas that these officials depended heavily on revenues generated from litigation and court fees stipulated in the regulations of the court itself. When the king provided compensation to the judiciary, it usually came from annuities he awarded from local taxes. High-ranking and favored officials such as the court president received a substantial annual income in the realm of 200,000 maravedís, while civil judges received around 120,000 maravedís.[55] In the second half of the sixteenth century, with rising inflation and a royal treasury strapped for resources, complaints about the judiciary suggest that low-level graft was endemic, especially at the appellate courts. These complaints led to efforts to implement set salaries, but it is unclear how regularly they were maintained.[56] Consequently, the regular gifts provided to Amezaga and his associates may not have been outside the norm of behavior.

Although Amezaga faced accusations that he had failed to protect the royal patrimony, his actions against Seville's city council suggest that he had aggressively defended the Crown's interests, albeit often to his own benefit. The rigorous audit of Amezaga's official behavior omitted mention of the prosecutor's audacious charges—made during this same period—denouncing councilmen and prominent citizens of Seville as fraudulent hidalgos, which straddled the threshold between zealous duty and impropriety. Diverse factors appear to have motivated Amezaga's unprecedented actions. Given the earlier efforts of Felipe II's government, Amezaga's denunciation of prominent Sevillanos appears as an extension of royal policy that sought to limit the proliferation of privilege, especially privilege bestowed under local auspices rather than through the

Crown's authorization. Nevertheless, his history of graft and extortion suggests that the charges served his own efforts to extort prominent wealthy individuals or to harass those who had resisted earlier demands for gifts.

The investigation of Amezaga reveals the range and possibilities for corruption in the judicial system of sixteenth-century Castile. Moreover, his actions suggest how corrupt officials influenced the outcome of lawsuits and the provision of justice, especially in issues of status. Richard Kagan, among others, has written about the dramatic growth in litigation in sixteenth-century Castile, a "legal revolution" common to other parts of Europe.[57] With the rapid growth in litigation came an accompanying growth in the possibilities for graft and illicit actions by the personnel who staffed the overworked judicial courts. A certain level of graft may have been necessary to the very functioning of Castile's legal apparatus to provide sufficient compensation and encourage the recruiting of legal talent. But to balance the excesses of misconduct and to ensure official compliance with royal interests, Castile had a long-standing system of oversight through periodic audits.

This chapter has focused in detail on a significant contest between the city council of Seville and royal officials over control of legal privileges based on status. But the arguments made by the two sides reveal that such conflicts occurred with some frequency, although they varied over time in their form and nature. In sixteenth-century Seville contingent factors related to the city's history of relations with the Crown influenced the outcome of these conflicts. Moreover, the nature of the political system and balance between municipal and royal prerogatives constrained the ability of Crown officials to freely impose their will concerning issues of status and privilege. At the same time the indeterminate nature of the law offered the royal government—particularly chancery judges—the flexibility to respond with diverse rulings to unique disputes and contests.[58] The judicial and administrative institutions and bureaucracy allowed claimants to privilege and the officials themselves to manipulate the filing of complaints and the presentation of evidence necessary for the confirmation of status. These disputes reveal the fragmented nature of royal government in a political system with multiple sites of Crown authority controlled by individuals with diverse interests and objectives, all claiming to speak and act for Crown interests and sometimes literally speaking as the monarch.

CONCLUSION

Most Spaniards and non-Spaniards, if they are familiar at all with the designation of hidalgo, know it in connection to Miguel Cervantes de Saavedra's novel *El ingenioso hidalgo Don Quijote de la Mancha*. Consequently, Cervantes's portrait of a country gentleman of modest means and addled psyche who embraced the identity and ideals of the knight-errant informs and overshadows whatever modern popular and literary understanding there is of hidalgo. Cervantes was born the son of a surgeon, fought in Castile's army in Italy and in the Mediterranean fleet, and served as a royal official charged with supplying the royal galleys and collecting revenues from the alcabalas. There is no evidence that Cervantes himself ever claimed to be an hidalgo. Nevertheless, he resided on and off in Seville in the 1580s and 1590s, when the city was experiencing its high point of lawsuits over hidalguía, and in an official capacity visited Granada, the seat of the chancery court. Additionally, he spent seven months in Seville's royal prison, when Crown monies in his care were lost in bankruptcy.[1] During this time some of his fellow inmates likely appealed to hidalguía to escape incarceration.

Cervantes, like his fellow Castilians, was certainly aware of the thousands of disputes that occurred between municipal councils and their citizens over hidalgo status and the subsequent litigation over it. When he chose to designate his protagonist as an hidalgo, he drew on diverse contemporary meanings that the term would have held for his readers. As evidence reviewed in this book suggests, some of these readers certainly would have associated hidalgos and hidalguía less with a rank in the nobility and more with efforts to obtain and enjoy tangible privileges, regardless of one's actual lineage or one's deeds and service. At the same time Cervantes contrasts hidalgo and caballero, he also conflates them in the figure of Don Quixote. In this manner the village hidalgo realizes, or at least aspires to, the knightly values and behavior championed in Diego de Valera's *Espejo de verdadera nobleza*. Quixote's adoption of the identity of knight-errant also paralleled the manner in which claimants in lawsuits of hidalguía cast themselves and their ancestors in the language and rhetoric articulated in ad hoc laws enacted in the Cortes and in the edicts of Castile's monarchs.

Late medieval monarchs generated these laws and rules in concrete political contexts, often to address the consequences of their, or their predecessors', authorization of hidalgo status to garner political support and reward service. This authorization was itself a statement of royal power. However, royal grants and confirmations of status were not the only means to obtain hidalguía, which also originated from local public reputation and from the assent of local municipal authorities. Moreover, a form of complicity existed in the recognition of hidalgo status between the monarch and local governments, who held the right to appeal and question royal authorization of hidalgo status and regularly challenged claimants possessing royal grants. Despite challenges to individual claimants, municipalities largely accepted the right of the monarchy to serve as final adjudicator of these disputes and to issue edicts and laws regulating the judicial determination of status at the appellate courts.

At the local municipal level great diversity existed among Castile's cities, towns, and villages concerning whether or not hidalguía bestowed legal privileges and the exact nature and material benefits of these privileges. Furthermore, the importance of hidalgo status changed over time as municipalities altered, with royal approval, their local ordinances, particularly those governing the collection of taxes and the holding of political office. In the early modern period the Castilian monarchy used tax farmers and municipal councils as agents to collect royal revenues. In the early decades of the sixteenth century some municipalities took a greater role in the collection of the servicio or altered how they would pay it. In the case of Seville these changes created new economic privileges for the city's ruling class, led to amendments in rules for holding public office, and consequently altered the customs for identifying elites. While the economic benefits were relatively modest, they proved sufficient to encourage the appropriation of hidalgo identity by those with the means to do so, particularly the members of the council and their dependents.

Just as changes in fiscal regimes and the rules for public office created the possibility for disputes over status, so too did migration and resettlement. The tangible enjoyment of hidalgo privileges was intimately tied to citizenship in a particular municipality. Municipal governments generally opposed the claims of new citizens to hidalgo status, unless these new citizens had first succeeded in assimilating with the local ruling elite. Typically, members of a family who gained recognition of their status in one municipality had to do so again if they resettled elsewhere. In the city of Seville the council challenged the hidalguía of individuals of diverse foreign origin, whether these foreigners came from other

Castilian municipalities, such as Burgos; from non-Castilian lands, like the Basque territories; or from outside the Iberian Peninsula, particularly the Genoese. Castilian merchants and those who were descendants of converted Jews also faced this opposition when they settled in new municipalities and sought to gain recognition as hidalgos. Conversely, when and if these new citizens sufficiently and successfully integrated themselves with the dominant ruling class of the city through holding lower political office, patronage, marriage, or business dealings, the city tacitly accorded them the status of hidalgo through provision of tax exemptions and access to political office.

Those who did not succeed in integrating themselves with the local municipal authorities and yet still sought recognition of hidalgo status faced stiff opposition. These individuals were left with the option of appealing to royal justice at the chancery courts' tribunals of the hidalgos. The nature of litigation made it difficult, expensive, and time consuming for claimants to receive a positive final verdict, especially when councils were free to appeal adverse rulings. Certain legal procedures and requirements, such as the plaintiff's burden of proof, made success difficult even for those litigants with seemingly justifiable claims based on multiple generations of public reputation in their home municipalities or on royal authorizations. Local authorities often knew little about the background of these claimants but could employ a barrage of formulaic oppositions requiring them to engage in the costly endeavor of producing evidence in the form of depositions and written documents. The long-term effect of this resistance to hidalgo claims was to limit the proliferation of individuals enjoying the legal privileges of hidalguía. This resistance and the language used in opposing hidalgo claims also served to define hidalguía as a status derived from one's blood and lineage. In the lawsuits of hidalguía the litigants drew from existing discourses concerning the basis of nobility to support their claims. Paradoxically, this emphasis on lineage directly contradicted royal and municipal practices of providing hidalgo status, whether overtly or in a hidden manner.

In the second half of the sixteenth century the monarchical government of Felipe II, faced with extraordinary fiscal demands, pursued diverse strategies for generating revenues. These strategies included the sale of council offices and the sale of hidalgo status. In an effort to make these sales more attractive and perhaps to limit the loss of tax revenue, royal prosecutors sought to impose old laws and ordinances restricting political office to those of hidalgo status or required municipalities to implement such laws. Consequently, the prosecutors of the chancery court denounced dozens of Seville's leading citizens as fraudulently enjoying privileges. Facing royal pressure, the city council attempted to maintain local prerogatives and defended those individuals who were part of its elite social networks. The actions of the prosecutors revealed members of Seville's council, and their dependents and clients, who had come to enjoy hidalgo privileges despite questionable origins. Moreover, they revealed how Seville's council, like many others, implemented rules concerning status at its own discretion. Although internal rivalry and disputes existed among individuals and factions on the city council, the council maintained a united front and resisted the demands of the prosecutors. In the end the city obtained a favorable ruling from the chancery judges, tacitly acknowledging the council's right to exercise such discretion over the provision of status.

The actions of the royal prosecutors generated complex interactions and negotiations between the city council and the various officials at the chancery court. These interactions and their judicial outcome demonstrated the broad collaboration in governance that existed between the different authorities that made up the Castilian monarchy. In particular, negotiation between council and court produced a compromise that reflected what these authorities viewed as good government and justice in the provision of hidalgo liberties, freedoms, and privileges. However, many factors existed to impede the realization of justice in the enjoyment of these liberties, not least the fraudulent production of evidence by claimants and the malfeasance of royal officials. These contingent factors could dramatically influence the degree to which an individual claimant succeeded or failed in gaining recognition of his or her hidalguía.

Cervantes was not unique in his use of the hidalgo as a fictional character or type. Other Spanish authors of the early modern period, both before and after Cervantes, presented the materially poor hidalgo zealously seeking to gain or maintain public recognition of his noble status.[2] Scholars have speculated about whether such characterizations reflect the downward mobility of the lesser nobility during the period, especially in the early seventeenth century, or anxiety about this mobility as experienced by those who sought to maintain it or those who disapproved of it. In his sweeping study of the Mediterranean world in the age of Felipe II, Fernand Braudel suggests that hidalgo status and privileges, whether pursued for material or honorific ends, had adverse consequences for Castile's cultural development: "In their thousands of sometimes tumbledown houses, often bearing 'gigantic scutcheons carved in stone', dwelt a race that sought to live 'nobly', not soiling its hands with dishonourable work, serving king and Church, sacrificing everything, even its life, to this ideal. If there was noble folly, it was at its worst in Castile, despite the misery it could bring and the popular ridicule which expressed itself in so many sayings."[3]

As this study has shown, the desires of Castilians to gain hidalgo status and live nobly had tangible economic and political ends and ramifications. This book has been about disputes over hidalguía as a means for understanding privileges in late medieval and early modern Castile and not about hidalgos as a coherent social group. Hidalgo status in fifteenth- and sixteenth-century Spain was fluid and contingent on circumstance, political networking, and the ability to successfully carry out lengthy lawsuits. Consequently, the privileges derived from hidalguía were not static, but rather a site for struggle. Those who gained municipal recognition of their status could enjoy certain locally specific privileges, but there was widespread resistance to the proliferation of privileges, and those who desired to continue enjoying them had to actively maintain their status.

NOTES

Archives

Archivo General de Simancas (AGS)
  Cámara de Castilla (CC)
  Mercedes y Privilegios (MP)
Archivo Municipal de Sevilla (AMS)
  Sección 1: Privilegios
  Sección 2: Contaduría y Junta de Propios
  Sección 3: Escribanías de Cabildo del Siglo XVI
  Sección 10: Actas Capitulares
Archivo de la Real Chancillería de Granada (ARCG)
  Colección de Hidalguías (H)

Archival Identifying Information

carpeta: carp.
documento: doc.
legajo: leg.
sección: sec.

Introduction

1. AGS, MP, leg. 393, doc. 112.

2. AMS, sec. 1, carp. 146, doc. 192.

3. Palma Chaguaceda, *Historiador*, 45–47, 41.

4. Thompson, "Purchase of Nobility," 339. While Thompson focused on the royal sale of patents of hidalguía in the late sixteenth and early seventeenth centuries, he recognized the statistically far greater phenomenon of lawsuits to gain the status at the chancery courts. Domínguez Ortiz, *Clases privilegiadas*, 31.

5. Domínguez Ortiz, *Clases privilegiadas*; Gerbet, *Nobleza*; A. MacKay, "Lesser Nobility"; Sánchez Saus, *Caballería y linaje*.

6. Domínguez Ortiz, *Clases privilegiadas*, 56; A. MacKay, "Lesser Nobility," 161; Ruiz, *Spanish Society*, 68, 74–75. Local and regional studies have pointed out the existence of hidalgo farmers, artisans, notaries, and other professionals. Altman, *Emigrants and Society*, 42, 48, 54; Torres Fontes, "Hidalgos murcianos."

7. These studies have emphasized significant regional and local variations for the number of hidalgos for the entire population, with far greater numbers in the northern regions of the Crown of Castile—particularly in Asturias, with 75.9 percent, and similar or higher percentages for Vizcaya and Guipúzcoa. In addition to regional variation, scholars have

noted differences between cities and their subject municipalities, with high numbers for certain cities, such as Burgos and León, between 40 and 50 percent. Gerbet, *Nobleza*, 67–72; Molinié-Bertrand, "Hidalgos," 68, 75.

8. Domínguez Ortiz, *Clases privilegiadas*, 25–27. Using the studies of Gerbet and Molinié-Bertrand, scholars have estimated figures of 440,000 hidalgos. A. MacKay, "Lesser Nobility," 160.

9. Dewald, *European Nobility*, 22–27.

10. Henry Kamen cites a petition from the Cortes of 1518 complaining that taxpaying farmers obtained privileges to be hidalgos and free of taxes, thereby bringing great harm to their villages. *Spain*, 107, 247.

11. For a review of these arguments and the scholars who promoted them, see Thompson, "Purchase of Nobility," 313, 314; and Bush, *Noble Privilege*, 59, 60.

12. For a detailed comparative examination of the types and nature of privileges among the European nobility, see Bush, *Noble Privilege*, 27–92.

13. For instance, municipal councils together with royal prosecutors denied and litigated against individual claims to hidalgo status, but municipal councils also opposed the rulings and decisions of royal judges. In the latter situation, resistance followed indirect forms similar to those described in Ruth MacKay's study of royal military recruitment, in which town councils engaged in "delay, pleading, squirming, and obstinacy" when faced with unwelcome and unwanted royal demands or decisions. *Limits of Royal Authority*, 3.

14. García de Valdeavellano, *Orígenes de la burguesía*, 69, 131. From a different perspective, Fernand Braudel describes the "defection of the bourgeoisie." *Mediterranean*, 725–33.

15. Sixteenth- and seventeenth-century treatise writers included Arce de Ortálora, *Summa nobilitatis hispanicae*; Guardiola, *Tratado de la nobleza*; and Moreno de Vargas, *Discurso de la nobleza*. Cited in Gerbet, *Nobleza*, 45.

16. Scholarly studies of aristocratic families date to the works of the famous seventeenth-century genealogist Luis de Salazar y Castro. Notable modern studies include the following works: Atienza Hernández, *Aristocracia, poder, y riqueza*; García Hernán, *Aristocracia y señorio*; Herrera García, *Estado de Olivares*; Mitre Fernández, *Evolución de la nobleza*; Molina Puche and Ortuño Molina, *Grandes*; Nader, *Power and Gender*; Quintanilla Raso, *Nobleza y señorios*; Boyden, *Courtier and the King*; and Salas Almela, *Medina Sidonia*.

17. Prior to the 1970s, treatment of the lower ranks of the nobility was confined primarily to the genealogical journal *Hidalguía*. Marqués de Siete Iglesias, "Hidalgo y el caballero"; Delgado y Orellana, "Noble."

18. Domínguez Ortiz, *Clases privilegiadas*, 10. Domínguez Ortiz suggested at least seven categories ranging from prenobles, who possessed legal privileges but no title of status, to the Grandes, titled nobles formally recognized by Carlos I in 1520 as the elite of the aristocracy (ibid., 49–52, 77–78).

19. Lucas, "Ennoblement"; Schalk, "Ennoblement in France"; Perroy, "Social Mobility"; Dewald, *Provincial Nobility*; Major, *Renaissance Monarchy*, 57–106; Heal and Holmes, *Gentry*.

20. In addition to late medieval royal grants, Gerbet argued that privileges, especially tax exemption, provided to nonnobles eventually allowed some individuals and their descendants to obtain recognition as hidalgos. *Nobleza*, 45, 46; and "Guerres." Her conclusion is similar to the position of Robert H. Lucas concerning increased social mobility into the French nobility during the Hundred Years War. "Ennoblement," 240.

21. Gerbet, *Nobleza*, 60.

22. For a magisterial demographic history of the city of Seville that addresses these problems, see Collantes de Terán, *Sevilla*.

23. To create consistent groups that allow for quantification, historians have had to reclassify their subjects. Angus MacKay's answer to the problem of identifying hidalgos was "to introduce an element of tidiness by excluding those *hidalgos* who were also *caballeros*." In his demographic study of Seville, Collantes de Terán proposes that we should not count as hidalgos all the families referred to as hidalgos in the lists of citizens, because in these sources the term has a wider meaning that includes superior groups of the noble estate. Gerbet employs a similar method for counting the number of nobles in Extremadura. A. MacKay, "Lesser Nobility," 161; Collantes de Terán, *Sevilla*, 231; Gerbet, *Nobleza*, 69.

24. Major, *Renaissance Monarchy*, 69–73; Perroy, "Social Mobility," 27; Heal and Holmes, *Gentry*, 11–15.

25. Pescador del Hoyo, "Caballería popular." By the late medieval period, especially in Andalusia, Murcia, and Extremadura, the requirements to maintain knighthood became obligatory and had ceased to provide significant if any beneficial privileges for the caballeros de cuantía and caballeros de alarde. González Jiménez, "Caballería popular en Andalucía." While fifteenth- and sixteenth-century writers often distinguished between hidalgos and caballeros, they just as frequently conflated the two groups and used the terms interchangeably and even created hybrid designations such as *caballero hidalgo*.

26. Quintanilla Raso and Asenjo, "Hidalgos," 420; Collantes de Terán, *Sevilla*, 228, 231.

27. Ruth Pike noted that sixteenth-century writers used the terms *hidalgo* and *caballero* in a generic sense to denote anyone with noble lineage, but they just as regularly employed these terms to refer to people of influence, power, and wealth without scrutinizing their descent. *Aristocrats and Traders*, 27.

28. In his survey of social conflicts in the fifteenth century, Julio Valdeón Baruque described the efforts of hidalgos in support of the popular elements of their communities to resist señorial expansion. In particular, he cites the case of hidalgos in Trujillo opposing the transfer of lordship from the royal domain to Álvaro de Estuñiga, Count of Plasencia. During the same period hidalgos in Córdoba provided protection to converted Jews and their descendants during the violent riots of 1473. The brief descriptions of these events have led to speculation about the sources of conflict between ranks of the nobility and the shared interests or antagonisms that existed between the nobility (both titled aristocrats and hidalgos) and converted Jews. Valdeón Baruque, *Conflictos*, 171.

29. Although detailed studies of the members of Spanish expeditions have recognized the problems with the use of the term *hidalgo* and claims to this identity, general studies continue to explain the motivation of these men in terms of their social status. Lockhart, *Men of Cajamarca*, 31, 32.

30. Castro, *Realidad histórica de España*, 266.

31. Bitton, *French Nobility in Crisis*; Stone, *Crisis of the Aristocracy*; Jago, "Crisis of the Aristocracy."

32. Dewald, *European Nobility*, xiv.

33. Ibid., 5.

34. Burke, *What Is Cultural History?*, 74–76.

35. Stedman Jones, *Languages of Class*; Cornfield, *Language, History, and Class*; Vernon, "Linguistic Turn"; Joyce, "End of Social History."

36. Thompson, "Neo-noble Nobility"; Altman, *Emigrants and Society*, 44–69.

37. Davis, *Fiction in the Archives*; Fenster and Smail, *Fama*; Martínez, *Genealogical Fictions*.

38. Nader, *Liberty in Absolutist Spain*; Owens, *Absolute Royal Authority*; R. MacKay, *Limits of Royal Authority*.

39. Thompson, "Crown and Cortes"; Jago, "Habsburg Absolutism"; Fortea Pérez, *Monarquía y cortes*. Domínguez Ortiz provides the older perspective of a passive Cortes, which, after the Comunero Revolt, willingly accepted the Crown's demands for subsidies. *Crisis y decadencia*.

40. Thompson, "Castile," 79; Jago, "Habsburg Absolutism," 310–12, 317.

41. Nader, *Liberty in Absolutist Spain*, 2–4, 7–9; Owens, *Absolute Royal Authority*, 4, 15. Particularly, Ruth MacKay notes contemporary expectations that "a just law must not only be given by a just ruler; it must also respond to the common good, *el bien común*." *Limits of Royal Authority*, 24.

42. R. MacKay, *Limits of Royal Authority*, 59.

43. For a discussion of this organization, see Nader, *Liberty in Absolutist Spain*, 8, 9; and Owens, *Absolute Royal Authority*, 29–31.

44. Gerbet, "Guerres."

45. Collantes de Terán, *Sevilla*, 223; Romero Romero, *Sevilla y los pedidos*, 19; Ulloa, *Hacienda real*, 468, 472.

46. Cadenas y Vicent, "Como se solventaban," 534–37; Fayard and Gerbet, "Fermeture de la noblesse," 52–55.

Chapter 1

1. For treatment of these conflicts, see Azcona, *Isabel la católica*; Liss, *Isabel the Queen*; W. Phillips, *Enrique IV*; Suárez Fernández, *Nobleza y monarquía*; and Valdeón Baruque, *Trastámaras*, 191–220.

2. Danvila y Collada, *Cortes* (hereafter cited as *CLC*), 3:864.

3. W. Phillips, *Enrique IV*, 63–79, 97–120; Valdeón Baruque, *Trastámaras*, 191–220; Liss, *Isabel the Queen*, 40–50.

4. For the claims made in the Cortes, see *CLC*, 3:839; for the surviving documents authorizing status, see AGS, MP, leg. 393.

5. *CLC*, 3:863.

6. For a discussion of the geographic distribution of royal authorizations, see Gerbet, "Guerres," 321, 324. Amalia Prieto Cantero's catalog of royal grants during the reign of the Catholic Monarchs, "Documentos referentes a hidalguías," reveals the widespread nature of this phenomenon and provides an indispensable guide for research.

7. The surviving sources for Seville make the city and its subject municipalities an ideal case for the examination of disputes over hidalgo status during the late fifteenth century. In addition to Crown documents surviving in the Sección de Mercedes y Privilegios of the Archivo General de Simancas, the city council of Seville kept a meticulous record of its official correspondence with the Catholic Monarchs. Carande and Carriazo, *Tumbo*.

8. Gerbet, *Nobleza*, 47; Gerbet, "Guerres"; A. MacKay, "Lesser Nobility," 176n16; Olivera Serrano, *Cortes de Castilla*, 132; Cadenas y Vicent, "Valor de los mercedes."

9. For the evolution of taxation in Castile, see Ladero Quesada, *Hacienda real* (1967), 15–17; and *Siglo XV*, 13–113.

10. For a detailed description of the overlapping of royal and municipal taxes in the city of Seville, see Romero Romero, *Sevilla y los pedidos*, 15–24.

11. AGS, MP, leg. 393, doc. 2.

12. In 1371, only a few years after his usurpation of the throne, Enrique II provided a criterion for determining the status of hidalgos at the Cortes of Toro. He did so in response

to complaints about disputes over status and letters issued by the royal court itself. Similarly, Juan I in 1379 issued a law nullifying his own knighting of pecheros. Díaz de Montalvo, *Ordenanzas reales*, 4.1.4, 11; 4.2.2, 6.

13. Enríquez del Castillo, *Crónica de Enrique IV*, 248–50; Layna Serrano, *Historia de Guadalajara*, 2:29, 30; W. Phillips, *Enrique IV*, 101, 102.

14. These favors included incomes from royal annuities, jurisdiction over communities alienated from the royal domain, offices in the royal government and on municipal councils, and grants of hidalguía. *CLC*, 3:777.

15. Azcona, *Isabel la católica*, 140–53; Olivera Serrano, *Cortes de Castilla*, 119–52.

16. Olivera Serrano, *Cortes de Castilla*, xii–xiv, xvi.

17. *CLC*, 3:783–84.

18. Ibid., 3:840, 863, 864.

19. Iglesia Ferreirós, *Creación del derecho*, 2:13, 39–42.

20. The authors of the *Siete partidas* provided a description of this legal diversity in their own treatment of thirteenth-century Castilian law (1.1.12, 17, 18). For modern treatments, see García-Gallo, *Manual de historia*, 1:387; Iglesia Ferreirós, *Creación del derecho*, 2:35, 355–56; and Van Kleffens, *Hispanic Law*, 120–35.

21. For references to the *Partidas*, see Gerbet, *Nobleza*, 45; A. MacKay, "Lesser Nobility," 161; and Márquez de la Plata and Valero de Bernabé, *Nobiliaria española*, 11.

22. Van Kleffens, *Hispanic Law*, 217–23; cf. Kagan, *Lawsuits and Litigants*, 25.

23. Iglesia Ferreirós, *Creación del derecho*, 2:35–36.

24. Almost every scholarly study of the Castilian nobility or hidalgos makes reference to this and related passages in the *Siete partidas* as the authoritative source for the meaning of the term as a racial nobility of blood: "fidalguía es nobleza que viene a los omes por manera de linage" (2.21.2–3). Gerbet, *Nobleza*, 45–46; A. MacKay, "Lesser Nobility," 162; Márquez de la Plata and Valero de Bernabé, *Nobiliaria española*, 11, 226; Marqués de Siete Iglesias, "Hidalgo y el caballero."

25. González Alonso, *Fuero viejo*, 1.1.3, 3.4.2, pp. 14–15, 27.

26. Ibid., 1.3.1.

27. Carlé, *Concejo*, 81–87; Keniston, *Fuero de Guadalajara*, 8; Múñoz y Romero, *Colección de fueros*, 179, 309.

28. Domínguez Ortiz, *Clases privilegiadas*, 32, 169–70; Díaz de Durana, *Otra nobleza*, 85–112.

29. Alfonso X granted Burgos an exemption from contributions to the servicio, which it maintained through the Trastamara period and the reign of Carlos I. Felipe II also recognized the privilege but required that it be reconfirmed every three years when it was due. The privilege applied to the citizens of the city itself and not the towns and villages under its jurisdiction. Hiltpold, "Noble Status," 31; Ulloa, *Hacienda real*, 407, 468–70.

30. Romero Romero, *Sevilla y los pedidos*, 19–20; Collantes de Terán, *Sevilla*, 223; Carrilero Martínez, *Reyes Católicos*, 123.

31. Gerbet, "Population noble"; Domínguez Ortiz, *Clases privilegiadas*, 26, 27.

32. An ordinance of 1286 stipulated that there should be twenty-four city councilmen, twelve caballeros, and twelve *omes buenos* (good men). Kirschberg Schenck and Fernández Gómez, *Concejo de Sevilla*, 45–47, 52, 57. When Pedro I reconfirmed the city's ordinances in 1351, the document introduced new designations specifying that the council should be composed of twelve fijosdalgo and twelve ciudadanos. García Fernández, *Reino de Sevilla*, 138. By the end of the fifteenth century, royal correspondence to the city of Seville regularly addressed the councilmen as caballeros hijosdalgo.

33. Díaz de Montalvo, *Ordenanzas reales*, 4.2.3–4.

34. Juan II enacted a law at the Cortes of Valladolid in 1417 denying tax exemptions to those caballeros who failed to attend musters and maintain proper arms. Ibid., 2.1.6, 9.

35. Cadenas y Vicent, "Como se solventaban," 538; *Nueva Recopilación*, 2, 11, 3.

36. Cadenas y Vicent, "Como se solventaban," 534–37; Fayard and Gerbet, "Fermeture de la noblesse." In contrast, the procedures governing these suits in the fourteenth and fifteenth centuries remained hazy. Pérez de la Canal, "Justicia," 401–3.

37. Díaz de Montalvo, *Ordenanzas reales*, 4.2.7.

38. AGS, MP, leg. 393, doc. 89.

39. Willard, "Concept of True Nobility," 34–39.

40. Rodríguez Velasco, *Debate sobre la caballería*.

41. Penna, *Prosistas castellanos*, c, ci.

42. Valera, *Espejo de verdadera nobleza*, 105.

43. Ibid., quoted in MacKay, "Lesser Nobility," 163.

44. Ibid. (author's translation).

45. AGS, MP, leg. 393, doc. 419.

46. AGS, MP, leg. 393, doc. 8.

47. *CLC*, 4:58; AGS, MP, leg. 393, doc. 6.

48. *CLC*, 4:58.

49. This edict copied almost to the word a law enacted by Isabel's great-grandfather, Juan I, in 1379. Whereas Juan had specified these requirements for the caballeros he had knighted, Isabel applied them to the hidalgos she and her half brother, Enrique, had created and confirmed. *CLC*, 4:59.

50. AGS, MP, leg. 393, doc. 59.

51. AGS, MP, leg. 393, docs. 66, 75, 81, 101, 102, 109, 110, 111, 116, 122, 133, 138, 142, 160; Carande and Carriazo, *Tumbo*, 1:258; 2:99, 2:115; 2:396.

52. Carande and Carriazo, *Tumbo*, 2:544–45; Liss, *Isabel the Queen*, 228.

53. For a brief description of the siege of Baza and the sacrifices Isabel made and required of her subjects to maintain the siege, see Liss, *Isabel the Queen*, 252–53.

54. Carande and Carriazo, *Tumbo*, 3:9, 10.

55. Cadenas y Vicent, "Como se solventaban," 540–44.

56. AGS, MP, leg. 393, docs. 65, 109, 111, 112, 116, 174, 419.

57. Prieto Cantero, "Documentos referentes a hidalguías"; Carande and Carriazo, *Tumbo*.

58. AGS, MP, leg. 393, docs. 543, 544.

59. AGS, MP, leg. 393, docs. 112, 116, 142, 284, 285, 392, 418.

60. Carande and Carriazo, *Tumbo*, 1:258.

61. "Pero si contra esto que dicho es alguna cosa quisieredes dezir e alegar en guarda de vuestro derecho porque lo asi non devades fazer e conplir por quanto vosotros dis que soys conçejo e todos unos e parte en el fecho e alla non podrian con vosotros alcançar conplimiento de justicia." Carande and Carriazo, *Tumbo*, 1:259, 3:95, 4:12, 4:66.

62. Cadenas y Vicent, "Valor de los mercedes."

63. The scribes variably designated "the privileges and liberties held by other hidalgos of their kingdoms" or specified the privileges hidalgos held in the given municipality. AGS, MP, leg. 393, doc. 182; Carande and Carriazo, *Tumbo*, 4:66, 155; Carrilero Martínez, *Reyes Católicos*, 121.

64. Using a chancery document produced sometime after 1592, Marie-Claude Gerbet sought to quantify the number of grants provided by Enrique IV and his successors. The source provides radical summaries of earlier chancery documents issued during the reigns of Enrique IV, Isabel and Fernando, and Carlos I. From the references in the document, she distinguishes between concessions (first-time grants of status) and confirmations of status.

Significantly, the individual entries in the document itself never refer to "concessions" but instead refer to letters, favors, and privileges (*cartas*, *mercedes*, and *privilegios*), and none of these terms necessarily implies a first-time grant. Considering the evidence without the assumption that some necessarily had to be first-time grants, there is no obvious distinction between concessions and confirmations, and this distinction is potentially erroneous. Gerbet, "Guerres."

65. Carande and Carriazo, *Tumbo*, 2:100.

66. Through the late medieval and early modern periods, monarchs in western Europe appealed to absolutist legal theory to justify royal expedients that broke the general or common law. In practice monarchs exercised their absolutist prerogative "when they wanted to violate the common law in a specific instance without contravening its principle." Nader, *Liberty in Absolutist Spain*, 80–81; Sánchez Agesta, "Poderío real absoluto," 439–60.

67. "Enbargante qualquier ley o prematica sancion que disen que non se den cartas de fidalguia a ninguna persona, e sy se dieren que non valgan." Carande and Carriazo, *Tumbo*, 2:100–101.

68. AGS, MP, leg. 393, doc. 112.

69. Carande and Carriazo, *Tumbo*, 4:169.

70. Liss, *Isabel the Queen*, 228.

71. AGS, MP, leg. 393, docs. 116, 118.

72. Carande and Carriazo, *Tumbo*, 4:154, 155.

73. Ibid., 3:307–8.

74. AGS, MP, leg. 393, doc. 347.

75. Carande and Carriazo, *Tumbo*, 4:52.

76. Ruiz, *Spanish Society*, 93, 108.

Chapter 2

1. Sánchez Saus, "Sevillian Medieval Nobility," 377, 378; *Élites políticas*, 151, 152.

2. Peraza, *Historia de Sevilla*, 65, 67.

3. The number of towns and villages fluctuated as new communities developed and others occasionally were alienated from Seville's jurisdiction. For a list of these municipalities, see Ladero Quesada, *Ciudad medieval*, 73–78; and Morales Padrón, *Ciudad del quinientos*, 211.

4. Ladero Quesada, *Ciudad medieval*, 161–70; Morales Padrón, *Ciudad del quinientos*, 211–21; Kirschberg Schenck and Fernández Gómez, *Concejo de Sevilla*.

5. For comparative descriptions of other municipal councils in the Crown of Castile, see Altman, *Emigrants and Society*, 33–34; Edwards, *Christian Córdoba*, 24–43; Guerrero Mayllo, *Gobierno municipal de Madrid*; Jara Fuente, *Concejo, poder, y élites*, 92–100; and C. Phillips, *Ciudad Real*.

6. Garriga, *Audiencia*, 147.

7. ARCG, H.

8. Additionally, both archives possess records of cases without final rulings or final rulings without preliminary documents. The loss of relevant sources makes a strict statistical study impossible, but the extant data suggests significant trends and patterns in the numbers of sixteenth-century lawsuits.

9. Díaz de Noriega y Pubal, *Blanca de la carne*, 25; Morales Padrón, *Ciudad del quinientos*, 68.

10. Edwards, *Christian Córdoba*, 60–62; Ladero Quesada, *Hacienda real* (1973), 21–32.

11. Edwards, *Christian Córdoba*, 58, 59, 66; Ladero Quesada, *Siglo XV*, 63.

12. After 1495 the cities and larger towns throughout Castile began to take charge of paying the incomes due from alcabalas in their communities, which tax farmers had traditionally collected. The municipalities paid the revenues owed to the Crown for these diverse sales taxes in one lump sum, in a procedure referred to as encabezamiento (Edwards, *Christian Córdoba*, 69). For a review of the difference between *arrendamiento* and the process of encabezamiento as it became regularized in the sixteenth century, see Nader, *Liberty in Absolutist Spain*, 195.

13. "En cada libra de carne se paga una blanca mas del precio que vale y esta blanca la pagan todos generalmente ansy hidalgos como pecheros e clerigos e al fin del año por mando de la cibdad se buelve la dicha blanca a todo lo que en ella an pagado a los fijosdalgo clerigos e religiosos e otras personas que por qualquyer otro previllego son libres de pechar e contribuyr en los pechos de pecheros" (AMS, sec. 1, carp. 37, num. 35, fol. 18).

14. Ortiz de Zúñiga, *Anales eclesiasticos*, 3:290, 291.

15. Díaz de Noriega y Pubal, *Blanca de la carne*, 21, 22.

16. In 1429, revenues from alcabalas supplied the royal treasury with 75 percent of its income. Ladero Quesada, *Siglo XV*, 45–47, 57.

17. For a full review of the types of goods taxed in Ciudad Real in the sixteenth century, see C. Phillips, *Ciudad Real*, 84.

18. Ibid. For the continued use of excise taxes on meat to pay municipal obligations, especially for military levies, see R. MacKay, *Limits of Royal Authority*, 66, 70, 72.

19. Edwards, *Christian Córdoba*, 70, 74, 75; Ladero Quesada, *Hacienda real* (2009), 61.

20. Nader, *Liberty in Absolutist Spain*, 56.

21. Collantes de Terán, *Sevilla*, 27, 223. The original fuero given to the city in 1250 makes no mention of the pecho, but states that all citizens and residents were required to pay the tithes on olive oil production and fig cultivation. Guichot y Parody, *Historia*, 1:29. For evidence that the hidalgos and caballeros in Andalusia contributed monies for the hermandad established by the Catholic Monarchs, see the summary of royal incomes ordered by Isabel in 1503. AGS, Diversos de Castilla, lib. 3, fol. 85, included in Azcona, *Isabel la católica*, 755.

22. Surviving sources provide contradictory pronouncements and have muddled the question of whether or not caballeros or hidalgos contributed in Seville's royal or council taxes. During the fifteenth century, generic royal letters sent to the cities of Castile notifying the respective councils of their share of the servicio often contained the formulaic statement that all citizens and residents should contribute in the tax except knights, squires, noble ladies, maidens, and hijosdalgo. Despite such letters, the tax records of the city of Seville for this period contained directives to the contrary, directing officials that "the masters of the military orders, counts, magnates, knights, squires, and hidalgos and all the other laymen should pay this tax according to the charter of the city." More conclusively, the accounts of the city's treasurers provide the amounts these individuals paid. Romero Romero, *Sevilla y los pedidos*, 19, 20.

23. *CLC*, 3:633. Disposición 42 from the 1451 Cortes of Valladolid, cited in Quintanilla Raso and Asenjo, "Hidalgos," 424.

24. Ibid., 424.

25. Collantes de Terán, *Sevilla*, 23.

26. Romero Romero, *Sevilla y los pedidos*, 37, 38.

27. Collantes de Terán, *Sevilla*, 23.

28. Romero stated that in most cases the direct estimation of the amount owed resulted in a quantity greater than the maximum established by the system of cuantías. Members of the council generated special padrones for the amounts owed by the regional aristocracy who

lived in Seville and the city's dominant families, who typically held the highest offices on the council. The padrones for the *ricos hombres* (magnates) and regidores survive for the years 1432, 1442, and 1445. Romero Romero, *Sevilla y los pedidos*, 71.

29. Juan II awarded Juan Alonso de Guzmán the title of Duke of Medina Sidonia in 1445. Pedro Ponce de León's famous grandson Rodrigo became the first Marquis of Cádiz in 1471. Sánchez Saus, *Caballería y linaje*, 215, 216, 349–51.

30. Collantes de Terán, *Sevilla*, 233–52; Romero Romero, *Sevilla y los pedidos*, 20.

31. Romero Romero, *Sevilla y los pedidos*, 15, 16.

32. Nader, *Liberty in Absolutist Spain*, 194, 195.

33. Collantes de Terán, "Mercados de abasto," 60–65.

34. Quintanilla Raso and Asenjo, "Hidalgos," 432.

35. Ibid., 431.

36. Pescador del Hoyo, "Caballería popular"; González Jiménez, "Caballería popular en Andalucía"; Powers, "Two Warrior-Kings"; A. MacKay, "Lesser Nobility," 160–61.

37. Edwards, *Christian Córdoba*, 143, 68.

38. Quintanilla Raso and Asenjo, "Hidalgos," 431. For a description of the factional divisions in Córdoba in the last quarter of the fifteenth century, see Edwards, *Christian Córdoba*, 148–53.

39. Edwards, *Christian Córdoba*, 21, 29, 30.

40. Quintanilla Raso and Asenjo, "Hidalgos," 431.

41. Edwards, *Christian Córdoba*, 141.

42. Porras Arboledas, *Ciudad de Jaén*, 21, 22.

43. AMS, sec. 1, carp. 175, doc. 48.

44. Of these four, three were members of seigneurial families and one was Don Juan de Silva, Count of Cifuentes, the asistente for the city, who received 1,394 maravedís. AMS, sec. 1, carp. 175, doc. 48. In the 1577 return only three individuals received more than 1,000 maravedís. AMS, sec. 3, tomo 4, doc. 1, fols. 22, 23.

45. The 1542 account of the blanca de la carne recorded a return of 11,000 maravedís to the Count of Gelves, Álvaro Colón y de Portugal, Christopher Columbus's great-grandson, but gave more modest amounts—250, 600, 1,700, 170, 700, 700, 600, 800, 1,800, 1,000, and so on—for those listed as hidalgos. AMS, sec. 1, carp. 178, doc. 95.

46. AMS, sec. 3, tomo 4, doc. 1, fols. 22, 23. The information in this document appears to be limited to the refunds for the parishes of San Esteban, San Lorenzo, Omnium Sanctorum, Santa Catalina, and San Roman.

47. AMS, sec. 3, tomo 4, doc. 4.

48. Nader, "Noble Income," 413, 426.; Ulloa, *Rentas*.

49. Hamilton, *American Treasure*, 393–401.

50. Ladero Quesada, *Ciudad medieval*, 129.

51. AMS, sec. 3, tomo 8, doc. 32, fol. 199.

52. Morales Padrón, *Ciudad del quinientos*, 239.

53. AMS, sec. 1, carp. 178, doc. 95, fol. 10.

54. AMS, sec. 3, tomo 4, doc. 1, fol. 7.

55. For a presentation of royal incomes (*rentas*) for the Crown of Castile by region and major municipality from 1429 to 1504 for alcabalas and tercias, see Ladero Quesada, *Hacienda real* (2009), 395–400.

56. Morales Padrón, *Ciudad del quinientos*, 233; Ulloa, *Hacienda real*, 283.

57. Morales Padrón, *Ciudad del quinientos*, 238–39. For a full list of the commodities taxed in Ciudad Real, see C. Phillips, *Ciudad Real*, 84.

58. Morales Padrón, *Ciudad del quinientos*, 239.

59. AMS, sec. 1, carp. 116, num. 69.

60. Ortiz de Zúñiga, *Anales eclesiasticos*.

61. AMS, sec. 3, carp. 10, doc. 7, fol. 13v.

62. Morales Padrón, *Ciudad del quinientos*, 68.

63. Isabel and Fernando authorized a compilation of the city's ordinances in 1502. The city began the collection and ordering of these laws in 1515 and finished the task in 1519. The finished collection included a number of rules originating from letters issued both by the Catholic Monarchs and by Juana I during these years. Guichot y Parody, *Historia*, 1:301n1.

64. Ibid., 1:27. The fuero did not provide a description of the city government, and scholars have speculated on and debated the nature of the city's earliest political institutions. Kirschberg Schenck and Fernández Gómez, *Concejo de Sevilla*, 21–25.

65. Kirschberg Schenck and Fernández Gómez, *Concejo de Sevilla*, 31; García Fernández, *Reino de Sevilla*, 133–36.

66. Edwards, *Christian Córdoba*, 143.

67. García Fernández, *Reino de Sevilla*, 138.

68. Ladero Quesada, *Ciudad medieval*, 133–36, 166; Sánchez Saus, "Sevillian Medieval Nobility."

69. Collantes de Terán, *Sevilla*; Sánchez Saus, *Caballería y linaje*. Sánchez Saus has pointed out the permeability that existed between caballeros de cuantía or caballeros ciudadanos and caballeros hidalgos. "Sevillian Medieval Nobility," 370.

70. García Fernández maintains that Pedro issued this letter to settle internal tensions in the oligarchy by providing equal seats to hidalgos and ciudadanos: "e que sea doze fijos dalgos e doze cibdadanos segun que lo husaron fasta aquy." Conversely, this may have been part of an effort to reduce the number of councilmen, an issue that concerned city and monarch through the medieval period. In either case, the order appeals to the way things had always been and served as a future precedent for how things should be. *Reino de Sevilla*, 138.

71. Some scholars have read this regulation and similar ones issued by Pedro's predecessor Alfonso IX as royal support for more noble control of the cities and towns in Andalusia. Kirschberg Schenck and Fernández Gómez, *Concejo de Sevilla*, 60–72.

72. Quintanilla Raso and Asenjo, "Hidalgos," 420.

73. Ladero Quesada, *Ciudad medieval*, 166.

74. A later ordinance recorded that during the reign of Juan II, it came to the king's knowledge that the city was appointing two hidalgos for the position in violation of the letter of Alfonso XI. Juan II consequently ordered the council to appoint a ciudadano to the office. Guichot y Parody, *Historia*, 349.

75. Kirschberg Schenck and Fernández Gómez, *Concejo de Sevilla*, 242–46, 254.

76. Juan II's original Spanish reads, "Un vecino abonado cuantioso." Guichot y Parody, *Historia*, 1:330, 333.

77. Ladero Quesada, *Ciudad medieval*, 172.

78. The letter was composed by Juana's secretary, Miguel Pérez de Almaçan, on May 19 and was signed in the presence of her father, Fernando, the governing regent: "Mando e defiendo que de aquí adelante no sean probeydos para los dichos officios de jurados e alguaziles de la dicha ciudad nynguna persona que sea pecheros salvo a personas que sean exsentas de los dichos pechos no enbargante que los dichos officos vaquen por muerte o rrenunciación o patrusque o permutación o en otra qualquier manera e si alguno de los dichos pecheros fuere probeydo para alguno delos tales officios mando que no sean rescevidos e que la tal eleción sea en si nynguna e de ningun valor y efecto." AMS, sec. 1, carp. 25, doc. 252, fol. 5. See Morales Padrón, *Ciudad del quinientos*, 212.

79. Guichot y Parody, *Historia*, 1:308.

80. "Por cuanto somos informados que la ciudad de Sevilla, no pudiendolo hacer, exenta y exime a muchos oficiales y otras personas, de pechos y servicios; y lo que aquellos habían de satisfacer carga sobre las viudas y huerfanos y otras personas miserables, lo cual es en perjuicio de la ciudad: Por ende, ordenamos y mandamos, que de aquí en adelante la ciudad no pueda dar exenciónes y libertades de ningunos pechos reales, ni concejales, ni mixtos; salvo aquellos que de derecho se deben dar: y si las dieren de hecho, mandamos que no valgan: y, sin embargo de ello, aquellos a quienes dieren las dichas exenciónes, pechen y contribuyan como los otros vecinos de la Ciudad. Y mandamos a los jurados de la ciudad, que no obstante tales exenciónes los empadronen y los hagan pechar" (Guichot y Parody, *Historia*, 1:308).

81. AMS, sec. 1, carp. 25, doc. 252, fol. 5. In the resulting city ordinances the section treating the alguaciles of the city ends with the statement that henceforth each parish should elect hidalgos for the office. Guichot y Parody, *Historia*, 337.

82. The second letter was issued on July 20, 1515, again in Juana's name, and signed by Fernando and the secretary Pedro de Quintana in the presence of Chancellor Castañeda. AMS, sec. 1, carp. 25, doc. 252, fol. 6.

83. "Y me fue suplicado cerca dello mandase proveer mandamyento que de aquí adelante no fuesen proveyidos de los dichos officios nynguno dellos dichos pecheros salvo personas hijosdalgo notorios porque desta manera se excusar a el dicho daño" (ibid.).

84. See note 78. For examples of royal mercedes granting permission to transfer council office, see the dozens preserved in the correspondence between the city of Seville and the Catholic Monarchs for the 1480s and 1490s, such as the authorization to convey the office of veinticuatro from Ruy Gómez de Ayala to his son Juan Ayala in 1489. Carande and Carriazo, *Tumbo*, 4:361.

85. "E si alguno de los dichos pecheros fuere probeydo para alguno delos tales officios mando que no sean rescevidos e que la tal eleción sea en si nynguna e de ningun valor y efecto e que declaro para que yo pueda proveer del dicho officio a personas esenta de los dichos pechos" (AMS, sec. 1, carp. 25, doc. 252).

86. AMS, sec. 1, carp. 175, doc. 48.

87. The family names listed in the record that included a council officer and another recipient without a stated reason for the return (such as hidalgo status) included Alcázar, Anosco, Briones, Cataño, Esquivel, Esteban, Fernández Marmolejo, de la Fuente, Fuentes, Guzmán, Mesa, Morales, Ortiz, Osorio, Pinelo, Pérez, Ramos Saavedra, and Vergara. Not all the city officials appeared in this record, but members of their family, or at least individuals sharing their name, were listed as receiving the refund, also without a stated reason. This group included the Alfaro, Melgarejo, Mexia, and Ribera (ibid.).

88. Morales Padrón, *Ciudad del quinientos*, 26, 27. In contrast to the 1515 account, the 1577 account is incomplete and lists only the returns for six of the city's jurados. AMS, sec. 3, tomo 4, doc. 1, fols. 7–21, 24.

89. Ortiz de Zúñiga, *Anales eclesiasticos*, 4:24.

90. Porras Arboledas, *Ciudad de Jaén*, 20, 74–76.

91. AMS, sec. 1, carp. 175, doc. 48.

92. Nader, *Power and Gender*, 3, 4, 13.

93. AMS, sec. 1, carp. 175, doc. 48. Sánchez Saus profiles ten of these families in his genealogical study of the principal caballero families of late medieval Seville, *Caballería y linaje*.

94. The clerk did not provide a reason for Doña Juana Mendoza's refund but did note that she was the mother of Pedro de Pineda. AMS, sec. 1, carp. 175, doc. 48.

95. *El poema de mio cid*, 210.

96. Quintanilla Raso and Asenjo, "Hidalgos," 423. The families included the Carranza, Cerezo, Cervantes, Esquivel, Gallegos, Medina, Montemolín, Ortiz, Quadros, and Santillán. Moreover, the claims of the Ortiz and Medina are questionable and possibly fabricated.

97. These numbers exclude many of the leading citizens and officeholders referred to specifically as caballeros hijosdalgo. Collantes de Terán, *Sevilla*, 231.

98. Sánchez Saus states that after the thirteenth century any professed link with the hidalgos of the city's conquest was no more than a genealogical fiction that all Seville's aristocracy aspired to whether or not such claims were well founded. "Sevillian Medieval Nobility," 368, 369.

99. Ibid., 377, 378.

Chapter 3

1. Technically the grant of privilege was made not only to Pedro Gonçalo de Caravajal but to him, his sons, his grandsons, and all his descendants: "Es que vos el dicho Pedro Gonçález Caravajal e vuestros hijos que ahora son o fueren de aquí adelante o nyetos o otros quales quieres decendientes de vuestra linaje e del dicho Pedro Gonçalo Caravajal vuestro padre seades y se an avidos por fijosdalgo notorios e de solar conocido e ayades e goçades . . . todas las honras e gracias e franquezas e esenciones e previllegios e libertades e preheminencias e ynmuydades . . . que gozan los otros omes fijosdalgo notorios" (ARCG, H, 4508–049).

2. Neither of these other lawsuits produced surviving verdicts, so it is impossible to know whether the claimants succeeded in gaining recognition of their status as hidalgos. ARCG, H, 5091–308, 4951–008.

3. Collantes de Terán, "Comerciantes y fianzas públicas," 317.

4. For a discussion of municipal citizenship and movement between municipalities, see Nader, *Liberty in Absolutist Spain*, 27–32; and Herzog, *Defining Nations*, 6–8, 17–19.

5. Richard Kagan has asserted that the principal reason for cases of hidalguía in the sixteenth century was the continuing geographic mobility of Castilians, especially the movement from the north to the south. *Lawsuits and Litigants*, 121.

6. Fayard and Gerbet, "Fermeture de la noblesse."

7. Ruiz, *Spanish Society*, 75–79. Hernando Alonso Chirino/Cherino, also known as Fernando Alonso de Guadalajara, held the office of regidor in Cuenca from 1421 until 1460, before passing it to his son Alonso de Cherino, who held the office until 1463. Jara Fuente provides a review of the city council of Cuenca in the fifteenth century, the office of regidor, and the relationship between council office and the status of hidalgo in the city. *Concejo, poder, y élites*, 99–113, 122–25. Jara Fuente also identifies the Guadalajara/Cherino family enjoying recognition of the status and privileges of hidalguía (355, 356, 423).

8. Altman, *Emigrants and Society*, 49–53.

9. Newberry Library, Ayer MS 1852.

10. Ibid., fols. 223–37.

11. "Lo otro porque en caso que los susodhos algun previlegxio tuviesen nunca lo avían mostrado ni usado del ni avía seydo obedecido ni conplido en la dicha villa y que sería de los previlexios rrebocados del dicho señor Rey Don Enrique mi tío del año de sesenta y quarto y que asi no les aprovechava ni valía derecho . . . e el previlegxio estava derogado por leyes e premáticas" (ibid., fols. 236–37).

12. Ibid., fols. 241–56v.

13. Ibid., fols. 263.

14. Pierson, *Commander of the Armada*, 30–34, 40.

15. "Filiación y linpieza de mi linaje y de la nobleza de mis padres y abuelos" (Newberry Library, Ayer MS 1852, fols. 264v–65).

16. For a discussion of efforts to substantiate or fabricate status as a means to secure offices or secure encomiendas, see McLeod, "Self-Promotion," 35.

17. McLeod, "Self-Promotion," 25–27; Restall, *Seven Myths*, 12–14. For a discussion of these relaciones as evidence of nobility and purity, see Martínez, *Genealogical Fictions*, 123.

18. "Porque soy caballero hijodalgo de padre e abuelos e no devo estar presso por deudas civiles y se me ha de guardar las libertades que a los tales cavalleros hijosdalgo se suelen e acostumbran guardar=pido e suplico a vuestra merced que . . . me mande soltar libremente de la dicha prición declarando dever yo gozar de las dichas libertades y exempciónes y no dever estar presso para lo qual y en la nesecario" (Newberry Library, Ayer MS 1825, fol. 3).

19. Ibid., fol. 51.

20. Ibid., fols. 34v, 35, 39.

21. Ibid., fol. 13. The edict Alonso complained about was either the order to implement the Leyes Nuevas of 1542 or a subsequent related edict. Burkholder and Johnson, *Colonial Latin America*, 138, 139.

22. Ladero Quesada, *Ciudad medieval*, 18; González, *Repartimiento*.

23. Ladero Quesada, *Ciudad medieval*, 157; Collantes de Terán, *Sevilla*, 212–18; Otte, *Sevilla y sus mercaderes*, 167–200.

24. Collantes de Terán, *Sevilla*, 213.

25. Pike, "Genoese in Seville," 349.

26. Collantes de Terán, *Sevilla*, 216.

27. Cristóbal de Grimaldo gained citizenship in 1483 and Flerigo Centurión in 1487. Ibid., 216.

28. Carande and Carriazo, *Tumbo*, 2:232, 233; 4:14.

29. Seville's city council records note Juan Cataño's presence on the council in 1473 and 1474, but it is not clear whether or when he renounced the office or to whom. Carande and Carriazo, *Tumbo*, 1:111.

30. Otte, *Sevilla y sus mercaderes*, 39.

31. Liss, *Isabel the Queen*, 251.

32. Pike, "Genoese in Seville," 351–53.

33. Pike, *Enterprise and Adventure*, 4.

34. ARCG, H, 5091–022.

35. ARCG, H, 5108–163, 4575–028.

36. Collantes de Terán, *Sevilla*, 227.

37. Pike, *Enterprise and Adventure*, 2, 147n8.

38. AMS, sec. 1, carp. 175, doc. 48.

39. Palenzuela Domínguez, "Mercaderes," 331–33, 344. Other prominent Burgalese merchants in early sixteenth-century Seville were the Santiago, Escalante, Gutiérrez, Astudillo, Jaymes, Medina, Villegas, Corona, Sandoval, Salinas, Ballasteros, Valmaseda, Najera, Castro, and Maluenda. Morales Padrón, *Ciudad del quinientos*, 75. Members of the Escalante family were repeatedly engaged in lawsuits over their hidalgo status with the city through the sixteenth century. ARCG, H, 4979–16, 4968–17, 185–19. In addition to the Escalante, the Gutierrez, Valmaseda, Salinas, and Astudillo have all left records of litigation for their hidalguía.

40. Palenzuela Domínguez, "Mercaderes," 335.

41. Pike, "Sevillian Nobility," 448, 449.

42. Palenzuela Domínguez, "Mercaderes," 348.

43. Pike, *Aristocrats and Traders*, 99, 100.

44. Palenzuela Domínguez, "Mercaderes," 334.

45. Ulloa, *Hacienda real*, 407, 468–69. In the lawsuit of hidalguía pursued by the converso councilman of Toledo, Pedro Franco, some of his fellow councilmen testified that all vecinos of Toledo were free and exempt from all taxes. Martz, *Network of Converso Families*, 277, 278.

46. Hiltpold, "Noble Status," 31.

47. Martz, *Network of Converso Families*, 184.

48. The order was issued August 8, 1515. AMS, sec. 10, caja 31, carp. 131, fol. 61v.

49. Ibid., fols. 3–4.

50. Ibid., fol. 28.

51. Pike, *Enterprise and Adventure*, 50, 52–54, 75.

52. "Vos hago naturales destos mys reynos de Castilla e de León" (AMS, sec. 10, caja 31, carp. 131, fols. 29, 29v, 30). The letter asserted the grant of naturalization regardless of any laws or edicts to the contrary, explicitly those issued by Isabel at the Cortes of Madrigal, and invoked Juana's "propio motu" to make the grant. Royal secretary Lope Conchillos signed the letter by order of King Fernando.

53. Pike, *Enterprise and Adventure*, 99, 100.

54. The witnesses were Bautista Centurión, Leonardo di Afascio, Andrea Doria, Gaspar de Spindola, Xpoval Mattuto, Pedro Gentyl, Nicolas Gentyl, and Juan Degracia. AMS, sec. 10, caja 31, carp. 131, fols. 31–44.

55. Ibid., fol. 46.

56. The final order was issued July 31, 1515. Ibid., fols. 54, 54v.

57. The following individuals of Italian origin or descent litigated at the chancery court for recognition of hidalgo status: Federico de Alborgo (1550), ARCG, H, 5090–190; Jeronimo de Italiano (1550, 1551), ARCG, H, 5090–166; Paris and Jeronimo Cataño (1550–55), ARCG, H, 5090–219, 4686–211, 5095–079; Jorge Negron (1550), ARCG, H, 5091–022; Luis de Spinola (1550), ARCG, H, 5090–158; Luis de Bocanegra López Lezcano (1571–76), ARCG, H, 5102–184, 5103–053, 4555–004; Luis Justiniano (1576), ARCG, H, 5104–232; Domingo de Corcuera (1579–83), ARCG, H, 5105–160, 4777–025, 4761–018, 4565–011; Sebastian Pinelo (1579), ARCG, H, 5105–158; Camilo Negron (1587–89), ARCG, H, 5108–163, 4575–028; Luis de Ricasoli (1587), ARCG, H, 5108–111; Augustin de Vivaldo (1590), ARCG, H, 4576–017.

58. Luis also had a company in 1549 with two other prominent merchant financiers, Cristóbal Centurión and Carlos Jufre de Lercaro. Not only was Luis a vecino of Seville, but so was his father. Pike, "Genoese in Seville," 366, 376, 377.

59. ARCG, H, 5090–158.

60. For a detailed review of the literature on universal Basque hidalguía, see Díaz de Durana, *Otra nobleza*, 51–76.

61. The first written version of the *Fuero viejo de Vizcaya* was produced in 1452 and a revised version was issued and confirmed in 1526. Collins, *Basques*, 263, 264.

62. Sarasola, *Vizcaya*, 57, 119–21. The most notable of these liberties was the practice of holding a general provincial assembly of representatives of the towns and villages of Vizcaya to recognize the new Lord of the Señorio of Vizcaya and to approve any changes or revisions to the territory's fueros. Collins, *Basques*, 256. Guipúzcoa developed similar practices and enjoyed similar liberties during this period.

63. Díaz de Durana, *Otra nobleza*, 61–63, 97–102, 105–12.

64. In towns that received the fuero of San Sebastian—one of the earliest charters and one that served as a model for later fueros—there are no references to hidalgos until the fourteenth century. In towns such as Rentería and Zumaya, the fueros (issued respectively in 1320 and 1347) made references to hidalgo citizens, but none established political or economic distinctions between vecinos. In contrast, in 1273 Alfonso X exempted hidalgo settlers of Vergara five years after it was founded, and his successors extended similar exemptions to

towns along the Navarrese border. Through the second half of the fourteenth century the petitions of municipal councils led to privileges from the Crown that either exempted all inhabitants or provided all inhabitants with the status of hidalgo. Ibid., 97–99.

65. Díaz de Durana notes that the document captures the culmination of a process, in which on one hand Basque hidalgos succeeded in maintaining their privileges, and on the other the document proclaimed the extension of hidalguía to the entire population of the lordship of Vizcaya. Ibid., 104, 105, 107–10.

66. The royal confirmation of the fuero stated that "cualquier hijo natural vizcayno, o sus dependientes, que estuviessen casados o avecindados habitants, o moradores fuera de esta tierra de Vizcaya en qualesquier partes, lugares, y provincias, de los reynos de España, mostrando, e probando ser naturales vizcaynos, hijos dependientes de ellos . . . , les valiesse la dicha hidalguía e les fuessen guardados los privilegios, franquezas, e libertades, que a home hijodalgo segun fuero de Espana, debian ser guardados enteramente." Poza, *Fuero de hidalguía*, xxiv, n. 74.

67. Carande and Carriazo, *Tumbo*, 5:106.

68. Collantes de Terán, "Comerciantes y fianzas públicas," 317; Ronquillo Rubio, *Vascos en Sevilla*.

69. AMS, sec. 3, tomo 4, doc. 4.

70. The following natives of the Basque provinces and citizens of Seville were involved in lawsuits of hidalguía with the city council of Seville in the decades immediately before and after the introduction of the blanca de la carne: Juan Pérez de Oyarazabal (1500), ARCG, 5210-001; Pedro de Larrinaga (1501), ARCG, 4901-002; Miguel Martín de Jauregui (1520, 1537), ARCG, 5106-153; Juan de la Rentería (1520-25), ARCG, 5074-134; Miguel Martínez de Jauregui (1525-37), ARCG, 4504-004; Bernardo de la Rentería (1529-36), ARCG, 4503-022; Pedro de Ysasaga (1523), ARCG, 4704-005; Antonio de Aguirre Vizcaíno (1533), ARCG, 4873-006; Fortún Avendaño Vizcaíno (1534), ARCG, 4502-011; Francisco de Zabala (1536-38), ARCG, 5091-242; Anton de Azoca (1536), ARCG, 5091-310; Juan López de Azoca (1536), ARCG, 5091-309; Esteban Vergara Martínez de Albisua (1536), ARCG, 4503-008; Juan Sánchez de Aramburu (1536), ARCG, 4504-038; Juan de Haro, (1537), ARCG, 4692-241; Juan Martínez de Balçola (1540), ARCG, 5087-014; Pedro de Urreta (1541), ARCG, 14527-018; Domingo de Lizarraras Artiga (1544-46), ARCG, 4511-012; and Francisco Ibáñez de Garagarza (1544, 1546), ARCG, 4742-003, 4511-032.

71. Díaz de Durana, *Otra nobleza*, 113–17.

72. AMS, sec. 1, carp. 176, doc. 71.

73. "ii. sy saben creen vieron oyeron decir y ello es notorio y dello pública boz e fama que la dicha casa e solar de Viquiça [Vequiça] que esta syta en la tierra llana e ynfançonadgo de Vizcaya es solar muy conoscido de cavalleros hijosdalgo e ynfancones senoría de vasallos fuera del dicho senorio de Vizcaya en la provincia de Alava y en otras partes cabeca de la proginje y naturaleza de los Avendaneses Ganboynos de Vizcaya Alaba y otras partes y que por tal es avido e thenido" (ibid.).

74. In addition to the questions used for these depositions, a 1503 summary of royal incomes alludes to the fees paid in Viscaya and Guipúzcoa from iron and steel, which in Guipúzcoa was the old tithe/tenth (*diezmo*) and in Trasmiera fifty sueldos. The report also mentions fees paid for the transport of goods in these provinces. Azcona, *Isabel la católica*, 754.

75. Ladero Quesada, *Hacienda real* (2009), 182, 184.

76. AMS, sec. 1, carp. 176, doc. 71.

77. AMS, sec. 3, tomo 8, doc. 32.

78. The responses of the witnesses verify that Pedro Ortiz had lived in Seville for at least sixteen years. The city refunded Ortiz 4,775 maravedís for the previous four and a half years,

suggesting that Ortiz had acquired citizenship only five years earlier. AMS, sec. 3, tomo 8, doc. 32.

79. Pike, *Linajudos and Conversos*.

80. The literature on Jews and conversos in medieval and early modern Spain is extensive. See, for example, Valdeón Baruque, *Judíos*; Baer, *History of the Jews*; Homza, *Spanish Inquisition*; Kamen, *Spanish Inquisition*; Netanyahu, *Origins of the Inquisition*; Domínguez Ortiz, *Clase social*; Roth, *Conversos*. For Seville, see Wagner, *Inquisición en Sevilla*; Gil, *Conversos*; and Pike, *Linajudos and Conversos*.

81. Quesada Ladero, *Historia de Sevilla*, 154; Collantes de Terán puts the number of Jewish households between 450 and 500, after the epidemics of the midcentury and before the riots of 1391. *Sevilla*, 209.

82. One beneficiary, Don Suleman (Soloman ibn Zadok de Toledo), received numerous valuable properties both in the city and in the countryside. Nevertheless, the majority of the twenty-seven Jews listed in the repartimiento received houses in the newly established Jewish quarter. Montes Romero-Camacho, "Anti-Judaismo," 86.

83. Collantes de Terán, *Sevilla*, 88, 89.

84. For a treatment of the conditions that contributed to the pogrom and its impact on Castile's Jewish community, see Mitre Fernández, *Judios*.

85. Ladero Quesada, *Ciudad medieval*, 154.

86. A. MacKay, "Popular Movements," 33, 35.

87. Ladero Quesada, *Ciudad medieval*, 155.

88. Montes Romero-Camacho, "Anti-Judaismo," 102, 112n130. Francisco's relative Alonso Fernández Melgarejo served as tax farmer of the almojarifazgo, obtained the office of jurado of the barrio de Génova, and even became a veinticuatro of the city and its contador mayor. Ibid.

89. Sánchez Saus, *Élites políticas*, 135, 136.

90. Ladero Quesada, *Ciudad medieval*, 132, 255. Collantes de Terán mentions these families and adds the Fernández Marmolejo and Martínez Medina, noting that Alfonso Fernández Marmolejo was a veinticuatro by 1384. *Sevilla*, 229.

91. A branch of the caballero family of the Esquivels was either converso or married converso families. Other notable converso families that rose into the ranks of the city's caballeros were the Medina and the Alcázar. There were multiple related and unrelated Medina families in Seville's elite. See Sánchez Saus, *Caballería y linaje*, 174.

92. The conversos Tomás de Jaén and Alemán Pocasangre held the positions of mayordomos of the city's rents in the 1470s and lost their positions at the instigation of the royal asistente immediately prior to the establishment of the Inquisition tribunal. Gil, *Conversos*, 1:42. For the violence against conversos and Jews in the fifteenth century, see A. MacKay, "Popular Movements," 33–35, 58–62.

93. Morales Padrón, *Ciudad del quinientos*, 96; Montes Romero-Camacho, "Anti-Judaismo," 149–51.

94. Ladero Quesada, *Ciudad medieval*, 235.

95. Gil, *Conversos*, 53, 54.

96. Collantes de Terán, *Sevilla*, 229.

97. Gil, *Conversos*, 67, 68.

98. Ladero Quesada, *Ciudad medieval*, 236.

99. Some of the more significant families listed in the *composiciones* were the Alcázar, Alemán, Baena, Bernal, Cazala, Franco, Las Casas, Roelas, Luque, Morcillo, Ortiz, Palma, Santaella, and Sisbón. Morales Padrón, *Ciudad del quinientos*, 97. For a detailed comparative

treatment of converso families in sixteenth-century Toledo, see Martz, *Network of Converso Families*.

100. Morales Padrón, *Ciudad del quinientos*, 97.

101. AMS, sec. 1, carp. 175, doc. 48. Some of these men were among those identified as conversos by the comunero rebels.

102. The four members of the Torres clan who received refunds were Tomas de Torres, Francisco de Torres, Catalina de Torres, the widow of Cristóbal de Espeso, and Gonzalo de Torres. Ibid.

103. ARCG, H. In addition to the Fernández Marmolejo there are surviving records for a lawsuit involving the Roelas family in 1554, descendants of the Aleman family in 1578 and 1580, and descendants of the Francos de Ríos.

104. ARCG, H, 4559-31, 4568-2.

105. ARCG, H, 4537-006.

106. Juan Nuñez de Illescas was also litigating against the town of Castillejo del Campo, and Francisco Nuñez de Illescas was in a suit against the town of Carmona. The surviving documents include the initial announcements of a complaint but neither the testimony presented nor the final ruling. ARCG, H, 5101-219.

107. ARCG, H.

Chapter 4

1. The formulaic legal phrase to express this notion of status was "hidalguía en propiedad y posesión" and was in use by at least the fifteenth century in royal pragmáticas. Cadenas y Vicent, "Como se solventaban," 540.

2. The earliest extant document of a lawsuit of hidalguía in the chancery archive of Valladolid dates from 1395. But references to judicial rulings on cases of hidalguía exist in edicts issued by Alfonso XI as early as 1334. A. MacKay, "Lesser Nobility," 161, 162.

3. Beginning in the late 1550s, the royal government sold letters granting the right of hidalguía to interested buyers. Thompson, "Purchase of Nobility," 339.

4. Like Thompson's estimate of the total number of lawsuits for the sixteenth and seventeenth centuries, this figure is probably low because it includes only the number of lawsuits preserved at the chancery archive in Granada and not those in Seville's municipal archive. ARCG, H.

5. Gerbet, *Nobleza*, 40; Fayard and Gerbet, "Fermeture de la noblesse," 60, 61.

6. Domínguez Ortiz, *Clases privilegiadas*, 34.

7. Ulloa, *Hacienda real*, 468.

8. For a treatment of how the Crown presented and justified hidalguía outside of court in the letters accompanying the purchased titles of hidalgo status between 1552 and 1700, see Thompson, "Neo-noble Nobility," 380, 381.

9. Martínez, *Genealogical Fictions*, 1, 19, 42, 44–49.

10. The chapter's description of the procedures followed in lawsuits of hidalguía draws not only from Sánchez Paneque's case but also from the dozens of other cases referenced throughout the chapter, the summary of similar suits from the municipalities of Extremadura described by Janine Fayard and Marie-Claude Gerbet, and seventeenth-century guides for court clerks. For Sánchez, see AMS, sec. 1, carp. 37, doc. 35; and Fayard and Gerbet, "Fermeture de la noblesse," 52–55. These procedures conform with the more thoroughly elaborated ones employed in the seventeenth century. González de Torneo, *Practica de escrivanos*, 12–14, 135–44.

11. Owens, *Absolute Royal Authority*, 9, 10.

12. The amount of time dictated by the court could vary considerably. In the case of Pedro Sánchez Paneque, the court provided eighty- and ninety-day deadlines and extended these deadlines on multiple occasions. AMS, sec. 1, carp. 37, doc. 35.

13. Pérez de la Canal, "Justicia," 438.

14. Fayard and Gerbet, "Fermeture de la noblesse," 58.

15. Romero Romero, *Sevilla y los pedidos*, 85, 88, 89.

16. AMS, sec. 1, carp. 37, doc. 35, fols. 1, 61.

17. Ibid., fols. 7, 12.

18. None of the letters bothered to provide any statement that the recipient was unconnected to "vile and mechanical arts." Thompson, "Neo-noble Nobility," 386.

19. AMS, sec. 1, carp. 37, doc. 35, fol. 4.

20. Pérez de la Canal, "Justicia," 429, 440.

21. Kagan, *Lawsuits and Litigants*, 122.

22. Ibid., 38–40. For a description of some of these costs for the chancery court in Granada, see De Mena, *Real audiencia*, 247, 248.

23. ARCG, H, 4568–4.

24. A. MacKay, "Lesser Nobility," 160.

25. In the case of Hernando and Melchor de Almansa, the city of Seville disputed with the court over who was responsible for paying the costs of investigating the claimants. ARCG, H, 5096–216.

26. AMS, sec. 1, carp. 116, doc. 69.

27. ARCG, H, 5074–134, 4681–311.

28. ARCG, H, 4681–209, 5074–172.

29. ARCG, H. The percentage of hidalguía lawsuits involving the city of Seville that had final verdicts is roughly 45 percent. While low, this figure is significantly higher than Kagan's estimate that only 10 percent of all suits brought to the chancery court in Valladolid in the year 1590 received final rulings and cartas ejecutorias. Kagan, *Lawsuits and Litigants*, 93.

30. ARCG, H.

31. AMS, sec. 1, carp. 40, doc. 90.

32. ARCG, H, 4566–031, 4577–011.

33. Fayard and Gerbet, "Fermeture de la noblesse," 62.

34. For a sense of the sums the city of Seville allocated for its litigation at the royal and chancery courts for the years 1585 to 1589, see AMS, sec. 2, carp. 201. In some of these years the city expended as much as a million maravedís for ongoing suits. Kagan, *Lawsuits and Litigants*, 12.

35. AMS, sec. 1, carp. 40, doc. 92.

36. Kagan, *Lawsuits and Litigants*, 42–49.

37. Fayard and Gerbet, "Fermeture de la noblesse," 61.

38. AMS, sec. 3, leg. 10, doc. 7.

39. ARCG, H, 4681–209.

40. These procedures are similar to those of civil suits, in which the parties have to provide the court with the full range of claims and objections that they might subsequently employ.

41. Domínguez Ortiz argues that the diversity of criteria for establishing hidalguía and the problems proving adherence to these criteria provoked innumerable lawsuits. Domínguez Ortiz, *Clases privilegiadas*, 33. I believe that the causal relationship between criteria and dispute worked the other way around. In the effort to deny a person's claim to status, the opposing party appealed to a diversity of rules that had been articulated in response to previous complaints and conflicts.

42. AMS, sec. 1, carp. 37, doc. 35 fol. 18.

43. A. MacKay, "Lesser Nobility," 162.

44. Angus MacKay argues that in this case and others like it the performance of military service was not a legal requirement, but simply additional evidence favoring the claim to noble status. Ibid. While this claim is true for the case in 1395, it did not apply to the situation in the sixteenth century.

45. Díaz de Montalvo, *Ordenanzas reales*, 6:381–82.

46. Collantes de Terán, *Sevilla*, 16, 17.

47. "E que oyó dezir algunos personas parientes del dicho Manuel Sánchez que al llamamyento general que se hizo de hidalgos para la guerra del reyno de Granada el dicho Manuel Sánchez padre del que litigava como tal hidalgo enbió en su lugar uno que syrviese en la dicha guerra segund que esto y otras cosas dixo e dipuso" (AMS, sec. 1, carp. 37, doc. 35, fols. 10–10v).

48. "Los hijos, ilegtimos, legitmados por cartas ó priviligios Reales, no se entiendan serlo para gozar de hidalguía ni exención de pechos." *Nueva recopilación.*

49. Altman, *Emigrants and Society*, 9–11. For information on Pizarro and a discussion of the hidalgo status of the men on his expedition, see Lockhart, *Men of Cajamarca*, 31–33, 135–57.

50. Lockhart, *Men of Cajamarca*, 136.

51. "Venga o descienda de bastardos o expurgeos o de casta de moros judíos conversos o penitenciados por el santo officio de la ynquisición" (AMS, sec. 3, tomo 9, doc. 5, fol. 286).

52. Martz, *Network of Converso Families*, 61–63.

53. "Sy saben creen vieron o an oydo dezir y dello ay pública boz e fama quel dicho Ortuño de Avendaño syendo onbre soltero hubo y procreó por su hijo natural al dicho Ortuño de Avendaño litigante de Mari Ortiz de Verayaga muger soltera thenyendola conoscidamente por su amiga y que por tal su hijo natural por el dicho su padre fue procreado" ("Probanza que hizo el año de 1533, Ortuño de Avendaño, vecino de esta ciudad sobre su hidalguía." AMS, sec. 1, carp. 176, doc. 71).

54. AMS, sec. 1, carp. 40, doc. 91.

55. In modern jurisprudence this practice is referred to as pleading in the alternative.

56. Domínguez Ortiz, *Clases privilegiadas*, 32. Marie-Claude Gerbet similarly asserted that old padrones were often destroyed at the time new ones were composed. *Nobleza*, 50.

57. Colmeiro, *Cortes*, 2:4, 5; 3:141, 144.

58. Espinosa, *Empire of the Cities*, 254; Kagan, *Lawsuits and Litigants*, 179.

59. AMS, sec. 1, carp. 40, doc. 90.

60. "Lo otro por que si en algún tiempo la parte contraria y sus passados abían dejado de pechar abía sido y fue por ser caballeros armadas y prebillegiados y por ser criados allegados y favorescidos de los arçobispos de Sevilla cuya abía sido y era la dicha villa" ("Ejecutoria declarando por hombre llano pechero á Pedro Hernández de Andrada vecino desta ciudad y de la villa de Umbrete," ibid.).

61. Nader, *Liberty in Absolutist Spain*, 115.

62. Ibid., 117; Herrera García, *Aljarafe sevillano*, 58–59, 104.

63. "Y por ser caballeros armadas y prebillegiados y por ser criados allegados y favorescidos de los concejos y de otras personas podersossas y por ser tan pobres que no tenían bienes de que pechar o otro por que la parte contraria y sus passados conpulsos y aprenyados abían ydo a nos serbir a las guerras y salido a los alardes como contiosos" (AMS, sec. 1, carp. 40, doc. 90).

64. AMS, sec. 1, carp. 37, doc. 35, fols. 35, 44, 55.

65. Ibid., fol. 23.

66. Ballesteros, "Don Yuçaf," 253; Netanyahu, "Conversion of Don Samuel."

67. "E que syenpre se razonaron por omes fijsdalgo seyendo judíos e que después ql dicho don Samuel paneque fue tornado xpiano que syenpre se razonó e estuvo en posesyón de ome fijodalgo" (AMS, sec. 1, carp. 37, doc. 35, fols. 23, 24).

68. Sánchez Saus, Élites políticas, 135, 136.

69. Netanyahu, Origins of the Inquisition, 238, 239. For a discussion of conversos who held the office of regidor in Toledo in the fifteenth and sixteenth centuries, see Martz, Network of Converso Families, 25, 33–36, 199–203.

70. Martz, Network of Converso Families, 25, 33–36, 199–203.

71. Thompson, "Neo-noble Nobility," 381, 382.

72. Siete partidas, 7.24.6, cited in Netanyahu, Origins of the Inquisition, 261. Netanyahu also cites the council of Basle's decree that converts should enjoy the privileges of those cities and localities in which they were regenerate (276).

73. "Porque aunque sus antepasados en los tienpos antiguos fueron judíos el y su padre y abuelo y otros sus antepasados fueron y avían sydo muy buenos xpianos y gente noble" (AMS, sec. 1, carp. 37, doc. 35, fol. 46).

74. "Lo otro porque ny se podía dezir que seyendo el ynycio vicioso e yncapaz de nobleza no se podía al dicho su parte ayudar de la posesyón en que avía estado el y su padre y abuelo de la libertad de fidalguía porque aunque el ynycio fuera viciosso convertiendose como se convirtieron sus antepasados a nuestra santa fee católica de su voluntad ellos e sus decendientes fueran y heran capaces de nobleza y la podían provar por la dicha prescripción ynmemorial o provando de padre e de abuelo conforme a las leyes destos reynos" (ibid., fol. 46).

75. Cadenas y Vicent, "Como se solventaban," 540, 541.

76. Sánchez Paneque's lawyer developed these arguments from fifteenth- and early sixteenth-century discourses about the ability and right of Jewish converts to participate fully in Christian society. Alfonso de Cartegena, the bishop of Burgos and son of the converted rabbi Solomon ha-Levi, argued in the Defensorium Unitatis Christianae that Jews did and could possess nobility. Cartagena defined Jewish servitude as a theological subordination, as opposed to a natural or civil servitude, and consequently one that ended when a Jew converted to Christianity. Netanyahu, Origins of the Inquisition, 563–69, 580.

77. "No se podía dubdar syno que todas las noblezas de fidalguya al principio tuvieron origen de previllejio la prescrivción de tiempo ynmemorial tenía fuerça de previllejo" (AMS, sec. 1, carp. 37, doc. 35, fol. 47).

78. "Querían dezir que tuvieron previllejo de los señores reyes que a la sazon heran les dieron y concordieron y quyen pretendía tener previllejo no se podía dezir honbre fijodalgo de sangre" (ibid., fol. 47).

79. Fifteenth-century petitions of the Cortes and royal letters commonly used the unqualified term hijodalgo, and the only extended formulation was hijodalgo de solar conocido. See CLC, 3:143–44, 539–40, 782, 802, 863–64.

80. "Si los recendientes o predecesores de la parte contraria fueron libres por privillejo no pudieron después adquerirlo por prescripción ques que una vez hera libre o libertado de la servidumbre en que nació o en que cayó no podía ser libertado más" (AMS, sec. 1, carp. 37, doc. 35, fol. 47).

81. The book of the 1518 composición for the city of Écija listed two members of the Paneque clan and the amounts they had contributed: Gonçalo Martyn Paneque for 3,572 maravedís and Pedro Gonçalo Paneque for 2,250 maravedís. Gil, Conversos, 1:238–48.

82. Thompson, "Purchase of Nobility," 324.

83. Kagan, Lawsuits and Litigants, 71.

84. Fayard and Gerbet, "Fermeture de la noblesse," 60.

85. Fenster and Smail, Fama, 1–4.

86. The expression is "ome hijodalgo notorio de padre y de abuelo devengar quinientos sueldos segun fuero de Castilla," and its source and meaning remain debated. It has been suggested that the expression refers to the right to be recognized as someone who received this quantity as a stipend when they went to war or that it designated those who could receive this amount as indemnity for the injuries they incurred in battle. Marqués de Siete Iglesias, "Hidalgo y el caballero," 615. See also *Nueva recopilación*, lib. 6, título 2, ley 8.

87. AMS, sec. 1, carp. 37, doc. 35, fols. 7, 18.

88. Ibid., fols. 13, 9.

89. "E que se acordava que podía aver más de veynte años que pasando un cogedor con un padrón que pensava que hera de las monedas foreras e yva con el otro honbre y llegando a la casa donde bivía el dicho Manuel Sánchez dixo el uno dellos por qué no entramos aquí e que dixo el otro que por que hera ensento e no debía aquel pecho diziendo que hera fijodalgo" (ibid., fol. 15).

90. Ibid., fols., 10, 11.

Chapter 5

1. The city's records of the case preserve a wide range of documents, including dozens of royal provisiones issued by the court at the request of the prosecutor, the court's numerous rulings, and minutes from the city council meetings. AMS, sec. 1, carp. 146, doc. 192.

2. The other two men were the citizens Francisco de Ugarte and a man with the surname Urquica (ibid.). Although the court's writs do not identify Mesa as a veinticuatro, he is listed as one in the records of the city council meetings; see AMS, sec. 10, 1583.

3. Montalvo provided the law with the title "Como fueron rebocadas todas las mercedes de noblezas y fidalguías, y quales deven ser guardadas." Díaz de Montalvo, *Ordenanzas reales*, lib. 4, título 2, ley 9.

4. The council initially resisted this expansion of the asistente's voting powers and gained assurances that they would be temporary. Ortiz de Zúñiga, *Anales eclesiasticos*, 3:99. For the introduction of the asistente in Seville, also see Lunenfeld, *Keepers of the City*, 16, 26–28; and Morales Padrón, *Ciudad del quinientos*, 215, 216.

5. For an excellent description of marriage practices among the urban elite of fifteenth-century Seville, see Sánchez Saus, *Caballería y linaje*, 41–48, 87–100.

6. This solidarity continued to be the norm despite the efforts of private genealogists to make a living out of testifying for or against the ancestry of important members of the city's elite, primarily in efforts to enter the prestigious Order of Santiago. Pike, *Linajudos and Conversos*.

7. Domínguez Ortiz, *Clases privilegiadas*, 10–12; Pike, *Aristocrats and Traders*, 21–23, 99, 100.

8. Although Cuartas Rivero focuses primarily on the Crown's efforts to sell council offices, she also treats the existing system and procedures for transfer of office and efforts by royal governments, notably the Catholic Monarchs, to regulate these transfers. "Venta de oficios públicos," 495, 496. For the transfer of office in the town of Madrid, see Guerrero Mayllo, *Familia y vida cotidiana*, xiii–xv.

9. Pike, *Aristocrats and Traders*, 99.

10. "Los susodichos por ser veinte y quartos oficiales rregidores y personas rricas y poderosas con favores y negociaciones que an tenido y tienen con los demás oficiales del cavildo de la ciudad de Sevilla pretenden goçar de ydalguía y siempre de no pagar ny pechar los pechos y deramas reales que los demas onbres llanos pecheros de la ciudad de la ciudad de Sevilla pagan a su magestad" (AMS, sec. 1, carp. 146, doc. 192).

11. Ibid.

12. For a detailed treatment of the assimilation of converso families in Toledo, see Martz, "Pure Blood Statutes," and Martz, *Network of Converso Families*.

13. "El que es hijodalgo notorio que tiene executoría e previlegio de hidalguía de su magestad piden que se les vuelva la blanca de la refación de la carne en el cavildo y regimiento desta ciudad y el cavildo y rregimiento le vuelve a cada uno la blanca de la carne por el título que tiene el hijodalgo notiorio por su notoridad y el de ehecutoría por su ehecutoría y a lo de previlegio por su previlegio" (AMS, sec. 1, carp. 146, doc. 192).

14. Pike, *Aristocrats and Traders*, 37–47; Pike, "Sevillian Nobility," 447, 454–56.

15. Sánchez Saus, *Caballería y linaje*, 121.

16. Ibid., 122, 123.

17. Pike, "Sevillian Nobility," 447, 450.

18. Cook and Cook, *Plague Files*, 24, 25; Pacheco, *Verdaderos retratos*, 286.

19. Cook and Cook, *Plague Files*, 24, 25.

20. Pike, *Aristocrats and Traders*, 44, 46.

21. Ibid., 44–46.

22. Lucas, "Ennoblement," 240–46; Perroy, "Social Mobility," 34, 35.

23. Nader, *Liberty in Absolutist Spain*, 71–91, 77.

24. Ibid., 1–7, 99–129.

25. Kamen, *Spain*, 166.

26. Sánchez Saus, *Caballería y linaje*, 124, 125.

27. Nader, *Liberty in Absolutist Spain*, 105, 107.

28. Infante-Galán, *Céspedes*, 43–46.

29. Ladero Quesada, *Ciudad medieval*, 77.

30. Vila Vilar, *Corzo y los Mañara*, 142–45.

31. AMS, sec. 1, carp. 178, doc. 95.

32. Ortiz de Zúñiga, *Anales eclesiasticos*, 4:50.

33. Another captain serving alongside Corzo in this enterprise was Don Juan de Céspedes y Figueroa, one of the sons of Gonzalo de Céspedes. Ibid., 4:162.

34. For the details of the dowry and the efforts of the count's creditors to obtain payment from the revenues of the dowry, see AMS, sec. 1, carp. 146, doc. 194.

35. "Sevilla no tiene obligación de seguir este pleyto con el dicho Juan Antonio Corço por rrazon de los susdicho y si el senor licenciado Diego de Amescga fiscal de su magestad en la dicha chançellería real de Granada lo quiere seguir no a de ser a costa de Sevilla" (AMS, sec. 1, carp. 146, doc. 192).

36. Of particular note is Gonzalo's edition of Juan Manuel's *Conde de Lucanor* (1575) and Ruy González de Clavijo's *Historia del Gran Tamorlán* (1582). He published his *Libro de la Montería* in 1582 and *Nobleza de Andaluzia* in 1588. López Martínez, "Gonzalo Argote de Molina"; Argote de Molina, *Nobleza de Andaluzia*.

37. Palma Chaguaceda, *Historiador*, 26.

38. For a surviving copy of the ordinances and their royal confirmation, as well as later complaints about the failure to implement them, see AMS, sec. 1, carp. 25, doc. 252.

39. Pacheco, *Verdaderos retratos*, 273.

40. Palma Chaguaceda, *Historiador*, 31.

41. In 1590 Gonzalo successfully negotiated the surrender of the outlaw captain Pedro Machuca and three hundred of his band of followers. Pacheco, *Verdaderos retratos*, 274.

42. Palma Chaguaceda, *Historiador*, 41.

43. Sánchez Saus, *Caballería y linaje*, 393–411.

44. The marquis's grandfather, Pedro Fernández de Saavedra, became involved in the colonization of the Canaries when he obtained the señorio of Lanzarote through marriage in 1478. Pedro married Constanza Sarmiento, whose grandfather, Diego García de Herrera, had traded his jurisdictional rights in the Canary Islands to the Crown in exchange for five million maravedís, the title of Conde de Gomera, and the lordships of Lanzarote, Fuerteventura, and Hierro. Felipe bestowed the title of Conde de Lanzarote on Augustin in 1567 and elevated it to marquis in 1584. Palma Chaguaceda, *Historiador*, 41, 42. Pedro Fernández de Saavedra also held the office of veinticuatro of Seville, which was passed down to his grandson Augustín. Sánchez Saus, *Caballería y linaje*, 409, 410.

45. AMS, sec. 1, carp. 146, doc. 192.

46. The peace treaty and formal agreement of the ransom terms identify the Muslim captain as Morato Arraez and provide a detailed description of the raid on Lanzarote, as well as an explanation for the raid itself. Palma Chaguaceda, *Historiador*, 45–47.

47. Palma Chaguaceda, *Historiador*, 26.

48. Pacheco, *Verdaderos retratos*, 286, 273.

49. Kevin Ingram describes Argote de Molina's history as an effort to invent a genealogy and compares it to his contemporary Rodrigo Caro's efforts to disguise the Jewish backgrounds of his family in *Varones insignes en letras naturales de la ilustrisima ciudad de Sevilla*. Ingram, "Secret Lives, Public Lies," 14.

50. AMS, sec. 3, tomo 4, doc. 4.

51. The records of the 1583 refund mention only jurados from eight of the city's thirty parishes, suggesting that the refunds listed were for purchases made at only one of the half dozen municipal slaughterhouses (*carnicerías*). Ibid.

52. ARCG, H, 5096–091.

53. ARCG, H, 4947–11, 4575–18.

54. ARCG, H, 5096–216.

55. AMS, sec. 3, tomo 8, doc. 34. See the discussion of this issue in chapter 3.

56. "Si alguna delación se a hecho de los susodichos fuera de la quel dicho señor fiscal hizo que conforme a las leyes y pragmáticas destos rreynos es necesaria a costa de los susodichos se puede seguir esto causa y no a costa de Sevilla" (AMS, sec. 1, carp. 146, doc. 192).

57. AMS, sec. 1, carp. 179, doc. 137.

58. Herrera García, *Estado de Olivares*.

59. ARCG, H, 4920–1, fol. 101v.

60. ARCG, H, 4756–6.

61. Lohmann Villena, *Espinosa*, 48.

62. His uncle Alonso the elder sued for recognition of his hidalguía against the town of Corral de Almaguer, a municipality in Castilla Nueva on the route south to Andalusia and Muria. ARCG, H, 4681–228.

63. Herrera García, *Estado de Olivares*.

64. Lohmann Villena, *Espinosa*, 50.

65. ARCG, H, 4920–001, fols. 90–100.

66. ARCG, H, 05144–025.

67. ARCG, H, 4603–012.

Chapter 6

1. Espinosa, *Empire of the Cities*, 11–14; Kagan, *Lawsuits and Litigants*, 101, 102; Owens, *Absolute Royal Authority*, 115, 120, 124–42.

2. Scholars have translated the verb *cumplir* used in this expression into English as "execute" and "implement," but "comply" also expresses the sentiment. R. MacKay, *Limits of Royal Authority*, 1, 2.

3. As Richard Kagan has observed, in sixteenth-century civil cases in Castile, the judge's freedom to give his decision with the simple statement that one party "proved their case" while the opposing party "did not" raised the potential for the arbitrariness of the presiding judges. *Lawsuits and Litigants*, 27.

4. Ibid., 175, 176.

5. R. MacKay, *Limits of Royal Authority*, 1, 2.

6. "Lo otro porque la dicha ciudad notoriamente alega cossas que después abiendosele notificado otras semjantes provisiones contra otros vecinos de la dicha ciudad rrespondió que las obedezía y mandava cumplir no solamente aquellas pero las que después dellas se obtubiesen como consta por las dichas provisiones originales notificaciones y rrespuesta a ellas dada por el dicho consejo de que hazemos presentación" (AMS, sec. 1, carp. 146, doc. 192).

7. García-Gallo, *Manual de historia*, 1:195–96, 215; González Alonso, "Formula 'obedezcase,'" 470.

8. González Alonso, "Formula 'obedezcase,'" 484.

9. Ibid., 487.

10. AMS, sec. 1, carp. 25, doc. 252.

11. Martz presents the division of the regidores into two benches as a traditional structure of the council. *Network of Converso Families*, 15, 200. Those on the noble bench were to be hijosdalgo of blood, whose parents had not held a "mechanical or vile office." Those on the commoner's bench had to be "hijosdalgo or at least Old Christians, of pure blood, with no trace of Moor or Jew." Martz speculates that the royal order was a stratagem for squeezing money from officeholders, who would have to have their lineage confirmed or would buy an hidalguía (199–202).

12. Ibid., 202.

13. Domínguez Ortiz, *Clases privilegiadas*, 262, 263.

14. AMS, sec. 1, carp. 25, doc. 252; Boyden, *Courtier and the King*, 61.

15. "Y me fue suplicado cerca dello mandase poveer mandamyento que de aquí adelante no fuesen proveydos de los dichos officios nynguno dellos dichos pecheros salvo personas hijosdalgo notorios" (And I was petitioned about the matter so that I might provide an order that from now on no pechero would be provided with this office, but only hijosdalgo notorios). "Y agora los procuradores de cortes de la dicha ciudad de Sevilla me suplicaron y pidieron por merced mandase que la dicha mi carta se extendiese a los officios de veintequatros fieles executores" (And now the representatives to the Cortes for the city of Seville petitioned me for a favor [*merced*] [that] I should order that the previous letter should be extended to the offices of councilman and fieles executors) (AMS, sec. 1, carp. 25, doc. 252).

16. Boyden, *Courtier and the King*, 82.

17. Martínez Millán and Morales, *Felipe II*. Eraso continued to serve as secretary of the Cámara despite being found guilty of peculation and misuse of official authority in 1566. Boyden, *Courtier and the King*, 129.

18. Espinosa, *Empire of the Cities*, 143, 144.

19. On March 7, 1581, Bartolomé de Hoces, the city's representative to the Cortes, presented a notarized copy of multiple documents to Juan de Aguilera, lieutenant to the asistente. The city clerk, Baltazar de Godoy, noted in his description of the event that the letter and writ required the attendees to verify and copy the documents so that the city might "possess" the law. Consequently, the letter ordered the clerk to produce his register so that any necessary copies could be made and so that these officials could establish that the documents

agreed in substance. The process of verification ended when the lieutenant of the asistente announced that the notarized documents from the king were authentic. AMS, sec. 1, carp. 25, doc. 252.

20. Ibid.

21. Martz, "Pure Blood Statutes," 93.

22. Martz, *Network of Converso Families*, 199–202.

23. Thompson, "Purchase of Nobility," 320, 321.

24. "Lo otro porque aunque las dichas provisiones se pudieran dar para otras partes no se avían de dar para la dicha ciudad por aver en ella como ay tanto número de forasteros e tener la dicha ciudad provisiones reales para que los tales no puedan adquirir posesión de hidalguía aunque esten mucho tienpo que la dicha ciudad" (AMS, sec. 1, carp. 146, doc. 192).

25. "Si se diese lugar aquellas provisiones qualquier forastero pudiese litigar con mi parte sobre hidalguía no serían bastantes los propios que tiene para los gastos delos dichos pleitos" (AMS, sec. 1, carp. 146, doc. 192).

26. "La dicha ciudad tiene en esto tanto cuidado e diligencia que no se le puede oponer lo contrario porque como es notorio siempre a mirado por lo que toca al servicio de vuestra alteza e pro común de la dicha ciudad" (ibid.).

27. AMS, sec. 3, tomo 8, doc. 34. Morales Padrón lists Don Fernando de Torres y Portugal, Count of Villar, as the asistente for the years 1579 and 1580, and Bernardino Suárez de Mendoza, the Count of Coruña, as the asistente for 1581. *Ciudad del quinientos*, 330.

28. The very cost of the "patents" were presented as monetary commutations for personal service in war, as the wages of a given number of soldiers, or appropriated to specified military purposes. In other words, the royal clerks drafted the patents as formal authorizations of status accompanied by a sort of monetary service offered by the recipient. Thompson, "Neonoble Nobility," 381, 383.

29. "El daño que a su real patrimonio se siguiría y los muchos inconvientes que a su servicio y al bien y benefficio público de aquella ciudad y su tierra resultarían de concederse los dichas previlegios por esta forma mayormente a los pobres y gente de menos sustancia y fuerça sobre cargarían todos los servicios y pechos que los hombres ricos heran los que habrían estos previlegios por este camino y sus decendientes para siempre que venían a ser gran número habrían de pagar y contribuir a que su majestad como principe tan xpiano y piadoso no debría dar lugar" (AMS, sec. 3, tomo 8, doc. 34).

30. "Que su magestad y sus subcesores no puede dar y ennoblecer con los dichos previlegios de hidalguía a las personas que en otras partes les hubieren servido de manera que merescan ser honrrados y noblecidos" (ibid.).

31. The text that outlined the agreement did not indicate if the ability to provide the status meant through a grant or through adjudication. Although the final document signed by Francisco de Eraso stated that the Crown "would not sell privileges of hidalgíua to the citizens of Seville," it specifically bound the king to other conditions listed in the proceeding agreement (*asiento*), which were broader in nature. Ibid.

32. Espinosa, *Empire of the Cities*, 252.

33. Kagan, *Lawsuits and Litigants*, 39–41.

34. Espinosa, *Empire of the Cities*, 252, 253. For the 1524–25 visita of the chancery court in Granada, see Garriga, *Audiencia*, 469–81.

35. Kagan, *Lawsuits and Litigants*, 178, 179. For a description of the auditing system for judges, see Espinosa, *Empire of the Cities*, 220. Espinosa argues that the reviews and audits succeeded in guaranteeing a meritorious and mostly honest cadre of judicial officials.

36. Extensive documentation of this review survives in the AGS, CC, legs. 2725, 2735.

37. AGS, CC, leg. 2725, fols. 1–41.

38. The latest date given in the judicial review of his time in office is from spring 1590. Likewise, a lawsuit from 1590 confirms that he was still actively acting in his capacity as chancery prosecutor at this time. AMS, sec. 3, tomo 9, doc. 5, fol. 281.

39. AGS, CC, leg. 2725, fols. 1, 1v.

40. "Por aver recevido del dicho Ventura Pretel cantidad de dadibas y joyas . . . ay cinco o seis testigos de publicidad que en Baeça se decia que Ventura Pretel avía dado al fiscal muchas joyas e cosas" (ibid.).

41. Domínguez Ortiz, *Clases privilegiadas*, 34n51.

42. AGS, CC, leg. 2725, fol. 4.

43. Ibid., fols. 2–3v.

44. Ibid., fol. 8v.

45. AGS, CC, leg. 2725.

46. Some of the citizens of Seville mentioned in the audit who either provided gifts to Amezaga or were the victims of extortion were Miguel de Jauregui, Joan de Oliver, Mateo de Oliver, Lorenzo de Vallejo, Francisco Hernández de Almeria and his brothers, Francisco de Cifuentes, Andres Ortega Cabrio, Pedro de Vertendona, Pedro Pérez de la Elguera, Licenciado Mosquera, and Juan Domingo de Tudela. Ibid., fols. 6v, 10v, 12, 13, 14, 19v, 24v, 35v, 41v.

47. Ibid., fol. 8.

48. AMS, sec. 3, tomo 4, doc. 39.

49. Ibid., fol. 208.

50. "El qual mostro a Anton Suaréz su solicitador un memorial de cosas de lencería y cosas que dixo aver dado al fiscal que le costaron mas de quarenta mill maravedís que se las avía hecho traer y dixo al dicho Anton Suaréz que de aquella manera se negociaba con brevedad y que otros andaban gastando su tiempo en Granada y no savían negociar como esto lo rrefiere en su dicho el dicho Anton Suaréz" (AGS, CC, leg. 2725, fol. 10).

51. Ibid., fol. 18.

52. Ibid., fols. 3, 3v.

53. AGS, CC, leg. 2735.

54. Espinosa, *Empire of the Cities*, 12–14, 220.

55. Ibid., 253.

56. Mena, *Real audiencia*, lib. 2, título 11, cédula 6.

57. Kagan, *Lawsuits and Litigants*, xx.

58. Jack Owens provides a detailed treatment of judicial flexibility in his account of how Carlos I and his chancery judges sought to handle the extended and politically complex lawsuit between the city of Toledo and the House of Béjar concerning the lordship of Pueblo de Alcocer in the wake of the comunero rebellion. *Absolute Royal Authority*, 115–42.

Conclusion

1. Cervantes, *Don Quijote*, 9–12.

2. Ruiz, *Spanish Society*, 68, 69, 74, 75.

3. Braudel, *Mediterranean*, 2:715.

BIBLIOGRAPHY

Primary Sources

Arce de Ortálora, Juan. *Summa nobilitatis hispanicae.* Salamanca: Andreas a Portonariis, 1559.
Argote de Molina, Gonzalo. *Nobleza de Andaluzia.* Seville: Extramuros, 2008.
Carande, Rámon, and Juan de Mata Carriazo, eds. *El tumbo de los Reyes Católicos del concejo de Sevilla.* 6 vols. Seville: Fondo para Fomento de la Investigacíon en la Universidad, 1968.
Carrilero Martínez, Ramón, ed. *Los Reyes Católicos en la documentación albacetense, 1476–1504.* Albacete: Instituto de Estudios Albacetenses, 2004.
Danvila y Collada, Manuel. *Cortes de los antiguos reinos de León y de Castilla.* 5 vols. Madrid: Imprenta de Rivadeneyra, 1861–1903.
Díaz de Montalvo, Alfonso, ed. *Ordenanzas reales de Castilla.* In Pacheco et al., *Códigos españoles*, vol. 6.
Enríquez del Castillo, Diego. *Crónica de Enrique IV.* Edited by Aureliano Sánchez Martín. Valladolid: Universidad de Valladolid, 1994.
Gómez, Marcos Fernández, Pilar Ostos Slacedo, and María Luisa Pardo Rodríguez, eds. *El tumbo de los Reyes Católicos del concejo de Sevilla.* 13 vols. Madrid: Editorial Centro de Estudios Ramón Areces, 1998–2007.
González Alonso, Benjamín, ed. *El fuero viejo de Castilla.* Salamanca: Junta de Castilla y León, Consejería de Educación y Cultura, 1996.
González de Torneo, Francisco. *Practica de escrivanos que contiene la judicial, y orden de examinar testigos en causas civiles, y hidalguías, y causas criminales y escrituras publicas, en estilo estenso, y quantas, y particiones de bienes, y execuciones de cartas executorias.* Valladolid: Pedro de Lasso, 1608.
Guardiola, Fray Benito de la. *Tratado de la nobleza y de los títulos y ditados que oi dia tienen los varones claros y grandes de España.* Madrid: Alonso Gomez, 1591.
Jordán de Asso y del Rio, Ignacio, and Miguel de Manuel y Rodriguez, eds. *Fuero viejo de Castilla.* Madrid: Viuda e hijos de Calleja, 1847.
Keniston, Hayward, ed. *Fuero de Guadalajara.* Princeton: Princeton University Press, 1924.
Leyes de Toro. In Pacheco et al., *Códigos españoles*, vol. 6.
Mena, Sebastián de, ed. *Ordenanças de la real audiencia y chancilleria de Granada.* Facsimile. Granada: Diputación de Granada, 1997.
Moreno de Vargas, Bernabé. *Discurso de la nobleza de España.* Madrid: Viuda de Alonso Martin, 1622.
Múñoz y Romero, Tomás, ed. *Colección de fueros municipals y cartas pueblas de los reinos de Castilla, León, Corona de Aragon, y Navarra: Coordinada y anotada.* Madrid: Ediciones Atlas, 1847.
Nueva recopilación. In Pacheco et al., *Códigos españoles*, vol. 12.
Ordenamiento de Alcalá. In Pacheco et al., *Códigos españoles*, vol. 1.
Ortiz de Zúñiga, Diego. *Anales eclesiásticos y seculares de la muy noble y muy leal ciudad de Sevilla.* 5 vols. Madrid: Imprenta Real, 1796.

Pacheco, Francisco. *Libro de descripción de verdaderos retratos de ilustres y memorables varones*. Edited by Pedro Piñero Ramírez and Rogelio Reyes Cano. Seville: Diputación Provincial de Sevilla, 1985.

Pacheco, Joaquín Francisco, Fermín de la Puente y Apezechea, Pedro Gómez de la Serna, Francesco de Paula Díaz y Mendoza, and Gregorio López, eds. *Los códigos españoles, concordados y anotados*. 2nd ed. 12 vols. Madrid: Antonio de San Martin, 1872–73.

Penna, Mario. *Prosistas castellanos del siglo XV*. Vol. 116 of *Biblioteca de autores españoles*. Madrid: Colección Rivadeneira, 1959.

Peraza, Luis de. *La historia de Sevilla*. Edited by Francisco Morales Padron. Seville: Artes Gráficas Salesianas, 1979.

Poza, Andres de. *Fuero de hidalguía: Ad pragmáticas de Toro et Tordesillas*. Edited by Carmen Muñoz de Bustillo. Translated by María de los Angeles Durán Ramas. Bilbao: Universidad del País Vasco, 1997.

Las siete partidas. In Pacheco et al., *Códigos españoles*, vols. 2–4.

Valera, Diego de. *Espejo de verdadera nobleza*. Edited by Mario Penna. In *Biblioteca de autores españoles*, vol. 116. Madrid: Colección Rivadeneira, 1959.

Secondary Sources

Altman, Ida. *Emigrants and Society: Extremadura and Spanish America in the Sixteenth Century*. Berkeley: University of California Press, 1989.

Atienza Hernández, Ignacio. *Aristocracia, poder, y riqueza en la España moderna: La casa de Osuna, siglos XV–XIX*. Madrid: Siglo XXI de España, 1987.

Azcona, Tarcisio de. *Isabel la católica: Estudio crítico de su vida y su reinado*. Madrid: Biblioteca de Autores Cristianos, 1964.

Baer, Yitzhak. *A History of the Jews in Christian Spain*. Philadelphia: Jewish Publication Society of America, 1978.

Ballesteros, Antonio. "Don Yuçaf de Écija." *Sefarad* 6 (1946): 253–87.

Bitton, Davis. *The French Nobility in Crisis, 1560–1640*. Stanford: Stanford University Press, 1969.

Boyden, James. *The Courtier and the King: Ruy Gomez de Silva, Philip II, and the Court of Spain*. Berkeley: University of California Press, 1995.

Braudel, Fernand. *The Mediterranean and the Mediterranean World in the Age of Philip II*. 2nd ed. 2 vols. New York: Harper and Row, 1976.

Burke, Peter. *What Is Cultural History?* Cambridge: Polity Press, 2004.

Burkholder, Mark, and Lyman Johnson. *Colonial Latin America*. 6th ed. New York: Oxford University Press, 2008.

Bush, Michael. *Noble Privilege*. Manchester: Manchester University Press, 1983.

Cadenas y Vicent, Vicente de. "Como se solventaban los pleitos de hidalguía y leyes por las cuales se han venido rigiendo." *Hidalguía* 22 (1974): 533–53.

———. "El valor de los mercedes enriqueñas de hidalguía." *Hidalguía* 14 (1969): 291–94.

Carlé, María del Carmen. *Del concejo medieval castellano-leonés*. Buenos Aires: Instituto de Historia de España, 1968.

Carrilero Martínez, Ramón. *Los Reyes Católicos en la documentación albacetense, 1476–1504*. Albacete: Instituto de Estudios Albacetenses, 2004.

Castro, Américo. *Realidad histórica de España*. 4th ed. rev. Mexico City: Editorial Porrua, 1971.

Cervantes, Miguel de. *El ingenioso hidalgo Don Quijote de la Mancha*. Edited by John Jay Allen. Madrid: Ediciones Cátedra, 1996.

Collantes de Terán, Antonio. "Comerciantes y fianzas públicas en Sevilla durante el reinado de los Reyes Católicos." In *Comercio y hombres de negocios en Castilla y Europa en tiempos de Isabel la católica*, edited by Hilario Casado Alonso and Antonio García Baquero, 310–29. Madrid: Sociedad Estatal de Conmemoraciones Culturales, 2007.

———. "Los mercados de abasto en Sevilla: Permanencias y transformaciones, siglos XV y XVI." *Historia Instituciones Documentos* 18 (1991): 57–70.

———. *Sevilla en la baja edad media: La ciudad y sus hombres*. Seville: Ayuntamiento de Sevilla, 1977.

Collins, Roger. *The Basques*. 2nd ed. Cambridge: Basil Blackwell, 1990.

Colmeiro, Manuel. *Cortes de los antiguos reinos de León y de Castilla*. 2 vols. Madrid: Sucesores de Rivadeneyra, 1883–84.

Cook, Alexandra Parma, and Noble David Cook. *The Plague Files*. Baton Rouge: Louisiana University Press, 2009.

Cornfield, Penelope, ed. *Language, History, and Class*. Oxford: Blackwell, 1991.

Cuartas Rivero, Margarita. "La venta de oficios públicos en Castilla-Leon en el siglo XVI." *Hispania* 44 (1984): 495–516.

Davis, Natalie Zemon. *Fiction in the Archives*. Stanford: Stanford University Press, 1987.

Delgado y Orellana, José Antonio. "El noble, el hidalgo, y el caballero." *Hidalguía* (1966): 461–80.

Dewald, Jonathan. *The European Nobility, 1400–1800*. Cambridge: Cambridge University Press, 1996.

———. *The Formation of a Provincial Nobility: The Magistrates of the Parlement of Rouen, 1499–1610*. Princeton: Princeton University Press, 1980.

Díaz de Durana, José Ramón. *La otra nobleza: Escuderos e hidalgos sin nombre y sin historia; Hidalgos e hidalguía universal en el País Vasco al final de la Edad Media, 1250–1525*. Bilbao: Universidad del País Vasco, 2004.

Díaz de Noriega y Pubal, José. *La blanca de la carne en Sevilla*. Madrid: Instituto Salazar y Castro (CSIC), 1975.

Domínguez Ortiz, Antonio. *La clase social de conversos en Castilla en la edad moderna*. Granada: Universidad de Granada, 1991.

———. *Las clases privilegiadas en el antiguo régimen*. Madrid: Ediciones ISTMO, 1973.

———. *Crisis y decadencia de la España de los Austrias*. Barcelona: Ariel, 1969.

Edwards, John. *Christian Córdoba: The City and Its Region in the Late Middle Ages*. Cambridge: Cambridge University Press, 1982.

Espinosa, Aurelio. *The Empire of the Cities: Emperor Charles V, the Comunero Revolt, and the Transformation of the Spanish System*. Leiden: Brill, 2009.

Fayard, Janine, and Marie-Claude Gerbet. "Fermeture de la noblesse et pureté de sang en Castille à travers les procès de hidalguía au XVIème siècle." *Histoire, économie, et société* (1982): 51–75.

Feldman, David. "Class." In *History and Historians in the Twentieth Century*, edited by Peter Burke, 201–6. Oxford: Oxford University Press, 2002.

Fenster, Thelma, and Daniel Lord Smail. *Fama: The Politics of Talk and Reputation in Medieval Europe*. Ithaca: Cornell University Press, 2003.

Fortea Pérez, José Ignacio. *Monarquía y cortes en la Corona de Castilla: Las ciudades ante la política fiscal de Felipe II*. Valladolid: Cortes de Castilla y León, 1990.

Gan Giménez, Pedro. *La real chancillería de Granada (1505–1834)*. Granada: Universidad de Granada, 1987.

García de Valdeavellano, Luis. *Orígenes de la burguesía en la España medieval*. Madrid: Espasa-Calpe, 1969.

García Fernández, Manuel. *El reino de Sevilla en tiempos de Alfonso XI (1312–1350)*. Seville: Diputación Provincial de Sevilla, 1989.

García-Gallo, Alfonso. *Manual de historia del derecho español*. Rev. 3rd ed. 2 vols. Madrid: Artes Gráficas y Ediciones, 1967.

García Hernán, David. *Aristocracia y señorio en la España de Felipe II: La Casa de Arcos*. Granada: Universidad de Granada, 1999.

Garriga, Carlos. *La audiencia y las chancillerías Castellanas, 1371–1525*. Madrid: Centro de Estudios Constitucionales, 1994.

Gerbet, Marie-Claude. "Les guerres et l'accès à la noblesse en Espagne de 1465 à 1592." *Mélanges de la Casa de Velázquez* 8 (1972): 295–326.

———. *La nobleza en la Corona de Castilla: Sus estructuras sociales en Extremadura (1454–1516)*. Translated by María Concepción Quintanilla Raso. Caceres: Diputación Provincial de Caceres, 1989.

———. "La population noble dans le royaume de Castille vers 1500." *Anales de historia antigua y medieval* (1979): 78–99.

Gil, Juan. *Los conversos y la Inquisición sevillana*. 8 vols. Seville: Fundación El Monte, 2000.

González, Julio. *El repartimiento de Sevilla*. Madrid: Consejo Superior de Investigaciones Científicas, 1951.

González Alonso, Benjamín. "La formula 'obedezcase, pero no se cumpla' en el derecho castellano de la Baja Edad Media." *Anuario de historia de derecho español* 50 (1980): 469–87.

González Jiménez, Manuel. "La caballería popular en Andalucía (siglos XIII al XV)." *Anuario de estudios medievales* 15 (1985): 315–29.

Guerrero Mayllo, Ana. *Familia y vida cotidiana de una elite de poder: Los regidores de Madrileños en tiempos de Felipe II*. Madrid: Siglo XXI, 1993.

———. *Gobierno municipal de Madrid*. Madrid: Instituto de Estudios Madrileños, 1993.

Guichot y Parody, Joaquín. *Historia del excelentísimo ayuntamiento de la muy noble, muy leal, muy heróica é invicta ciudad de Sevilla*. 4 vols. Seville: Ayuntamiento de Sevilla, 1896–1903.

Haliczer, Stephen. "The Castilian Aristocracy and the Mercedes Reform of 1478–1482." *Hispanic American Historical Review* 55 (1975): 449–67.

Hamilton, Earl J. *American Treasure and the Price Revolution in Spain, 1501–1650*. Cambridge: Harvard University Press, 1934.

Heal, Felicity, and Clive Holmes. *The Gentry in England and Wales*. Stanford: Stanford University Press, 1994.

Herrera García, Antonio. *El aljarafe sevillano durante el antiguo régimen: Un estudio de su evolución socioeconomica en los siglos XVI–XVIII*. Seville: Diputación Provincial, 1980.

———. *El estado de Olivares: Origen, formación, y desarrollos con los tres primeros condes, 1535–1645*. Seville: Diputación Provincial de Sevilla, 1990.

Herzog, Tamar. *Defining Nations: Immigrants and Citizens in Early Modern Spain and Spanish America*. New Haven: Yale University Press, 2003.

Hiltpold, Paul. "Noble Status and Urban Privilege: Burgos, 1572." *Sixteenth Century Journal* 12 (1981): 21–44.

Homza, Lu Ann. *The Spanish Inquisition, 1478–1614: An Anthology of Sources*. Indianapolis: Hackett, 2006.

Iglesia Ferreirós, Aquilino. *La creación del derecho: Una historia de la formación de un derecho estatal español*. 2nd ed. 2 vols. Madrid: Marcial Pons, 1996.

Infante-Galán, Juan. *Los Céspedes y su señorio de Carrión, 1258–1874*. Seville: Diputación Provincial de Sevilla, 1970.

Ingram, Kevin. "Secret Lives, Public Lies: The Conversos and Socio-Religious Non-Conformism." PhD diss., University of California, San Diego, 2006.

Jago, Charles. "The 'Crisis of the Aristocracy' in Seventeenth-Century Castile." *Past and Present* 84 (1979): 60–90.

———. "Habsburg Absolutism and the Cortes of Castile." *American Historical Review* 86, no. 2 (1981): 307–26.

Jara Fuente, José Antonio. *Concejo, poder, y élites: La clase dominante de Cuenca en el siglo XV*. Madrid: Consejo Superior de Investigaciones Científicas, 2000.

Joyce, Patrick. "The End of Social History." *Social History* 20 (1995): 73–91.

Kagan, Richard. *Lawsuits and Litigants in Castile: 1500–1700*. Chapel Hill: University of North Carolina Press, 1981.

Kamen, Henry. *Spain, 1469–1714: A Society of Conflict*. 3rd ed. London: Longman, 2005.

———. *The Spanish Inquisition: A Historical Revision*. New Haven: Yale University Press, 1997.

Kettering, Sharon. *Patrons, Brokers, and Clients in Seventeenth-Century France*. Oxford: Oxford University Press, 1986.

Kirschberg Schenck, Deborah, and Marcos Fernández Gómez. *El concejo de Sevilla en la edad media (1248–1454): Organización institutional y fuentes documentales*. Seville: Ayuntamiento de Sevilla, 2002.

Ladero Quesada, Miguel Ángel. *Castilla y la conquista del reino de Granada*. 2nd ed. Granada: Diputación Provincial de Granada, 1993.

———. *La ciudad medieval (1248–1492)*. Rev. 3rd ed. Historia de Sevilla. Seville: Universidad de Sevilla, 1989.

———. *La hacienda real castellana entre 1480 y 1492*. Valladolid: Departamento de Historia Medieval, 1967.

———. *La hacienda real de Castilla, 1369–1504*. Madrid: Real Academia de Historia, 2009.

———. *La hacienda real de Castilla en el siglo XV*. Tenerife: La Universidad de la Laguna, 1973.

———. *El siglo XV en Castilla: Fuentes de renta y política fiscal*. Barcelona: Editorial Ariel, 1982.

Lalinde Abadia, Jesus. "Los gastos del proceso en el derecho historico español." *Anuario de Historia Español* 34 (1964): 248–316.

Layna Serrano, Francisco. *Historia de Guadalajara y sus Mendozas en los siglos XV y XVI*. 3 vols. Madrid: Aldus, 1942.

Liss, Peggy. *Isabel the Queen: Life and Times*. Rev. ed. Philadelphia: University of Pennsylvania Press, 2004.

Lockhart, James. *The Men of Cajamarca: A Social and Biographical Study of the First Conquerors of Peru*. Austin: University of Texas Press, 1972.

Lohmann Villena, Guillermo. *Les Espinosa, une famille d'hommes d'affaires en Espagne et aux Indes à l'époque de la colonisation*. Paris: SEVPEN, 1968.

López Martínez, Celestino. "Gonzalo Argote de Molina, historiador y bibliófilo." *Archivo Hispalense* 58 (1953): 187–208.

Lucas, Robert H. "Ennoblement in Late Medieval France." *Medieval Studies* 39 (1977): 239–60.

Lunenfeld, Marvin. *Keepers of the City: The Corregidores of Isabella I of Castile, 1474–1504*. Cambridge: Cambridge University Press, 1987.

MacKay, Angus. "The Lesser Nobility in the Kingdom of Castile." In *Gentry and Lesser Nobility in Late Medieval Europe*, edited by Michael Jones, 159–80. New York: St. Martin's Press, 1986.

———. "Popular Movements and Pogroms in Fifteenth-Century Castile." *Past and Present* 55 (1972): 33–67.

MacKay, Ruth. *The Limits of Royal Authority: Resistance and Obedience in Seventeenth-Century Castile.* Cambridge: Cambridge University Press, 1999.

Major, James Russell. *From Renaissance Monarchy to Absolutist Monarchy: French Kings, Nobles, and Estates.* Baltimore: Johns Hopkins University Press, 1994.

Marqués de Siete Iglesias. "El hidalgo y el caballero." *Hidalguía* (1955): 615–24.

Márquez de la Plata, Vicenta María, and Luis Valero de Bernabé. *Nobiliaria española: Origen, evolución, instituciones, y probanzas.* Madrid: Prensa y Ediciones Iberoamericanas, 1995.

Martínez, María Elena. *Genealogical Fictions: Limpieza de Sangre, Religion, and Gender in Colonial Mexico.* Stanford: Stanford University Press, 2008.

Martínez Millán, José, and Carlos de Carlos Morales. *Felipe II (1527–1598): La configuración de la monarquía hispana.* Vol. 4. Salamanca: Junta de Castilla y León, 1998.

Martz, Linda. *A Network of Converso Families in Early Modern Toledo.* Ann Arbor: University of Michigan Press, 2003.

———. "Pure Blood Statutes in Sixteenth-Century Toledo: Implementation as Opposed to Adoption." *Sefarad* 54 (1994): 83–108.

McLeod, Murdo. "Self-Promotion: The *Relaciones de Méritos y Servicios* and Their Historical and Political Interpretation." *Colonial Latin American Historical Review* 26 (1998): 25–42.

Mitre Fernández, Emilio. *Evolución de la nobleza en Castilla bajo Enrique III, 1396–1406.* Valladolid: Universidad de Valladolid, 1968.

———. *Los judios de Castilla en tiempo de Enrique III: El pogrom de 1391.* Valladolid: Universidad de Valladolid, 1994.

Molina Puche, Sebastián, and Jorge Ortuño Molina. *Los grandes del reino de Murcia, los Marqueses de Villena.* Murcia: Real Academia Alfonso X el Sabio, 2009.

Molinié-Bertrand, Annie. "Les 'hidalgos' dans le royaume de Castille à la fin du XVIe siècle: Approche cartographique." *Histoire, économie et société* (1974).

Montes Romero-Camacho, Isabel. "El anti-judaismo o anti-semitismo Sevillano." In *Los caminos de exilio,* edited by Juan Carrasco, 73–157. Conference Encuentros Judaicos de Tedula. Pamplona: Gobierno de Navarra, 1996.

Morales Padrón, Francisco. *La ciudad del quinientos.* Rev. 3rd ed. Historia de Sevilla. Seville: Universidad de Sevilla, 1989.

Nader, Helen. *Liberty in Absolutist Spain: The Habsburg Sale of Towns, 1516–1750.* Baltimore: Johns Hopkins University Press, 1990.

———. "'The More Communes, the Greater the King': Hidden Communes in Absolutist Theory." In *Theorien kommunaler Ordnung in Europa,* edited by Peter Blickle, 215–23. Schriften des Historischen Kollegs Kolloquien 36. Munich: Oldenbourg, 1996.

———. "Noble Income in Sixteenth-Century Castile: The Case of the Marquises of Mondéjar, 1480 to 1580." *Economic History Review* 30 (1977): 411–28.

———, ed. *Power and Gender in Renaissance Spain: Eight Women of the Mendoza Family, 1450–1650.* Urbana: University of Illinois, 2004.

Netanyahu, Benzion. "The Conversion of Don Samuel Abravanel." In *Toward the Inquisition: Essays on Jewish and Converso History in Late Medieval Spain.* Ithaca: Cornell University Press, 1997.

———. *The Origins of the Inquisition in Fifteenth Century Spain.* New York: Random House, 1995.

Olivera Serrano, César. *Las cortes de Castilla y León y la crisis del reino, 1445–1474.* Burgos: Instituto de Estudios Castellanos, 1986.

Otte, Enrique. *Sevilla y sus mercaderes a fines de la edad media.* Seville: Fundación El Monte, 1996.

Owens, Jack B. *"By My Absolute Royal Authority": Justice and the Castilian Commonwealth at the Beginning of the First Global Age.* Rochester: University of Rochester Press, 2005.

Palenzuela Domínguez, Natalia. "Los mercaderes y hombres de negocios burgaleses en Sevilla en tiempos de Isabel la Católica." In *Comercio y hombres de negocios en Castilla y Europa en tiempos de Isabel la católica,* edited by Hilario Casado Alonso and Antonio García Baquero, 331–52. Madrid: Sociedad Estatal de Conmemoraciones Culturales, 2007.

Palma Chaguaceda, Antonio. *El historiador Gonzalo Argote de Molina.* Madrid: Consejo Superior de Investigaciones Científicas, 1949.

Pérez de la Canal, Miguel Angel. "La justicia en la corte de Castilla durante los siglos XIII al XV." *Historia Instituciones Documentos* 2 (1975): 387–481.

Perroy, Edouard. "Social Mobility Among the French Noblesse in the Later Middle Ages." *Past and Present* 21 (1962): 25–38.

Pescador del Hoyo, Carmela. "La caballería popular en Castilla y León." *Cuadernos de Historia de España* 33–34 (1961): 101–38; 35–36 (1962): 56–201; 37–38 (1963): 88–198; 39–40 (1964): 169–200.

Phillips, Carla Rahn. *Ciudad Real, 1500–1700: Growth, Crisis, and Readjustment in the Spanish Economy.* Cambridge: Harvard University Press, 1979.

Phillips, William D., Jr. *Enrique IV and the Crisis of Fifteenth-Century Castile, 1425–1480.* Cambridge: Medieval Academy of America, 1978.

Pierson, Peter. *Commander of the Armada: The Seventh Duke of Medina Sidonia.* New Haven: Yale University Press, 1989.

Pike, Ruth. *Aristocrats and Traders: Sevillian Society in the Sixteenth Century.* Ithaca: Cornell University Press, 1972.

———. *Enterprise and Adventure: The Genoese in Seville and the Opening of the New World.* Ithaca: Cornell University Press, 1966.

———. "The Genoese in Seville and the Opening of the New World." *Journal of Economic History* 22 (1962): 348–78.

———. *Linajudos and Conversos in Seville: Greed and Prejudice in Sixteenth- and Seventeenth-Century Seville.* New York: Lang, 2000.

———. "The Sevillian Nobility and Trade with the New World in the Sixteenth Century." *Business History Review* 39 (1964): 439–65.

El poema de mio cid / The Poem of the Cid. Translated by Rita Hamilton and Janet Perry. A bilingual edition with parallel text. London: Penguin, 1975.

Porras Arboledas, Pedro. *La ciudad de Jaén y la revolución de las communidades de Castilla, 1500–1523.* Jaén: Diputación Provincial de Jaén, 1993.

Porro, Nelly. "Tres documentos sobre fijosdalgo castellanos." *Cuadernos de historia de España* 33 (1961): 355–66.

Powers, James F. "Two Warrior-Kings and Their Municipal Militias: The Townsman-Soldier in Law and Life." In *The Worlds of Alfonso the Learned and James the Conqueror,* edited by Robert I. Burns. Princeton: Princeton University Press, 1985.

Prieto Cantero, Amalia. "Documentos referentes a hidalguías, caballerías, y exenciones de pecho de la época de los reyes católicos, entresacados del legajo num. 393 de la sección mercedes y privilegios, del Archivo General de Simancas." *Hidalguía* 21, 22, nos. 121, 122, 123 (1973, 1974): 885–916, 113–44, 161–97.

Quintanilla Raso, María Concepción. *Nobleza y señorios en el reino de Córdoba: La casa de Aguilar, siglos XIV y XV.* Córdoba: Publicaciones del Monte de Piedad, 1979.

Quintanilla Raso, María Concepción, and María Asenjo. "Los hidalgos en la sociedad andaluza a fines de la Edad Media." In *Las ciudades andaluzas, siglos XIII–XVI,* edited by José E. López Coca Castañer and Ángel Galán Sánchez, 419–33. Málaga: Universidad de Málaga, 1991.

Restall, Matthew. *Seven Myths of the Spanish Conquest.* Oxford: Oxford University Press, 2003.

Rodríguez Velasco, Jesús D. *El debate sobre la caballería en el siglo XV: La tratadística caballeresca castellana en su marco europeo.* Estudios de Historia. Valladolid: Junta de Castilla y León, 1996.

Romero Romero, Francisco José. *Sevilla y los pedidos de cortes en el siglo XV.* Seville: Colleción Giralda, 1997.

Ronquillo Rubio, Manuela. *Los vascos en Sevilla y su tierra durante los siglos XIII, XIV, y XV: Fundamentos de su éxito y permanencia.* Bilbao: Diputación Foral de Bizkaia, 2004.

Roth, Norman. *Conversos, Inquisition, and the Expulsion of the Jews from Spain.* Madison: University of Wisconsin Press, 2002.

Ruiz, Teofilo F. *Spanish Society, 1400–1600.* London: Longman, 2001.

Salas Almela, Luis. *Medina Sidonia: El poder de la aristocracia, 1580–1670.* Madrid: Marcial Pons Historia, 2008.

Sánchez Agesta, Luis. "El 'poderío real absoluto' en el testamento de 1554: Sobre los orígens de la conepción del estado." In *Carlos V, 1500–1558: Homenaje de la Universidad de Granada,* edited by Antonio Gallego Morell, 439–60. Granada: Universidad de Granada, 1958.

Sánchez-Albornoz, Claudio. *España, un enigma histórico.* Buenos Aires: Editorial Sudamericana, 1962.

Sánchez Saus, Rafael. *Caballería y linaje en la Sevilla medieval: Estudio genealógico y social.* Seville: Diputación Provincial de Sevilla, Servicio de Publicaciones Universidad de Cádiz, 1989.

———. *Las élites políticas bajo los Trastámara: Poder y sociedad en la Sevilla del siglo XIV.* Seville: Universidad de Sevilla, 2009.

———. "Sevillian Medieval Nobility: Creation, Development, and Character." *Journal of Medieval History* 24 (1998): 367–80.

Sarasola, Modesto. *Vizcaya y los Reyes Católicos.* Madrid: Consejo Superior de Investigaciones Científicas, 1950.

Schalk, Ellery. "Ennoblement in France from 1350 to 1660." *Journal of Social History* 16 (1982): 101–10.

———. *From Valor to Pedigree: Ideas of Nobility in France in the Sixteenth and Seventeenth Centuries.* Princeton: Princeton University Press, 1986.

Stedman Jones, Gareth. *Languages of Class.* New York: Cambridge University Press, 1983.

Stone, Lawrence. *The Crisis of the Aristocracy, 1558–1641.* Oxford: Clarendon Press, 1965.

Stone, Lawrence, and Jeanne Fawtier Stone. *An Open Elite? England, 1540–1880.* New York: Clarendon, 1987.

Suárez Fernández, Luis. *Nobleza y monarquía: Entendimiento y rivalidad; El proceso de construcción de la corona española.* Madrid: La Esfera de los Libros, 2003.

Thompson, I. A. A. "Castile." In *Absolutism in Seventeenth-Century Europe,* edited by John Miller, 69–98. New York: St. Martin's Press, 1990.

———. "Crown and Cortes in Castile, 1590–1665." *Parliaments, States, and Representation* 2, no. 1 (June 1982): 29–45.

———. "Neo-noble Nobility: Concepts of *Hidalguía* in Early Modern Castile." *European History Quarterly* 15 (1985): 379–406.

———. "The Purchase of Nobility in Castile, 1552–1700." *Journal of European Economic History* 8 (1979): 313–60.

Torres Fontes, Juan. "Los hidalgos murcianos en el siglo XV." *Anales de la Universidad de Murcia* 22 (1964): 5–22.

Ulloa, Modesto. *La hacienda real de Castilla en el reinado de Felipe II.* 2nd ed. Madrid: Fundación Universitaria Española, 1977.

———. *Las rentas de algunos señores y señoríos castellanos bajo los primeros Austria.* Montevideo: Martínez Recco, 1971.

Valdeón Baruque, Julio. *Los conflictos socials en el reino de Castilla en los siglos XIV y XV.* Madrid: Sigloveintiuno, 1975.

———. *Los judíos de Castilla y la revolución Trastámara.* Valladolid: Universidad de Valladolid, 1968.

———. *Los Trastámaras: El triunfo de una dinastía bastarda.* Madrid: Ediciones Temas de Hoy, 2001.

Van Kleffens, E. N. *Hispanic Law Until the End of the Middle Ages.* Edinburgh: Edinburgh University Press, 1968.

Vernon, James. "Who's Afraid of the 'Linguistic Turn'?" *Social History* 19 (1994): 81–97.

Vila Vilar, Enriqueta. *Los Corzo y los Mañara: Tipos y arquetipos del mercador con Indias.* Seville: Escuela de Estudios Hispano-Americanos, 1991.

Wagner, Klaus. "La Inquisición en Sevilla." In *Homenaje al profesor Carriazo*, ed. Juan de Mata Carriazo, 3:441–60. Seville: Universidad de Sevilla, 1973.

Willard, Charity Cannon. "Concept of True Nobility at the Burgundian Court." *Studies in the Renaissance* 14 (1967): 33–48.

Dewald, Jonathan, 7
Díaz de Montalvo, Alfonso, 136
Díaz de Santa Cruz, Fernando, 59, 112
Díaz Roldán, Juan (*escribano*), 165,
Diosdado (family), 72–76
Domínguez Ortiz, Antonio, 4–6, 26, 104, 120,
    198 n. 18, 214 n. 41
Doria, Andrea, 85, 89
Doria, Francisco (banker), 89
Drake, Francis, 152, 155

Écija, 109, 124, 125, 133, 185
elites, political, 4–6, 8–10, 16
    municipal, 3, 12, 141–42; and conversos, 95,
        97; and refashioning identity, 65–68, 192;
        in Seville, 49, 60, 63, 65, 82, 84
ennoblement, 4, 17, 38, 143, 181
Enrique II (king of Castile, 1369–79), 28, 117,
    148, 200 n. 12
Enrique III (king of Castile, 1390–1406), 28, 96
Enrique IV (king of Castile, 1454–74), 10,
    17–18, 20–23, 121
    edict of, 135
    grants of hidalguía, 31–32, 69, 74, 202 n. 64
    laws enacted by, 32, 34, 172
Enríquez, Fadrique, 17
Eraso, Francisco de (royal secretary), 175–76
Eraso, Luis de (*regidor*), 187
Espejo de verdadera nobleza, 29–31, 191
Espinosa (family), 161–66
Espinosa, Alonso de, 161–66
Espinosa, Alonso de (the elder), 163
Espinosa, Juan Bautista, 161, 165–66
Espinosa Polanco, Juan Bautista, 119
Espinosa y Guzmán, Francisco Andrés de, 166
evidence (*probanza*), 14, 76, 100, 130–33
Extremadura, 5, 72, 74, 107, 113, 130

Fayard, Jaine, 113
Felipe II (1556–98), 87, 155, 174–77, 179, 193
    and sale of hidalguía, 88
    and sale of towns, 122, 149
Fernando II (king of Aragon, 1479–1516) and V
    (king of Castile, 1474–1504), 11, 31, 33, 88
Fernando III (king of Castile, 1217–52), 60, 81,
    83, 156
Ferrándes Campón, Gonzalo, 39
Fernández Cansino, Pedro (*veinticuatro*), 97
Fernández de Córdoba y Figueroa, Pedro
    (fourth Count of Feria), 75
Fernández Marmolejo (family), 99.

Fernández del Marmolejo, Francisco, 96
fiel ejecutor. See municipal councils: inspector
Fortea Pérez, José Ignacio, 9
fueros. See charters
Fuero viejo de Castilla, 25, 42
Fuero viejo de Vizcaya, 91, 92
French Revolution, 6
Fregenal, 39–40
Frexno, 31
Fuente, Gonzalo de la Fuente, 158
Fuentes, Pedro de (Señor de Fuentes), 84
Fuentes, Pedro de (*jurado*), 136

García-Gallo, Manuel, 172–73
genealogy, 4, 156, 219 n. 49
Genoese, 83–85, 88–90, 101
gentry (Britain), 6
Gerbet, Marie-Claude, 5–6, 113
Gerena, 1, 38
Gómez de Silva, Ruy (prince of Eboli), 176
Gonçales Trapero, Sancho, 38
González Alonso, Benjamín, 173
González Paneque, Hernando, 125 (Samuel
    Paneque)
González Paneque, Juan, 124–25
government, royal. *See also* municipal
    councils
    limits of, 169, 170
    officials, 181; corruption of, 180–89; remu-
        neration, 188; reviews of (*visitas*), 182
Granada. *See also* courts, royal appellate:
        chancery of Granada
    conquest of, 10, 31, 33, 39, 48, 51, 117–18
Guerreros (family), 93
Guipúzcoa, 26, 90–91
Gutiérrez de Madrid, Alonso, 99
Guzmán (family), 108
Guzmán, Alonso Pérez de (seventh Duke of
    Medina Sidonia), 163, 165
Guzmán, Clemencia, 56
Guzmán, Enrique (second Count of Oliva-
    res), 161–64, 166
Guzmán Inés, 163
Guzmán, Juan, 56
Guzmán, Juan Alonso de (third Count of
    Niebla), 52
Guzmán y Pimentel, Gaspar de (first Count-
    Duke of Olivares), 166

Habsburgs, 55, 103, 148, 162, 170–71
Heredia, Dr. (royal prosecutor), 136, 168, 172